NE
APPROAC
CRIME IN THE
1990s

Planning responses to crime

by **Trevor Locke**

Longman

Published by Longman Industry and Public Service Management, Longman Group (UK) Limited
6th Floor, Westgate House, The High, Harlow, Essex CM20 1YR
Telephone: Harlow (0279) 442601
Fax: Harlow (0279) 444501

First published 1990

British Library Cataloguing in Publication Data
Locke, Trevor
New approaches to crime in the 1990s.
1. Great Britain. Crime and punishment
I. Title
364'.941

ISBN 0-582-05124-X

0-582-05124-X

Typeset by Communitype Communications Ltd
Printed and bound in Great Britain by
Biddles Ltd, Guildford and King's Lynn

Contents

Foreword ix

Preface xi

1 Crime and responses to crime 1
  Do we need a new approach to crime? 1
  Rising crime? 3
  The rising cost of crime 7
  Responses to crime 9
    Types of response to crime 10
      National responses 14
        The Crown Court 21
        The Crown Prosecution Service 21
        The Prison Service 22
      Local responses 23
        Probation Services 24
        The Magistrates' Courts 26
        The Police 27
  The relationship between national and local responses 28
  The failure thesis 29
  Can crime be reduced? 30
  Appendix: Criminal justice legislation (England and Wales) in the twentieth century that has affected crime rates and the criminal law 31

2 Analysing the response 34
  The fragmentation thesis 34
    Organisational fragmentation 35
    Political fragmentation 36
    Geographical fragmentation 37
    Fragmentation of functions 38
    The consequences of fragmentation 39

Are there any advantages to fragmentation? 40
Integration 40
The autonomy thesis 41
Accountability 42
Professional autonomy 43
The depth of autonomy 43
How autonomous are the courts? 44
Pros and cons of autonomy 47
The interdependence of crime responses 47
The concept of collaboration 51
Why is collaboration necessary? 51
Why do agencies not collaborate? 53
Factors in collaboration 56
Subject boundaries 56
Geographic boundaries 57
Boundaries around functions 58
Constituent agencies 58
Level of representation 59
Levels of collaboration 60
Liaison 60
Coordination 60
Cooperation 61
Partnership 61
Consortium 62
Corporation 62
Models of collaboration 63
Structures for collaboration 66
Cooperation in juvenile justice 66
Discussion: the lessons of history 70
Conclusions: towards an integrated response 71

3 The strategic approach 73
Introduction 73
What is strategy? 73
Strategic thinking 76
Components of strategy 77
The scope of a strategy 78
Vision and mission 78
Policy 80
Planning 81
Information 81
Strategic planning 82
The process of strategic planning 85
Strategy and decision making 88
Strategic choice 88
Effectiveness, efficiency and economy in strategic planning 91

Does strategic planning work? 94
Strategy, policy and planning 96
Strategy and the management of change 97
Planning in a changing environment 101
Developing an environment scanning process 105
Using the results of environment scanning 106
Organisation and management 108
A strategic response to crime 109
The concept of a criminal justice strategy 112
Applying strategic thinking to responses to crime 118
The scope of a crime response strategy 119
Conclusions 119
Suggested reading 121

4 A matter of policy 123
Introduction: policy in responses to crime 123
Why policy is important 124
What policy is 125
Policy and planning 127
What policy does 128
Types of policy 129
Policy as product 131
The scope of policy 131
Components of policy 132
Goals 135
Principles 135
Requirements 137
Mandates and sanctions 137
Levels of policy 138
Public policy 139
Policy and politics 141
Corporate policy 142
Agency policy 142
Policy formulation 143
The process of policy formulation 144
Boundaries and limits 145
Policy formulation and decision making 146
Evaluating policy 147
Policy analysis 149
Policy statements 151
Policy and organisations 154
Putting policy into practice 155
Policy in criminal justice systems 158
Conclusions 158
Suggested reading 160

5 Planning for justice 161
Introduction 161
What is planning? 161
Why is planning important? 162
Why planning is important in criminal justice systems 162
So what does planning achieve? 164
Resistance to planning 165
The case against planning 166
Can responses to crime be planned? 167
At what level should planning be undertaken? 169
Macro-planning 170
Local planning 172
Micro-planning 172
What is the right level? 174
What would local planning look like? 175
Theories *of* planning. Theories *for* planning 176
A general approach to planning 177
Planning as a process 180
Designing a planning process 181
Structures for planning 183
Cooperation among agencies 183
The cooperative infrastructure 184
The practice of planning 184
Operational planning 185
Techniques in planning 187
Maps, charts and diagrams 187
Critical path analysis 188
Planning and training 190
A groupwork approach to planning 191
Problems in planning 191
Planning and uncertainty 191
Predicting out-turns 193
Values in planning 196
Politics and planning 196
Boundaries and logistics 197
Suggested reading 198

6 Information for planning 200
Policy, planning and information 200
Information and knowledge 202
What are models? 202
How can models be used in criminal justice planning? 203
What types of model will be needed? 204
Modelling crime 210
Constructing crime models 211
What information should be collected for local crime models? 212

Modelling influences on crime 214
How crime models can be used 214
Response models 215
Constructing response models 217
Using response models 218
Criminal justice models as diagnostic devices 218
Relating crime models to response model 220
Using models 221
Using information locally 222
Area profiling and modelling 223
Contextual information 224
Boundaries, scales and maps 225
Profiles and surveys 226
Choice of data 226
Making use of area profiles 227
Information, monitoring or research 228
Computers, modelling and simulation 228
Trends and developments in criminal justice computing 230
From databases to information resources 234
Planning information systems 235
Strategic information systems 237
Conclusions 238
Suggested reading 238
Appendix: Example of a local area profile 240

7 A strategy for the the 1990s 244
The prospects for controlling crime in the 1990s 244
The need for a new crime response strategy 246
A strategy of reduction 246
Decriminalistion 247
Depenalisation 249
Increasing the integration of responses 251
Integration through collaboration 252
National/local integration of strategies 252
Structures for local planning 253
Crime response commissions 255
The functions of commissions 255
The membership of commissions 257
Commission secretariats 259
The costs of commissions 261
The way forward 262
Strategic planning of local responses 263
The missions of crime response agencies 266
Defining missions 267
Development work and local initiatives 269

Crime and justice policy for the 1990s 272
Maintaining the quality of justice 272
Privatisation of criminal justice 273
The challenge of reducing imprisonment 275
A sentencing strategy 276
Conclusions 279

Bibliography 281

Foreword

Crime is a very widespread problem; only a proportion of it ever comes to the attention of the police or the courts. Those who do come before the courts very often bring with them a variety of needs and problems as well as their offences. The conditions that produce levels of crime are rooted deep within our society. They are particularly rooted in our cities and towns where poverty, disadvantage and discrimination create the outlook of an urban society unable to cope with crime.

Criminal justice systems need to be regulated and evaluated; there is constant need to improve and develop the ways in which they are managed and operated. If we are to be more successful in our responses to the problems of crime then we need to look beyond the system of criminal justice. We need to target our policies on those problems that affect offenders: problems of employment, housing, mental health, racial and sexual inequality, social security and family welfare.

We cannot tackle the problem of crime in isolation, through criminal justice policies alone. Many things have to be done about the problem of crime but few of these are to do with the system of criminal justice. We need a criminal justice system and we need it to work effectively. Most of our criminal justice system is, like our decaying prisons, a Victorian legacy. No one thought up our system for dealing with crime; it was not planned but grew piece by piece. In order to cope with the complexities and demands of the modern world, planning and strategy should now be used to make that system more rational and to give it more sense of purpose.

Much can be done to improve the way that crime is responded to and much of this needs to be done at a local level. Many of these improvements do not cost a great deal of money. Local strategies for dealing with crime need to incorporate several levels. Dealing with crime is a difficult and complex problem. There is a pressing need for public policy to give those who work with offenders and who confront the problem of crime a clear sense of what they should be doing. What we need is a clear and effective strategy for responding to crime.

Our work in NACRO gives us a unique view of the processes of crime and punishment. We have the privilege of working across the spectrum of crime responses, from crime prevention through to the rehabilitation of sentenced prisons. We work both at the national level and at that of the smallest neighbourhoods. Therefore we are in a very good position to see the disproportionate use of resources and often misplaced priorities in our criminal justice system.

The time has come for a shift in penal and criminal justice policies. It is time that we began to think again about how we respond to crime.

Vivien Stern
Director of NACRO October 1989

Preface

This book is about crime and justice; it is also about strategic planning. It is an attempt to apply the concepts of strategic planning to the problem of crime. It argues that if we are to increase the impact made on crime by the various organisations that respond to this problem, and if we are to improve the effectiveness of the criminal justice system, then we should engage in a strategic planning approach.

The material for this book was assembled over a long period of time, beginning several years ago, when I worked mainly in the field of juvenile justice. When I was an Information Officer at the National Youth Bureau, during the late seventies, I handled several enquiries about methods of organising schemes of intermediate treatment. In preparing answers to these enquiries, I gradually became aware of the many problems and dimensions of the design of such schemes. The late seventies, the era of President Carter, was a golden age of activity in the United States Department of Justice. A series of major publications arrived on my desk from the United States Criminal Justice Reference Service. Many of these dealt with fundamental issues in the policy and planning of criminal justice in the United States but their underlying ideas were equally relevant to the situation in this country. Various issues – interagency cooperation, the development of intermediate treatment schemes, the design of policy and planning processes – were brought together in two publications that laid the foundations of my interest in and understanding of strategic planning in criminal justice – Gregory Falkin's book on a strategic planning approach to delinquency [Falkin, 1979] and Robert Cushman's report on local government planning of criminal justice [Cushman, 1980].

In 1983, I joined NACRO's Juvenile Offenders Team, a government-funded programme set up to monitor and develop alternatives to custody for younger offenders. It was during this period that I worked extensively on monitoring and information systems and began to appreciate the role of policy in underpinning arrangements for juvenile justice work in local authority areas. This link between policy and information was further developed through the work that the Team did in the North East of England during 1987 to 88. Our work there (in collaboration with Save the Children Fund) led to the publication *Policy and Information in Juvenile Justice Systems* [Britton et al, 1988] which consolidated a mixture of ideas, theories and learnings that had developed over the previous years. Now that I have moved into the arena of young adult offenders, the relevance of these ideas for the wider criminal justice system has become established. As I shall argue later on, the field of juvenile justice has generated many of the most innovative concepts and practices to be found in the criminal justice field in this country.

By the time I began to bring together the outline of this book, I had pursued the concept of strategic planning into the business world, partly through becoming a member of the Strategic Planning Society and partly because the only reading available to me at the time was to be found in economics and management studies. This confirmed that the theory and practice of strategic planning was being effectively used in a wide range of private and public sector organisations and convinced me that if it could work for them then it could work for the criminal justice system. Whether it will work depends very much on there being a commitment, on the part of those involved in responses to crime, to finding more effective ways of tackling the problem.

Whatever I may have borrowed from academic studies, my main perspective on crime and justice remains rooted in the practical day to day concerns and activities of working to change the way in which society responds to crime. As will be very clear from the discussion that follows, I believe very fundamentally in the reciprocation of theory and practice. In researching material for this book, I have not drawn to any great extent on sociology or on criminology; in fact, I found these disciplines surprisingly unhelpful in my search for the kind of material I knew I was looking for. The 'theory' on which this book draws most heavily comes from the world of business studies and management science, as well as from social policy studies and such diverse fields as urban studies and economics. Its theoretical roots are decidedly eclectic. The book also has other roots that draw on day to day experiences of servicing the information needs of those who worked in juvenile justice, and on the development work that has been done in the fields of criminal justice and social work.

There are very many people that I should thank, whose contribution has helped to created this book. I should thank those who contributed their ideas and experience through the many seminars and workshops in which the ideas contained in these pages were first tried out. The enormously valuable conferences and meetings of the

Strategic Planning Society have been of great benefit in understanding the way in which strategic planning is a universal language for those who are organising complex systems. I am very grateful indeed to Vivien Stern for her comments on an early draft of the book and to my colleagues in the Juvenile Crime Section of NACRO who have shared with me their reactions to my ideas. I am also particularly appreciative of what I have learned from two of my colleagues, Liz Wainman and Alison Taylor, whose experience and clarity of vision have reassured me on many occasions that tentative ideas about theory have groundings in practical reality. I am also very thankful for the patient and detailed advice of Alan Dearling over a long period of time. Lastly, I owe a enormous debt to Tina and Matthew, in whose time most of this book has been written.

Trevor Locke, Leicester *October 1989*

Acknowledgements

The publishers would like to thank the following authors for their kind permission to reproduce their illustrations:
Figure 4.6 William H. Dunn [1981] *Public Policy Analysis: an introduction. Englewood Cliff, Prentice Hall*
Figure 6.1 and **Figure 6.2** Patricia Morgan [1985] *Modelling the Criminal Justice System.* Home Office Research and Planning Unit

1 Crime and responses to crime

Do we need a new approach to crime?

We begin with the concept that crime is a problem and that society responds to that problem in a variety of ways. The general pattern of responses to crime in England and Wales and the responses of the criminal justice system in particular need a new approach if they are to become more effective in reducing crime. That new approach is beginning to emerge, slowly and incrementally and as fragmentary as always. There is also a view, however, that, at the threshold of the 1990s, we are witnessing a revolution in approaches to offending and punishment. Just as the legal system is being turned on its head, so the criminal justice system seems to be set to undergo fundamental changes, both to its structure and to many of the principles and values on which it has been operating. There is, I believe, in the criminal justice system a widespread sense of unease about the changes that are taking place. One Clerk to the Justices wrote recently that he believed that

> 'the criminal justice system of this country is in urgent need of reform root and branch, overburdened and distorted as it is by a gross unjustifiable bias in favour of suspected and convicted criminals and having almost abandoned the concern (with which less recent judgements are clearly imbued) for the rights of the victims and for the need to protect society by simple deterrence and, where necessary, custodial curtailment of criminals, particularly the violent' [Burriss, 1989, p 655].

Will the changes being considered or which have been proposed be for the better? Or will they further fragment and inhibit the effectiveness of the criminal justice system? Some will regard these changes as undermining the cherished values and traditions of the English system of justice. Others might regard them as being the logical extension of the broader social and technological changes that have been taking place in modern society. Is the criminal justice system being dragged, kicking and screaming, into the twenty-first century?

That the criminal justice system is in need of reform is clearly a view that is shared by the present author; but, is it in need of structural reform? Or, should that reform be made more to its method of operation? Its procedures and functions? This is not an essential distinction, since structures and functions go together and cannot always be changed independently. Mr. Burriss's proposition may be accepted but his suggested conclusions demand some thought: have deterrence and custody worked? We have had such measures for a very long time but to what extent have they been effective? Are the courts sufficiently empowered to assist victims in such ways as victims would wish to be assisted? To what extent do *criminal* justice responses to crime protect society?

Like many others who work in and around crime and the systems of law enforcement and justice, I share this concern with protecting society against crime. By 'society' we should surely mean *everyone*, offenders included, since, in a sense, they too need to be protected from their own crime to the extent that if no one is prepared to do anything to assist them to stop offending then they and their families will continue to suffer the consequences. Some people would prefer not to share my concern for wishing to protect people from the consequences of their own actions. That is perhaps one of the dilemmas of our society: we insist on there being a wide variety of measures to protect people from the consequences of their actions (seat belts, warnings about smoking, crash helmets, advertising warnings about drink-driving, etc.) but when it comes to the criminal law, ignorance is not regarded as being an excuse and we shy away from wishing to interfere too much in the behaviour of offenders. The work of probation, social services and of NACRO and some of the work done by prison officers is geared to assisting offenders to stop offending. There is a lot of activity that is intended to prevent crime, some of it under the banner of social crime prevention, which is geared to avoiding crimes taking place. Rehabilitation, resettlement, social work and preventive measures represent, in effect, attempts to protect criminals from the effects of their own behaviour. Do we respond to offenders as criminals or should we assist them with the problems that they often face – addictions, unemployment, homelessness etc?

In our struggle to maintain a stable, peaceful and ordered society we have responded to offenders, sometimes with an attitude of justice, fairness and equality, at other times with attitudes of discrimination, vengeance and vindictiveness that are as harmful and appalling as the crimes we were supposed to be redressing. The value of punishment is still widely held in our society; only the manner of its implementation is beginning to change. But what are we punishing offenders for? Many offenders could be regarded as being victims of poverty, unemployment, multiple deprivations, possibly a number of problems that they inherited from the backgrounds into which they were born. Crime and poverty have been associated for a long time but not all those who suffer from poverty respond to their situation by committing crime. Similarly, there are many offenders amongst the affluent. Whilst crime and social policy have been linked together for many years, there now seems to be a trend away from looking at the broader social contexts of crime, back to the much older notion of viewing crime as an individual pathology, as something that is personal rather than social.

If we wish to protect society from crime, then we must find the best way of doing that; we must choose those methods that will have the most effect within the constraints of accepted social values and principles, in particular those of justice. But before we can turn our attention to the means of social protection, we must first consider what crime is and what we might *want it to be.*

All this is background to the task of considering how we can make responses to crime more effective. Before we can decide how best to plan responses to crime, we must understand the nature of the problem and what influences changes in rates of crime. As the Home Office's latest strategy statement says 'tackling crime involves having a clear idea of the nature of the problem' [Home Office, 1989c p9]. Moreover, such considerations suggest other fundamental questions: does society want to reduce crime? Which reasons are offered for wanting to reduce crime? To what extent is a desire to reduce crime reflected in public policy?

Rising crime?

Our criminal law and system of justice have roots that go back a very long way in our history; but crime also has roots that extend back far into our social past. Crime and justice, it could be said, have developed together, in some kind of relationship, over a long period of time. Changes to the institutions of justice have often been motivated by fears and panics. There have been periodic panics about 'crime waves' since the middle ages and these have continued up to the present day. Many people believe that we face a 'rising tide of crime', both those who read the popular newspapers and those who read the learned journals.

It is widely believed that crime has been rising steadily for a very long time. Crime reported to the police has been increasing steadily in post war years: 'it has been increasing all over the Western world for the last 30 years, in this country on average by between five and seven per cent a year' [Home Office, 1989c p9]. Many explanations have been put forward to account for this increase and some would have us believe that we are now living in an increasingly lawless society. This is not a view that I would support; if anything, people are more concerned now about law and order than they were in pre-Victorian times, during the inter-war years or during the sixties. Certainly fear of crime is now more widespread than ever before. The permeation of everyday life by the mass media and its ubiquitous preoccupation with crime, has made people more conscious not only of crime generally but also of particular types of crime. Rape, child abuse, drugs and street disorder are now more frequently reported to the police and this is partly due to the exposure of these crimes in the media.

Concern for crime as a political issue has had its ups and downs but there are few radical differences between party manifestos when it comes to criminal justice policies. In 'Losing the fight against crime', Kinsey, Lea and Young begin their analysis of crime and policing with the argument that

> 'The failure of Mrs. Thatcher's law and order programme is plainly visible. The Conservatives claim to be the natural party of law and order, yet since they returned to power in 1979, reported crime has gone up by almost 40 per cent' [Kinsey et al, 1986 p1].

Certainly the annual *Criminal Statistics* published (since 1857) by the Home Office suggests that an increasing amount of crime is being reported to the police. Not all crimes that are committed are reported; the proportion of reported to unreported crimes is known to vary considerably by type of crime. An apparent increase in crime might be due only to an increase in the rate at which crime is reported or to increased efficiency of police operations. The Home Office acknowledges that

> 'this means that the figures of recorded crime can vary considerably, depending on how much the public is reporting, or how many police there are to write crimes down, without any change in the underlying amount of crime actually experienced by the public' [Home Office, 1989c, p 11].

The same source goes on to suggest that the increase in reported crime is almost certainly connected to the growth in the number of telephones (used to report crimes) and the requirement that property insurance policy holders report any thefts or damages to their property when making claim.

During the 1960s and 70s recorded crime increased by about 200% in relation to the population although the number of offenders found guilty by the courts over the same period increased by only 75% [Faulkner, 1983]. In the last 35 years recorded offences in England and Wales have increased sevenfold, although there was a drop of 5% in 1988 [Home Office, 1989c, p9]. This is the national average for all types of crime; particular crimes have changed at different rates and the increase has been considerably higher in Scotland and the

London Metropolitan Police area [Kinsey et al, 1986]. It is quite possible that the proportion of people who commit crime on a regular basis has not increased very much but that their crimes have been recorded to a greater extent.

Not all crime is common crime: theft, burglary, robbery and so on. There has been a notable increase in commercial crimes [Committee of Public Accounts, 1982] some of which, such as fraud [Mars, 1983], have taken on international proportions. Insider trading is a new crime. Many people now end up with criminal convictions because they have fallen foul of the law, not the traditional criminal law but of customs, immigration, environmental, trade union and many other laws that have brought aspects of human activity into the remit of the criminal law that traditionally were never part of its historical jurisdiction. The revenues derived from drug trafficking, illicit financial dealings, corporate crime and illegal arms trading dwarf those of common crimes. Yet the public is much less aware of these so-called 'white collar' crimes and business crimes, partly because the media does not give them as much attention as it does to the more familiar activities of rogues and villains.

There are clearly a variety of explanations for the trends in crime rates that we see over the past century; in particular there are structural reasons for the changing pattern and rates of crime. *Firstly*, as noted earlier, there are more laws to break. The number of criminal offences, that is the number of laws which can be broken, have grown dramatically since Victorian times. No one knows exactly how many criminal offences there are in English law but one estimate has put the number in excess of 8,000 [White, 1985 p 22]. The Home Secretary was asked recently to list all new criminal offences enacted over the past ten years. In reply, Mr John Patten MP said 'no running record of criminal offences created or abolished was maintained. The information requested could be extracted from the statutes themselves only at disproportionate cost' [Justice of the Peace, 1989b]. There has been, over the past century at least, a process of expansion in what we define as being criminal. The process of criminalisation has extended the jurisdiction of the criminal law over an increasingly wide range of social problems. There are many examples of problematic interfaces between criminal justice and social needs, as for example child care, mental health and drug abuse. There is some evidence that where officials or families cannot bring their troublesome adolescents under the control of the criminal law, they resort to the freedoms to restrict liberty available under mental health law. Adolescent or delinquent behaviour, in particular that of children and females in general, has historically often been considered to be mental (or moral) rather than criminal. The shift from criminal justice to mental health in respect of troublesome adolescents has been identified both in the United States and in this country [Rutherford, 1986].

Whilst many new laws have been added to the statute book, some have been deleted or have fallen into disuse. Over the course of this century a number of behaviours have been put forward for decriminalisation: suicide (removed from the criminal law by the Suicide Act of 1961) homosexuality between consenting adults (decriminalised by the Sexual Offences Act of 1967), the smoking of marijuana, vagrancy, prostitution, public drunkenness (currently, it seems, in process of being *en*criminalised) and certain categories of road traffic offences. There is a range of behaviours that could arguably be transferred from criminal jurisdiction to other systems of regulation and some deserve to be removed altogether from public control.

More crimes have been added, however, than have been subtracted; some of these additions reflect social and technological change: computer fraud, laws relating to drug addiction, business and commercial crimes, offences of environmental pollution and so on. Has the increase in the number of criminal offences been a response to increasing disorder and unlawful behaviour or has it in fact fuelled an artificial inflation in crime rates?

Secondly common crimes, such as burglary and theft have become insurable and as insurance has increased so too has the tendency to report crimes to the police in order to make a claim against loss. As pointed out above, the growth in the amount of domestic contents insurance has increased the rate of reporting of crimes of burglary and theft because insurance companies require policy holders to report such crimes to the police in order to make a claim. Also, the value of goods reported as stolen has increased more than the rate of inflation because of the need to value goods at their replacement cost for insurance purposes. This has generated a rise in the cost of insurance particularly in the inner cities. Insurance costs drain expenditure away from other things that people would have spent money on and from investment. The vast increase in the number of motor vehicles has seen an associated escalation in thefts of and thefts from cars, motoring offences and other traffic violations that have added to the overall volume of detected crimes. This represents increasing opportunities for crime in an era of post-war consumer boom prosperity.

Crime has been steadily increasing in most West European countries and this has followed trends in increasing postwar prosperity. Even after we have allowed for the deficiencies and shortcomings of the official crime statistics, we are left with the conclusion that crime *rates* have increased in post war history and that our attempts to stem this increase have largely failed. 'Britain in the 1980's', argue Kinsey et al, 'faces a crime problem and a crisis in policing that are unique in the history of the country' [Kinsey et al, 1986]. Despite these changes, many crimes have exhibited a relatively stable pattern in comparison to other major social problems, such as unemployment (which has risen and fallen), homelessness (which shows considerable fluctuations over the long term) or disease. Common crimes are still the largest proportion of crime and of these the proportions of theft, burglary and violence, though subject to trends and variations, have remained largely similar over a long period of time. The amount of crime committed by juveniles, young adults and adults, by males and females has remained fairly constant. It is only recently that the proportion of young people in the population has dropped and the crime rate has begun to go down.

Despite the relative stability of crime, our responses to crime have not been so stable. The broad infrastructure of criminal courts and police forces has been reformed considerably over the twentieth century. The criminal justice system and the policies and practices within which it operates have been subject to almost continuous revision, reform and, to some commentators, revolution. In appendix one to this chapter a list of Acts of Parliament is given; these have either amended the criminal law, altered sentencing or have affected criminal statistics. What will be apparent from this list is the steady growth in the number of laws concerning crime and justice that have been passed in recent years. What it does not show is the increasing volume and complexity of criminal legislation.

The rising cost of crime

Crime is mainly characterised as being a social problem. It can also be characterised as being an *economic* problem. The economic costs of crime are considerable. Although most crime is property related, such as theft or burglary, the financial costs of crime are difficult to measure. Once goods have been stolen, they are then disposed of. Some writers have portrayed crime as an economic activity [e.g. Henry, 1978; Smithies, 1984]. It has been suggested that there exists a *hidden economy* 'operating in the shadow of the formal, measured economy' [Smith, 1986, p1]. Others have defined the *black economy* of concealed fraud and tax evasion [Smithies, 1984]. These studies suggest economic activity of considerable dimensions operating outside the formal infrastructure of the state controlled, public economy but with a considerable impact on it. The relationship between this illegal economic system and the official one has not been fully researched or understood but most commentators agree that it undermines the official economy to a considerable extent [Henry, 1978; Ditton, 1979]. Some policemen and probation officers talk of certain deprived housing estates as surviving on trade in stolen goods.

There seems to be a well organised infrastructure for the distribution of stolen commodities. The more stolen goods people take into their homes, the less new or legitimate goods they will purchase. This reduction in demand affects manufacturing and retail industries. It also reduces income from taxation; one estimate held that tax evasion probably accounts for loss of revenue in the region of £4,000 million a year whilst social security fraud accounts for some £200 million a year [Downs, 1983].

It has been suggested that the size of the 'black' economy is between 2 and 15% of GDP [Smith, 1986] but, as this writer argues, the problem is not so much its size as the degree to which it substitutes or displaces the official economy. The concept of sub-economies is not wholly accepted however. A recent work has suggested that the social science community has created the notion of a hidden economy in error [Harding and Jenkins, 1989]. Disputes about the size or even the existence of unofficial or illegal economic activities leave us with no clear picture about the economic consequences of crime, though the figures available on the costs of the criminal justice system are not quite so difficult to evaluate. As crime has increased so too has expenditure on the justice system. The current budget (1989/90) for the criminal justice system as a whole is £6 billion a year with at least £2 billion being spent on private security measures; public sector spending on crime prevention is round £30.5 million plus unknown amounts spent by voluntary sector and community groups on preventive action, assistance to victims and work with offenders.

Increasing numbers of police, court, prison and probation officers and lawyers place an increasingly heavy burden on public expenditure. The total amount of money spent on the security industry by the public and by organisations has grown considerably and reached £1.3 billion in 1986 [Home Office, 1989c, p18] though I suspect this is a conservative estimate. Money spent on crime and responses to it is money that cannot be spent on housing, education, health and other vital public services.

Justice and law enforcement have other effects on the economy. Fines taken from offenders reduces their purchasing power as consumers. While people are in prison they are taken out of productive labour in the market both as producers and as consumers. The costs of insurance premiums, security devices and systems and the cost of repairing damage caused by crime also diverts money away from more useful economic activities. Pouring more and more money into the criminal justice system and into security measures does not appear to have had a proportionate effect on the crime rate.

Responses to crime

Most societies like our own respond to crime and offenders through the functions of law enforcement, justice, imprisonment and, in most West European countries at least, a probation service of some kind. The organisations that perform these functions (or 'agencies' as they are often called) constitute a criminal justice system. Not everyone would agree that these agencies constitute a 'system'; in some respects they are more appropriately thought of simply as a 'network'. Crime prevention has now developed in many West European countries, our own included, to tackle the problem of crime before it occurs. Many other areas of social policy, such as social security, unemployment schemes, housing, drug rehabilitation, mental health services and child care also impact on crime and offenders. This broad picture of functions, agencies and systems that relate to crime and offenders I refer to as '*responses to crime*'. Responses can take many forms and are aimed at different targets. The system of responses to crime and offenders can be viewed as a continuum ranging from prevention through to imprisonment and including functions of security, policing, prosecution, justice, sentencing, probation, social work, custody, rehabilitation and supervision.

Discussions of the purposes of these responses have used four main concepts: prevention, reduction, control and management. *Prevention* attempts to reduce opportunities for criminal behaviour in the physical environment and to reduce motivations in the social environment. *Reduction* generally refers to measures that will reduce the number of crimes committed, including both preventive measures and rehabilitation practices that seek to reduce recidivist crime. Crime *control* suggests direct and immediate responses to offenders through policing, sentencing and imprisonment but this is limited to those offenders who come into the formal system of law enforcement and justice. *Management* takes a wider view and might deal also with the victims of crime, fear of crime and some of the wider, social aspects of responses such as probation and social work.

Added to the crime response systems of the state are those of the private sector: security firms, security guards employed within companies, private detectives, store detectives, police forces employed by transport companies and also the considerable body of work with offenders that is undertaken by voluntary agencies, trusts and charities. The total system of security, detection, control, prevention, rehabilitation and reduction that constitutes organised responses to crime is varied and of considerable proportions. Added to organised responses are those of parents, friends, workmates and a broader network of people with whom offenders come into contact. *Informal* responses, effected through attitudes, social relationships, culture, language and actions, often exert more powerful influences on offenders than the formal responses of the criminal justice system. People also respond to the fear of crime by changes in their life-style, such as locking their doors, not going out late at night, avoiding certain areas of cities and being mistrustful of strangers.

As the former Chief Constable of Devon and Cornwall wrote:

> 'In a modern developed democratic society it should be possible to articulate a concept for the control of crime. The traditional idea that the key to control lies mainly with the system of criminal justice must now be seriously questioned in the light of our new and growing understanding of the nature of unreported crime, the complicated web or pattern of behaviour defined as criminal, and the probability that most people are or will be guilty of committing at least minor criminal offences' [Alderson, 1979, p130].

It is now widely accepted that policing, sentencing, imprisonment or probation cannot alone make anything more than a marginal impact on crime. Adding more resources or finance or personnel to criminal justice agencies will not of itself increase the effectiveness of these agencies in reducing crime. But added, in a strategic way, to other social policies, they can and do substantially affect crime, for better or worse.

Types of response to crime

Some responses are *definitional*: they define crime as a problem and define the types of behaviour that are to be marked out as being criminal. This is the function of Parliament and the courts in making the laws that define certain behaviours as crimes. Other responses are *reactive*: policing, sentencing and probation are functions that respond to offenders, to apprehend them, bring them to justice and set out perhaps to supervise or rehabilitate them.

Some responses are *direct* such as policing or sentencing, but others are *indirect* in that they are not themselves concerned with crime but they nevertheless affect people generally, offenders included. Some responses, such as the law, are *universal*, affecting everyone in society; some affect the poor, deprived, alienated, disaffected or disorderly and thereby affect some offenders. Local authorities can affect crime through some of their policies or lack of policies. Housing, education, employment and many other local government policies indirectly affect crime but these are seldom looked at to see what such effects might have on the local crime rate. These are not direct responses to crime, as such, but to some of the conditions that are believed to affect or influence crime rates. We might perhaps call these *influences* on crime.

Responses to crime can be typified by the length of *time* they take to have any affect on crime rates. Some responses to crime are immediate (arrest) whilst others probably affect crime only in the long term (e.g. urban development). Other responses are *preventive*, seeking to reduce opportunities for crime, alter the environmental conditions that contribute to crime or intervene in social processes that lead to offending behaviour.

On the one hand we can identify crime-specific responses, such as components of the criminal justice system and on the other a set of social policy measures which affect people generally, offenders included, and thus affect crime without intending to specifically do so. It is widely though not universally accepted that there is a relationship between crime and poverty, though the exact nature of this relationship is debated. The view is frequently encountered that the majority of those who pass through the criminal justice system are poor, deprived and disaffected from the social and economic bonds that bind citizens to a law-abiding way of life. If we take account of the picture of crime that emerges from the British Crime Surveys and the work on hidden and black economies, we should weigh against this view the understanding of crime as being a wider phenomenon and one that is not necessarily reflected by the characteristics of those passing through the justice system.

A countervailing view suggests that

> 'in many communities there may have been brought together the necessary ingredients of formal and informal social regulation in a way which kept crime rates down to tolerable levels, which did not induce fear or damage communities and which ensured a reasonable measure of support for the rule of law, despite severe poverty and lack of opportunity' [Hope and Shaw, 1988a, p 5].

Studies of white-collar crime and tax evasion throw such views into relief. If we accept that such a relationship exists (at least for some offenders and types of crime) then we can argue that crime is affected both by immediate responses and by the indirect and often long term influences of social and economic policies (accepting that some of these influences might in fact have more immediate and short term impacts on crime than many of the more direct interventions).

As suggested above these general social and economic policies might be referred to as *influences* on crime and offenders, their families, neighbourhoods and friends and on their lifestyles and opportunities. Such influences can operate either directly or indirectly. In dealing with, for example, young offenders, some youth workers prefer to work with young people as young people (rather than as offenders) and maintain that if offending is reduced then that is a secondary effect of their work, rather than a primary goal. Some social workers and probation officers share similar attitudes to their clients who are offenders. Some crime prevention work, particularly that which is focused on social measures, can also be seen to fall within this type of influence.

Some would also argue that any social policy or measure that promotes social cohesion and conformity will impart a positive influence on offenders. It is often claimed that improvements to standards of social morality or parenting will help to reduce crime and that crime represents a 'weakening of the moral fabric of society'. A similar argument has run through economic analyses: if crime is bred by poverty, then the distribution of wealth will reduce acquisitive crime. This view holds little attraction for those who recognise the association between crime and increasing prosperity.

Several indirect and long term influences on crime can be identified, such as employment services. Whilst the relationship between levels of crime and unemployment is very complex, there is a more discernable relationship between unemployment schemes and work training for offenders and their subsequent level of offending. Helping offenders to find employment is rehabilitative, increasing their commitment to society, reducing their alienation from it and enhancing their chances of not reoffending. Some researchers have found that education can help to reduce offending in both young and adult people. Education can offer a pathway to employment or can enhance an individual's sense of self-worth. One study concluded that schools should be a prime target for organised prevention strategies but argued that some changes to educational policy and methods would be required to achieve preventive goals [United States Department of Justice, 1980 and also 1981]. Similar conclusions have been put forward by those working in educational projects with juvenile offenders in this country and by Rutherford, who sees the school and the family as being the main institutions through which responses to juvenile offending should be delivered [Rutherford, 1986]. Literacy programmes for offenders have a beneficial effect, especially in enabling their access to employment.

Recreation and leisure services and the youth service can provide young people with opportunities for social education and what is often referred to as 'constructive use of leisure time'. Helping offenders to use their time positively, is often claimed to help them stay out of trouble. Homelessness and unemployment are often seen as leading to 'survival crimes' in which desperate people steal or commit fraud to stay alive. Helping homeless and rootless offenders has a long tradition. Even the design of housing estates has a bearing on the pattern and level of crime in a local area. There are, therefore, many areas of public policy that can affect crime, sometimes very indirectly but also in some instances as directly as more immediate responses. At the back of these broader approaches to work with offenders, is a trend towards looking at the way that organisations treat offenders, both with regard to their policies and practices and to the decisions that are made within them about individuals. In the United States, in parts of Western Europe and this country the concepts of 'systems management' and 'gatekeeping' are becoming established as essential elements in organisational responses to offenders. This has thus drawn the focus away from a purely individualised concept of dealing with offenders towards seeing how disadvantage and discrimination have been institutionalised and that improvements in responses require selective organisational change as well as good practices at the 'face to face' level.

We can therefore begin to identify three levels of social and economic influences on crime: *primary responses* that are direct and crime-specific, *secondary responses* that are both direct and indirect but not usually crime-specific and *tertiary responses* that are usually indirect and long term and generalised. This is not a wholly satisfactory classification and objections to it can readily be found. A similar classification has been used but in reverse order. Brantingham and Faust divide preventive activity into *primary* measures (conditions in which the physical and social environments facilitate criminal acts and alter those conditions); *secondary* measures (which identify potential offenders and intervene in their lives) and *tertiary* measures (which seek to keep people from committing further offences) [quoted in Hope and Shaw, 1988a p 237]. Whilst this typology makes sense in the context in which these authors have used it, the alternative that I have suggested is more logical in the context of policy and planning. Certain social values can have a more immediate effect on some kinds of behaviour than can policing or sentencing. We should not therefore regard such analytical devices as being cut and dried. The value of this type of classification is that it begins to address the boundaries of strategic planning of responses and where priorities should lie.

Wider social processes can also affect crime and responses to it. The media, for example, has been extensively researched; some have claimed that films can encourage crime. Alternatively, the media can foster and promote public involvement in law enforcement (e.g. 'Crime Watch') and stimulate public awareness of crime prevention. The media frequently sensationalise crime, particularly in those interminable soap operas about policing, monotonously set in either New York or London and which generate distorted images of crime and police work. The news media also present a distorted view of crime, focusing very largely on violence, terrorism, drugs, murder and rape. It may be right that these crimes should be reported and discussed and they are matters of public concern but the absence of objective and representative reporting of crime leads to biased public opinion about how crime should be responded to. Heightened public anxiety about the more serious crimes leads to illegitimate diffusion of punitive responses to crime in general. The news media's attempts to report criminal statistics, both nationally and at local level, often is unskilful and ill-informed and further leads to an unrealistic impression of the nature and scope of crime.

Under the headings of national and local responses, I now go on to offer a '*rough guide*' to the criminal justice system of England and Wales, mainly for the benefit of readers who are not familiar with it.

National responses

Another dimension of responses to crime is that they are organised at both national and local levels. There is a sense in which the courts system does not directly respond to crime but processes offenders that are brought to it by the prosecution service. A similar view can be expressed for the Prison Service. Some would prefer to regard the police as being the only agency that *responds* to crime. The purpose of arranging various criminal justice agencies under the heading of *national responses* is to say that there are nationally run agencies and that they are part of the overall system that we have labelled *responses to crime.* Nationally, the criminal law (which officially defines what crime *is*) is laid down by Parliament, interpreted and modified by the courts and implemented through the offices of central government departments and agencies. National responsibility for crime and justice policies is divided among the Home Secretary, the Lord Chancellor and the Attorney General although other Departments of Government are also involved in a variety of related policy fields. The Department of Health is involved because it has responsibility for child care, which is the system through which juvenile justice and intermediate treatment schemes are delivered, though the Home Office also includes responsibilities for juvenile crime. The Lord Chancellor's Department shares responsibilities for the magistrates' courts service with the Home Office, each department being responsible for different aspects of administration and management. The Home Office is responsible for the finance of the Magistrates' Courts service, whilst the Lord Chancellor's Department is responsible for the appointment and training of magistrates. The Lord Chancellor's Department is responsible for criminal court operations, practices and procedures. Both departments share responsibilities for criminal justice policy. The running of the Criminal Injuries Compensation Board is located in the Home Office whilst responsibility for legal aid rests with the Lord Chancellor's Department. The Home Office does not have any direct control over the operational functions of local police forces, the courts or the Crown Prosecution Service. It exercises management control over only the Prison Service but the most vital part of that system – the prison gate – is controlled by another part of the system: the courts. A rough breakdown of central government responsibilities for criminal justice is given in **Figure 1.1.**

This list shows the main relevant responsibilities of the Government Departments that are centrally concerned with the criminal justice system and crime.

Home Office

Police Department
- H.M. Inspectorate of Constabulary
- Crime prevention/Crime Prevention Unit

Prison Department
- Prison Service
- H.M. Inspectorate of Prisons

Criminal Policy Department
- Co-ordination of criminal justice policy and management of the criminal justice system
- Sentencing powers
- Relations with Crown Prosecution Service
- Juvenile crime
- Attendance Centres
- Mentally disordered offenders
- Royal prerogative of mercy
- Criminal Law and procedure, etc.
- Criminal Injuries Compensation Board
- Drugs

Criminal Justice and Constitutional Department
- H.M. Inspectorate of Probation
- Probation Service
- Magistrates' Courts Service (overall responsibility and finance)

Statistical Department

Research and Planning Unit

Lord Chancellor's Department
- Judicial Studies Board
- Magistrates (appointments, training)
- Judges (appointment, administration of circuits)
- Criminal courts and legal services (strategy, policy, operations, practice, procedure)
- Legislation and legal aid

Attorney General
- Crown Prosecution Service (independent but reports to A.G.)
- Law Officers' Department
    - Solicitor General

Department of Health
- Child Care
    - Juvenile Crime/intermediate treatment

Figure 1.1 The response system.
National agencies, Government Sector

Although many branches of central government are involved in criminal justice policy and planning (in one way or another), it is the Home Office which takes the lead responsibility. As Douglas Hurd, Home Secretary until October 1989, stated in the crime strategy document which went out under his signature, 'I am clear that our main job is to lead and co-ordinate the effort against crime' [Home Office, 1989c p3]. The strategy document acknowledged that the five main branches of the criminal justice system are interdependent and that the system is decentralised. Despite the use of the term 'strategy' in this document, there was almost no mention of planning: either the need for more effective planning or of how planning can be improved at either national or local level.

The Home Office has maintained a Unit concerned with planning since the early 1970s. A Crime Policy Planning Unit was set up in 1984 following the recommendation of the Fulton Report [Fulton, 1968] that government department's responsibility for policy planning should be allocated to a planning unit. During the 1970s, and I would guess over much of the 1980s, the Unit's work has been around policy analysis rather than corporate planning [Morris, 1980 p 135]. There was however a long-term planning exercise which sought to project the trends of 1977 into the next decade [Home Office, 1976a, 1980]. Whilst the current Research and Planning Unit makes a very considerable contribution each year to research (its programme being published in an annual document), its contribution to planning of the criminal justice system remains somewhat obscure. Some articles have been published on its emergence [e.g. Train, 1977]. It is said that the RPU 'provides a service of research and advice to the Home Office on issues relevant to policy and planning, especially as concerns the criminal justice system' [Research and Planning Unit, 1987 p3] although some aspects of research are undertaken by other units such as the Scientific Research and Development branch of the Home Office. As we shall see in chapter six, on information for planning, it has developed some models of the criminal justice system and some of its members of staff periodically produce analyses of policy issues. But as far as an outsider can tell, there is no developed methodology of strategic or corporate planning in the Unit and certainly they have published nothing on either the theory or practice of this subject. Even if the Unit did not contribute directly to the corporate planning processes of the Home Office, it could have undertaken research into the role of planning in local systems. Apart from Moxon's collection of papers on interdependence [Moxon, 1985] and the work on the criminal justice models, nothing on planning of criminal justice appears in the Unit's considerable body of published work. Criminal justice planning is not, it would appear, in the forefront of the Unit's prime concerns.

The Home Office Statistical Department produces the annual

Criminal Statistics and the supplementary volumes, the *Statistical Bulletins* and a range of other regular reports such as *Prison* and *Probation* statistics. The Statistical Department, the Research and Planning Department and the Criminal Policy Department are all separate pieces of the Home Office structure, although they all report to the same Deputy Under Secretary of State. These apparent structural fragmentations need not be given too much significance, however, since functions can and are performed across departmental and sectional boundaries and effective policy and planning practices are not always developed simply through having seemingly rational structures.

It is not only Government that occupies the national arena of response policies; voluntary organisations and pressure groups (such as NACRO, the Howard League, the Prison Reform Trust and so on), professional bodies (e.g. Magistrates' Association, Association of Chief Officers of Probation, Association of Chief Police Officers, Justices Clerks Society etc.) also participate in a complex network of policy debate and formulation (see **Figure 1.2**). The media, too, plays a role in shaping the measures taken in response to crime.

Whenever the Government publishes proposals for law reform or announces a criminal justice initiative, dozens of national organisations respond with their reactions, alternative proposals, criticisms and occasionally support. This undoubtedly improves the quality of government policy as well as improving public debate on crime and justice issues. But it is rare to find these organisations collaborating in the promotion of a comprehensive strategy. That is sad, because there are certain issues which command widespread support and could be pushed forward if there was a collective strategy amongst the various pressure and policy bodies. There are however a few examples of voluntary organisations coming together to promote various aspects of policy and reforms, such as the seven organisations that formed New Approaches to Juvenile Crime, the group of nine organisations that launched a 'joint manifesto for prison reform' and later the fifteen organisations grouped into the Penal Affairs Consortium or the five organisations that have formed Action on Youth Crime.

It can be seen therefore that the task of coordinating policy across several government departments and of responding to the proposals and demands of a large number of professional associations, voluntary bodies and research centres poses considerable challenges to ministers and civil servants alike. National government already has a number of interdepartmental groups of ministers and civil servants meeting to coordinate policy and planning. There are for example tripartite group meetings involving representatives from the Home Office, the Lord Chancellor's Department and Crown Prosecution Service; these are concerned with criminal justice issues. Indeed

Figure 1.2 The response system.
National organisations, Voluntary Sector

This list illustrates the range of bodies in the voluntary sector that are either wholly or partly concerned with crime and criminal justice issues. It is a selective rather than definitive listing.

Professional and representation bodies

Association of Chief Police Officers
Association of Chief Officers of Probation
Association for Juvenile Justice
Association of Senior Probation Officers
Central Council of Magistrates' Courts Committees
Central Council of Probation Committees
Justices' Clerks' Society
Law Society
Magistrates Association
National Association of Probation Officers
National Association of Probation and Bail Hostels
National Intermediate Treatment Federation
Police Federation
Prison Officers Association
Standing Conference of Clerks to MCCs
Superintendents Association
The Police Advisory Board
The Police Council

Reform and pressure groups/service providers

Action on Youth Crime
Apex Trust
Children's Society
Community Service Volunteers
Crime Concern
Howard League for Penal Reform
Intermediate Treatment Fund
Justice
Legal Action Group
National Association for the Care and Resettlement of Offenders
National Association of Victims Support Schemes
National Association for Prison Visitors
National Children's Home
National Council for Civil Liberties
National Council for the Welfare of Prisoners Abroad
National Youth Bureau
New Approaches to Juvenile Crime
Preservation of the Rights of Prisoners
Prison Reform Trust
Prisoners Wives and Families Society
Prisoners Wives Service

Cont.

Reform and pressure groups/service providers (cont.)
- Radical Alternatives to Prison
- Rainer Foundation
- Save the Children
- Society of Voluntary Associates
- Women in Prison

Academic/Research bodies
- British Psychological Society (Division of Criminological and Legal Psychology)
- British Society of Criminology
- Institute for the Treatment and Study of Delinquency
- Police Foundation

Several centres for criminology or police studies based at Universities and Polytechnics such as

- Centre for Criminological Research (Oxford)
- Centre for Police Studies (Strathclyde)
- Centre for Socio-Legal Studies (Sheffield)
- Centre for Youth Crime and Community (Lancaster)
- Institute of Criminology (Cambridge)

Figure 1.2 The response system.
National organisations, Voluntary Sector (cont.)

the government acknowledged in its *Expenditure Plans* published in January 1989 that

> '...if the different services are to contribute efficiently and effectively to achieving the objectives of the system, they must understand and take account of the interactions with the other services' [Chancellor of the Exchequer, 1989, para 8 p 5].

The interdependency of the criminal justice system was recognised at both national and local levels. It went on to observe that

> 'Growing awareness of these interactions has led to much closer contact, both Ministerially and officially, between the Home Office, the Lord Chancellor's Department and the Crown Prosecution Service in recent years. For example, there is now a committee chaired by the Director of Public Prosecutions with representatives of the Crown Prosecution Service, the Law Officer's Department, the Home Office, the Justices' Clerks' Society and the Magistrates' Association, which provides an opportunity for discussion of issues of common interest. Regular meetings have been held in each court region which bring together representatives of the three departments, police and probation services and the magistrates' courts' [ibid.].

There are regular meetings at ministerial and official level and frequent informal contacts between those in the departments most directly concerned with the criminal justice system. Annual tripartite seminars have been held for the senior managers in the police, prison and probation services and in July 1989, magistrates and members of the CPS were also included [Home Office, 1989c p 70]. There are many opportunities for inter and multiagency gatherings, not least at the conferences regularly run by NACRO and other associations in the field.

There is also a ministerial group on crime prevention chaired by the Minister of State at the Home Office. The second progress report of this group (published in June 1989) outlines the activities of 13 government departments. Whilst the Home Office has launched a number of crime prevention initiatives, the work of other government departments includes

> 'moves by the Department of Education and Science to tackle vandalism and arson and encourage police/school liaison. Work to combat crime on housing estates by funding crime prevention activity and encouraging neighbourhood watch and concierge schemes has been undertaken by the Department of Environment, while the Department of Employment contributed to crime prevention through the Health and Safety Executive, the Training Agency and Employment Service. The Department of Health has been working with the Home Office to develop policies to tackle juvenile delinquency, and Trade and Industry's inner city task forces and action teams have been actively promoting crime prevention. The Department of Transport is increasing numbers of police officers on London's underground system and is funding passenger security measures there' [Home Office , 1989b p 4].

Such evidence as can be gleaned about the interface between central government and local justice systems suggests that there is a trend towards a greater degree of collaborative and coordinative planning. Conflicts and disagreements still occur, of course, so that the strength and significance of this trend should not be overemphasised. The size and complexity of the machinery of central government policy and planning for crime and criminal justice should be borne in mind when we come on to looking at these issues later in the chapter on policy, that on planning and indeed in the final chapter where proposals are put forward for improving the strategic planning of the system.

The division into national and local responses is by no means watertight. Some of the work of the police necessarily takes place at a national level and internationally (e.g. dealing with organised crime and terrorism). The Crown Prosecution Service is nationally organised but operates as part of local criminal justice systems. Similarly the Crown Court is a national institution that operates in local areas, albeit with often a wider catchment than most local systems.

The Crown Court

The Crown Court is a recent invention being established in 1972 (under the Courts Act of 1971) to replace the Courts of Assize (or 'assizes') and Quarter Sessions. It is part of the Supreme Court of Justice. Unlike the magistrates' courts, Crown Court trials can include a jury. There are about 90 centres in England and Wales where the Crown Court sits, the most widely known being the 'Old Bailey' (in London) which was established in 1834. England and Wales are divided into six circuits. The Crown Courts are staffed by over 300 High Court and Circuit Judges and 450 Recorders [White, 1985 p 16]. Generally these courts deal with the more serious offenders. They deal mainly with cases committed for trial from, appeals from and committals for sentence from the magistrates' courts. There has been a substantial increase in the workload of the Crown Courts, from about 73,000 cases in 1985 to 100,000 in 1988 [Home Office, 1989c, p 47]. The Crown Court is administered and financed by the Lord Chancellor's Department. Above the Crown Court is the Court of Appeal (Criminal Division), established in 1907, to hear criminal cases on appeal from the lower courts.

The Crown Prosecution Service

The Crown Prosecution Service commenced its operations in England and Wales in October 1986. The Service resulted from recommendations made by the Royal Commission on Criminal Procedure which were accepted by the government and enacted in the Prosecution of Offences Act of 1985. The CPS has, up to now (October 1989) been run by a Board of Management and four Regional Directors under the direction of the Director of Public Prosecutions who is appointed by the Attorney General (a political office). However, it seems that the regional managers are to be axed, leaving the service with a Director and 31 Chief Crown Prosecutors and, it seems, two new field director posts are to be created [Justice of the Peace, 1989a p 633]. The Service is obliged by the 1985 Act to report annually to Parliament. The same Act also provides for the publication of a code of practice for prosecutors which sets out the principles on which the duties of the Service are based.

The workload of the service is indicated by the fact that in 1988/89 they received 1,574,000 defendants who were prosecuted in magistrates' courts and 158,000 defendants received and prosecuted in the Crown Courts. The number of lawyers employed by the Service as prosecutors at 1st December 1986 was 1,229. By the end of March 1989, the service had 1,398 staff in post (78% of its total manpower requirement). The total staff establishment of the service for 1989/90 is put at 5,543 [Home Office, 1989c]. Expenditure on the CPS is running at about £173 million a year. The service is divided into 31 areas grouped into four regions. Unlike the police, the CPS is not regulated by any inspectorate although they do have internal procedures intended to ensure that their work is efficient. Crown Prosecutors are responsible for each decision they make.

The Prison Service

Although not strictly a local element of criminal justice systems, the Prison Service nevertheless links into local systems. Since 1361 magistrates have been able to send all sorts of people to prison [Stern, 1987 p 21]. The various local prisons that were run by local authorities came under the central control of the Home Secretary in 1877 [op cit p 23]. There are now about 129 prisons in England and Wales (117 for men and 12 for women). These held about 50,000 prisoners in September 1987. 'Including remand prisoners, the prison population per 100,000 inhabitants in February 1986 was 94 for the United Kingdom and 92 for England and Wales' [Windlesham, 1987 p 211]. The Service had 18,887 prison officers in 1986. By 1989, total personnel had risen to 32,910 [Home Office, 1989c]. In August 1985 the prison population was 48,200, compared to a certified normal accommodation of 40,283 (that is, a 120% occupancy) [op cit p 38]. The CNA for 1989/90 is planned at 48,934 and for 1991/92 is currently planned to be 55,436 [Chancellor of the Exchequer, 1989, p 8].

In 1986/87 the total running cost of the prison system was nearly £700 million. The current budget for the Prison Service is £1140 million (1989/90) and for 1991/92 is planned to rise to £1,290 million. The average cost of keeping a prisoner was about £252 a week (costs vary according to the type of prison). According to government figures, the 'real operating cost per inmate' was £13,970 a year in 1983/84, £12,800 a year in the current (1989/90) period and is planned to become £12,740 a year in 1991/92 (expressed at 1987/88 prices using GDP deflator) [Chancellor of the Exchequer, 1989 p 8]. Expenditure on prisons has risen by 36% in real terms (156% in cash terms) between 1978/79 and 1985/86. The Government is embarked on a major programme of rebuilding of prisons that is intended to 'produce a further 3,000 places by 1993', the number of places being estimated to increase by 16,335 over the period 1985/86 to 1991/92 [Chancellor of the Exchequer, 1989 p 9]. The Home Office estimated that the cost of the prison building programme would be over £700 million by the end of this century [Home Office, 1986].

The Home Secretary is responsible for the Prison Service. The Prison Department of the Home Office has a management committee (the Prisons Board) which includes the Director General for Prisons (who is head of the Prison Department), the heads of four directorates, four regional directors and two non-executive members [NACRO, 1987c, p 5]. Since 1981 the prison service has been subject to inspection by Her Majesty's Inspectorate. The Chief Inspector of Prisons is a Crown appointee. 'Although within the Home Office, the Chief Inspector is not part of the Prison Department' [Zellick, 1983 p 61]. The Chief Inspector publishes a full inspection of about 14 establishments each year. An annual report is published each year by the Home Office. Each prison is run by a governor and has its own Board of Visitors composed of lay people.

Local responses

The same fragmentation of responsibilities is found at local level. Here there is no overall body with responsibility for policy and planning of either responses to crime as a whole or of the local criminal justice system. Some may wish to argue that this is done by central government and to a certain extent it is true that a degree of policy and planning is carried out by central government with respect to local systems of justice. But various local services are run independently of government and, in terms of the underlying concepts put forward in this book, it is not acceptable to think of local systems of criminal justice as capable of being run by 'Whitehall'. Local systems are not coordinated locally in any organised and structured sense. What adds to this lack of coordination is that various parts of the local justice system are funded through a variety of channels. The local authorities' expenditure on the police, the magistrates' courts and the probation services is financed partly by central government through specific grants so that 'four-fifths of Home Office expenditure is spent by local authorities' but 'decisions on expenditure are largely a local responsibility' [Chancellor of the Exchequer, 1989, p 3]. Thus, in 1987–88 the Home Office spent, for example, £24 million on the probation services and local authorities spent £196 million, and for the police, the Home Office spent £105 million and local authorities spent £3,309 million (current rather than capital expenditure). It has been argued that 'the Home Office has no power to determine the amount and direction of probation service spending, either by individual services or in total' [Fowles, 1989, p 16]. Against this we might note that 'much of total Home Office expenditure is subject to cash limits' and that the total block grant for local authority current expenditure is also cash limited [Chancellor of the Exchequer, 1989, p 5]. We also learn that 'consideration is being given to cash limiting the specific grants for magistrates' courts and the Probation service' [ibid]. Further details on central government funding of specific services have been given above under sections dealing with these services.

Local authorities have committees concerned with various aspects of local responses to crime: a police authority, sometimes a public protection committee, social services are concerned with juvenile offenders and the probation service is run by a committee made up of magistrates and others. In this sense, local authorities are concerned with crime indirectly through a variety of duties and responsibilities that influence crime rates or that affect offenders in common with local people generally. Housing, for example, is a local authority service that can be seen to affect the life chances of certain vulnerable groups, such as young people, who might be at risk of offending through either being homeless or through not having stable accommodation. Local authority management of public housing estates can also be seen to contribute to crime prevention [NACRO/SOLACE, 1988 and NACRO, 1988a]. Many responses need to be made at local level, partly because crime is a very localised problem. It is true that international and national criminal activities are increasing but the bulk of criminal offences are committed by offenders within their own territory, their own town, neighbourhood or estate.

If we take a typical local authority, we can list the agencies and bodies that constitute the local, organised response system (see **Figure 1.3**). Services such as the Crown Courts, Crown Prosecution Service and the Prison Service add to the local crime response system but are run centrally rather than locally. Criminal justice systems are thus of a two-tier nature, some being part of the national provision and some provided at local levels.

Probation services

The probation service began as a voluntary initiative (the 'police court missionaries') but was given a statutory basis by the Probation of Offenders Act, 1907 and later in the Criminal Justice Act of 1925. The main duties of the probation services are set down in the Powers of Criminal Courts Act 1973. There are 56 probation services in England and Wales varying in size from the Inner London Probation Service, which employs over 1,000 staff, down to the City of London which employs just five. The largest twelve services employ more than half of all the staff in the country. There are 6,500 probation officers in England and Wales [NACRO, 1988b] though the total staffing amounts to 12,092 [Home Office, 1989c]. Many probation services also use accredited volunteers and there is a national association for them, the Society of Voluntary Associates. The budget for the service was £225 million in 1987/88 (a third of the expenditure on Prisons), compared to £277 million in the current (1989/90) financial year and to £290 million planned for 1991–92. The Home Office states that expenditure on the service has grown by 50% in real terms since 1979 [Home Office, 1989c]. The estimated annual cost of a probation order was £900 and a community service order was £800 in 1986/87. In 1987, 137,550 people began criminal supervision under the probation services, 41,020 began probation orders and 66% of probation orders ran their full course. In the same year, 35,490 people

This list illustrates the range of bodies that might be included in overall crime response systems at the local level.

Police Forces (43)

Magistrates Courts (700)

Probation Services (56)

Local Authority Departments

- Social Services Departments (juvenile offender schemes)
- Education Departments
  - Education Welfare Service
  - Schools Psychological Service
  - Units for disruptive pupils
- Housing Departments
  - Council estates management
- Leisure/recreation Departments
- Chief Executive's Department
- Research/Information Departments

Area or District Health Authorities

- Drugs/Alcohol schemes

Voluntary projects and services

- Crime prevention schemes/panels (unknown number)
- Rape crisis centres
- Victims support schemes
- Juvenile offender projects
- National charities providing local projects
- Solicitors/Law Society
- Law Centres

Figure 1.3 The response system. Local agencies

began community service orders and 74% of such orders were completed. For every 100 offenders under supervision there were 37 on probation, 18 on community service orders, 39 on supervision following release from custody and 6 subject to other forms of supervision [Chancellor of the Exchequer, 1989, p 10].

Probation services are financed by their local authorities and the Government pays a specific grant of 80% of their expenditure [Chancellor of the Exchequer, 1989, p 10]. In 1987 nearly 300,000 reports of various kinds were produced (such as social inquiry reports on offenders). Each service is governed by an independent probation committee made up of lay magistrates and co-optees from the local authority, together with others and often a Crown Court Judge [NACRO, 1988b]. All these local committees are members of the Central Council of Probation Committees. Probation officers are represented by the Association of Chief Officers of Probation and the National Association of Probation Officers.

Some effort has gone into setting down national standards for probation services: a Statement of National Objectives and Priorities (SNOP) has been devised and all local services have drawn up corresponding statements. However, the equation between the distribution of resources and need is open to debate. Many will claim, quite rightly, that there is variability of resources, that finance is distributed unequally and not always according to the needs of local areas. The annual budgeting system of the probation services involves negotiations between them and their local authorities. This leads to considerable variations in resourcing of services. The Audit Commission has commented that these variations are 'more the result of past opportunism of former chief officers than of any rational assessment of current local need' [Audit Commission, 1989].

The Magistrates' Courts

Justices of the Peace (or lay magistrates as they are otherwise known) came into being in the middle ages. The office of magistrate can be traced back to the twelfth century [White, 1985, p 13]. One of the authorities on the Justices of the Peace noted that 'it was under the threat of a mounting crime wave ... that the Justices of the Peace was instituted in the 14th century' [Moir, 1969]. The term 'petty sessions' was in use by the end of the sixteenth century, the petty sessional division being the smallest organisational unit of the service. Juvenile courts were established in 1908 to deal with children who formerly were tried in the adult magistrates' courts. Since 1933 magistrates sitting in the juvenile courts have been required to undergo special training for that type of work [Moir, 1969].

Magistrates' courts as courts of summary jurisdiction were constituted under the Summary Jurisdiction Act of 1848 and the Petty

Sessions Act of 1849 [Home Office, 1989a Vol.2]. The current legislative framework for the management and funding of magistrates' courts was laid down by the Justices of the Peace Act of 1949 [Home Office, 1989a para 2.1]. There are about 28,000 lay magistrates and 63 paid stipendiary magistrates [Home Office, 1989a]. They sit in about 700 courts [White, 1985, p 14] accommodated in about 640 court buildings [Fitzgerald and Muncie, p 84]. The system is divided into 58 Commission of the Peace areas and these are divided into 549 petty sessional divisions [Home Office, 1989a para 3.3]. The magistrates' courts service employed nearly 9,687 permanent staff in 1987/88, made up of 285 Clerks to the Justices, about 1,800 court clerks, about 6,700 administrative and clerical staff, roughly 600 ancillary staff and 400 ushers. The service is run by 105 Magistrates' Courts Committees [Home Office, 1989a]. Although the costs of running these courts is initially met by the local authorities, the Home Office reimburses them 80% of their costs through a specific grant and a block grant is paid towards the remainder [Chancellor of the Exchequer, 1989 p12]. Expenditure on magistrates' courts amounted to £209 million (local government, current and capital) and £9,687 on manpower in 1987–88 and the current budget is about £249 million and £10,065 million respectively (1989/90) [ibid]. Fines and fees collected by the courts are paid to central government. Some 1.8 million defendants were proceeded against in magistrates' courts in England and Wales in 1987.

The Police

Unlike many European countries, the United Kingdom has no national police force. The idea that there should be one has been put forward many times but has so far been rejected (e.g. by the Royal Commission on the Police in 1962). There are today 43 police forces in England and Wales. The first police force was established in 1829 in London under the Metropolitan Police Act following the initiative of Sir Robert Peel, although the 'Bow Street Runners' had been set up in 1749. The first detectives appeared when the CID was founded at its offices in Scotland Yard, London, in 1878. Other areas of the country set up their own police forces following legislation in 1835 and 1856. Each force has a Chief Constable (in the Metropolitan Police he is called a Commissioner) who is appointed by a police authority made up of local councillors and magistrates (except in London where the Home Secretary acts as the police authority). The Home Secretary exercises a range of powers over local police forces including approving pay rates and conditions of service and controlling police officer establishments. Police forces are inspected by Her Majesty's Inspectorate of Constabulary.

'The Inspectorate annually inspects and produces (unpublished) reports of all forces, including the Metropolitan Police – at the invitation of the commissioner and in co-operation with its internal inspectorate; and makes a (published) annual report to the Home Secretary' [NACRO, 1989d].

The Inspectorate plays a key role in efforts to improve management of police resources and computers are used to store, analyse and present statistical data about police activities, enabling trends to be monitored from year to year and among groups of forces [Chancellor of the Exchequer, 1989 p 6].

Funding on the police service in 1988-89 was estimated at about £3.8 billion and the budget for 1989/90 is £4,115 million with 51% in specific grants coming from central government and 49% from local authority rates. Local authorities are responsible for deciding an annual budget for the local force and for meeting the cost with assistance from central government. The average number of serving police officers has risen by 3,568 in the last five years [Chancellor of the Exchequer, 1989, p6]. On 31st December 1987 there were 124,102 police officers, approximately one officer to every 400 people. There were also 41,399 full and part-time civilian staff, including 4,754 traffic wardens and 16,209 special constables. The total workforce of the police forces for 1989/90 was 175,000 [Home Office, 1989c].

The relationship between national and local responses

The higher courts, prison, and Crown Prosecution services are part of a national infrastructure of justice. But most of the immediate responses to crime are made by local organisations, such as the police, magistrates' courts and probation services. Clearly there are important connections between national and local levels of response. But if we wish to increase the overall effectiveness of responses to crime, should we concentrate on national or local levels, or both? Can local responses be effective without national support?

National government sets many of the parameters under which local bodies act and provides them with most of their financial resources. But, owing to the autonomous nature of these local bodies, it cannot manage them directly; it can only lay down policy and planning to a limited extent and must otherwise rely heavily on persuasion and promotion. Nationally run agencies are not easily incorporated into local justice networks even though they affect and are in turn affected by local agencies in operational terms. Local agencies act as 'pressure groups' on central government policy, through their associations and representative bodies and through the influence of individuals. There is a network of policy and issue forums involving many national organisations that filter local opinion into national government policy processes. This presents complex problems to the processes of policy formulation and implementation and planning. In devising a national strategy, account needs to be taken of the local level, because it is there that criminal justice services will be delivered. International and national crime is something that requires a different approach but crime is on the whole a localised problem and one that is arguably best responded to by local agencies which are best placed to understand the nature and problems of their locality. Political differences are involved in the relationship between national and local relationships in this field as in any other aspect of public administration and government. The issues of coordination and integration that arise in strategic planning of crime responses will be returned to but our task for now is to pursue the analytical framework within which these issues can be addressed.

The failure thesis

We have so far considered the problem of crime and have described the responses that are made to it. The growth in crime over the last century suggests that responses that have largely been restricted to the police, the courts and the prisons have largely failed to control the problem of crime. The traditional response to offenders has been to reinforce the capacity of the criminal justice system to deal with the individual offender through detection, prosecution, conviction and punishment and, if possible, rehabilitation [Faulkner, 1983]. These responses together with those of deterrence, tougher sentencing and harsher penal regimes have failed to reduce crime [Clarke, 1981]. Research into the comparative effectiveness of various sentences has produced few reliable conclusions. This has lead to what has been called the 'nothing works pessimism of the 1970s' [Bottomley and Pease, 1986]. This pessimism has now given way to a plethora of over-confident measures such that one commentator believes that 'the framer of penal policy today needs to steer a course between the twin perils of nihilism (nothing that has been tried works) and unwarranted optimism (halve the prison capacity and hope for the best)' [Windlesham, 1987, p 314]. The 1980s have contributed much that is successful, in work with juvenile offenders and in various aspects of probation and policing. But we are concerned here mainly with the effectiveness of the criminal justice system as a whole and with the out-turns for crime of wider social policies. Crime prevention strategies appear to offer additional modes of response but they are *relatively* new and their effectiveness is not as yet established. Some prevention schemes have demonstrated considerable success; others have proved to be failures. Insufficient application of crime prevention has so far been undertaken and we have still a good deal to learn before we can fully evaluate its contribution to reducing crime.

The growth in crime has been described partly as a gradual increase in the number of crimes reported (and there are several explanations for this) and partly because the jurisdiction of the criminal law has been inflated as more and more offences are added to the statute book and a growing number of behaviours and targets of crime control have been drawn into the net of criminal justice. An idea to which we will return several times is that the criminal justice system has itself increased crime in addition to failing in its effectiveness to reduce crime. The consequences of this failure can be viewed in social, political and economic terms.

If responses to crime have been a failure then how are they to be made more effective? This book offers a *recipe* for increased effectiveness that begins with the assumption that crime should be reduced and that a new strategic approach to achieving that reduction must address the problems of fragmentation, lack of coordination and insufficiency of common purpose that we can see in the current set of responses to crime. One well known ex-policeman has suggested that a strategy to control crime must begin with the diminution of poverty, discrimination, injustice and urban decay [Alderson, 1979, p130]. That comment appeared as this country's political climate was heading into a period of dramatic turbulence and change. Poverty has by no means diminished; in the view of many, it has increased. Discrimination has been highlighted as one of the most endemic and tenacious problems in our society generally and in our criminal justice system. Injustice, some of it committed in the 1970s, is currently a topical concern and is no less an issue now than it was ten years ago. Urban decay has been tackled in many ways over many parts of the country but is undoubtedly a problem that we will be taking with us into the next century. Over the past ten years crime rates have continued to increase until only very recently.

Can crime be reduced?

There is still considerable doubt amongst many who research into, make policy about or work in the justice system that crime can be reduced. The 'nothing works' attitude of the 1970s has not been altogether defeated. Where it has been replaced by a degree of optimism and confidence is in particular elements of the system. The Home Office strategy for tackling crime 'looks beyond the formal structures of the criminal justice system to the role of the wider community' and 'explores the scope for closer partnerships between the various structures and agencies which can check and then reverse the upward spiral of crime' [Home Office, 1989c, p 3]. The strategy assumes that the task of responding to crime is shared between the criminal justice system, local government and the community and that the work of these parties 'is part of a coherent and increasingly effective whole'. Only days after that document was released, Douglas Hurd left Queen Anne's Gate for the Foreign Office. That parting note of optimism will hopefully ring soundly in the ears of his successor.

Appendix: Criminal justice legislation (England and Wales) in the twentieth century that has affected crime rates and the criminal law

1907 Probation of Offenders Act (statutory probation service)
1907 Criminal Appeal Act (Court of Criminal Appeal)
1908 Prevention of Crime Act
1908 Punishment of Incest Act
1908 Childrens Act (established juvenile courts)
1908 Child Care Act
1911 Official Secrets Act
1911 Perjury Act
1913 Forgery Act
1914 Criminal Justice Administration Act
1915 Indictments Act
1920 Official Secrets Act
1925 Criminal Justice Act
1925 Supreme Court of Judicature (Consolidation) Act
1929 Infant Life (preservation) Act
1933 Children and Young Persons Act
1933 Administration of Justice (Miscellaneous Provisions) Act
1934 Incitement to Disaffection Act
1936 Coinage Offences Act
1936 Public Order Act
1938 Infanticide Act
1948 Children Act
1948 Criminal Justice Act (introduction of attendance centres)
1948 Indictable Offences Act
1949 Justices of the Peace Act
1952 Prison Act
1955 Children and Young Persons (Harmful Publications) Act
1956 Magistrates' Courts (Appeals from Binding Over Orders) Act
1956 Sexual Offences Act
1957 Homicide Act
1958 First Offenders Act
1959 Mental Health Act
1959 Street Offences Act
1959 Obscene Publications Act
1960 Administration of Justice Act
1960 Indecency with Children Act

1961 Criminal Justice Act
1961 Suicide Act
1963 Children and Young Persons Act
1964 Administration of Justice Act
1964 Criminal Procedure (Insanity) Act
1964 Criminal Procedure (Right of Reply) Act
1964 Police Act
1964 Malicious Damage Act
1965 Murder (Abolition of Death Penalty) Act
1965 Criminal Evidence Act
1965 Criminal Procedure (Attendance of Witnesses) Act
1966 Criminal Appeal Act
1967 Criminal Justice Act (introduction of parole)
1967 Criminal Law Act
1967 Road Safety Act
1967 Sexual Offences Act
1968 Criminal Appeal Act
1968 Theft Act
1968 Firearms Act
1968 Justices of the Peace Act
1969 Children and Young Persons Act
1969 Administration of Justice Act
1970 Administration of Justice Act
1971 Attachment of Earnings Act
1971 Courts Act (Crown Courts)
1971 Criminal Damage Act
1971 Misuse of Drugs Act
1972 Criminal Justice Act
1972 Road Traffic Act
1973 Costs in Criminal Cases Act
1973 Children and Young Persons Act
1973 Powers of Criminal Courts Act (introduction of CSO)
1973 Administration of Justice Act
1974 Juries Act
1974 Legal Aid Act
1974 Rehabilitation of Offenders Act
1975 Criminal Jurisdiction Act
1976 Bail Act
1976 Prevention of Terrorism (Temporary Provisions) Act
1976 Police Act
1976 Sexual Offences (Amendment) Act
1977 Criminal Law Act
1978 Oaths Act
1978 Protection of Children Act
1979 Prosecution of Offences Act
1979 Justices of the Peace Act

1979 Criminal Evidence Act
1980 Child Care Act
1980 Magistrates' Courts Act
1980 Imprisonment (Temporary Provisions) Act
1981 Contempt of Court Act
1981 Criminal Attempts Act
1981 Forgery and Counterfeiting Act
1981 Supreme Court Act
1982 Criminal Justice Act
1982 Administration of Justice Act
1982 Legal Aid Act
1982 Mental Health (Amendment) Act
1983 Mental Health Act
1984 Police and Criminal Justice Act
1984 Juries (Disqualification Act)
1985 Prosecution of Offences Act (established CPS)
1985 Sexual Offences Act
1985 Sporting Events (control of alcohol, etc.) Act
1986 Children and Young Persons (Amendment) Act
1986 Drug Trafficking Offences Act
1986 Public Order Act
1988 Criminal Justice Act
1989 Childrens Act

2 Analysing the response

Having argued that society responds to crime in a number of ways, more broadly than through policing and the system of criminal justice, we now consider how that response can be analysed, as preparation for our subsequent task of discussing strategy, policy, planning and information. The first chapter considered the extent to which our approach to crime has largely failed in controlling and managing the problem both in the way that the problem has been defined (through legislation) and in the operations of the essential agencies that have a mission to deal with crime and offenders.

In this chapter that failure is explained by the fragmentation of response system and the associated concepts of response functions lacking integration. The analysis also uses the concepts of autonomy and interdependence as underlying ideas in the fragmentation theses. Lastly, collaboration is suggested as a concept through which these processes can be challenged within the framework of a strategic approach.

The fragmentation thesis

The argument of this thesis is that our systems of response to crime are fragmentary both in their organisation and functions. The criminal justice system is fragmentary because it has evolved in a piecemeal way over a long period of history and this evolution has been driven by pragmatism rather than by a planned and strategic approach to dealing with the problems of crime. Policing, sentencing, crime prevention and incarceration have developed in isolation from each other. The processes of policy formulation, management and operation involved in the system as a whole lack a framework of coherent purposes and principles.

Organisational fragmentation

The foremost problem facing policy makers and those responsible for planning response organisations is that there has been little in the way of a coherent, systemic approach to responding to crime. Those in criminal justice agencies have to work within a system that is fragmented into a range of separately managed organisations rather than in an environment where integrated management and organisation can be readily achieved across agency boundaries. Each of the response functions is necessary to dealing with crime and offenders; but responding to individuals alone will not reduce crime in the population as a whole. The systems of law enforcement, prevention and justice are unable to respond to crime collectively and the criminal justice system lacks coordination with the wider agencies and policies that address the problems that both victims and offenders face. A strategic approach attempts to build into each of these separate functions the capacity to work together, in an integrated way, to achieve an effective system of response. As we shall see later, each of the organisations in the criminal justice system and the functions they perform are interdependent; they cannot function in isolation from each other. Actions taken in one part of the system will affect activities in various other parts. The criminal justice system, similarly, operates within an environment of social policy and programmes that have consequences both for crime rates and for the effectiveness of its responses.

Because each of the law enforcement and justice organisations has developed separately, no overall authority (particularly at the local level) has been created in order to achieve integrated, strategic management of the response system as a whole. The Home Office takes a leading responsibility for the police, probation and prison services but shares its central responsibility with a range of other departments. At local level, there is no one person or body with overall responsibility for responses to crime. Each of the law enforcement and justice agencies has responsibility for various aspects of the response; they cooperate with each other over specific operational issues and procedures but there is seldom any attempt, at local level, to engage in corporate strategic planning. Chief Officers occasionally discuss high-level organisational policies; most Chief Constables meet periodically with other chief executives in a local area. There is a certain amount of to-ing and fro-ing between council houses and Whitehall but this does not result in the formulation of strategic policies and plans. Magistrates sit on a number of committees, such as probation committees and police authorities. But the agendas for meetings and discussions of this kind are mainly concerned with sorting out issues for individual agencies. There is little sense of a group of heads of agencies and public representatives systematically working out a corporate approach to crime in a locality except perhaps in a few isolated areas. Cooperation between organisations at local level very much depends on the good will, enthusiasm and foresight of individuals. In some areas a collective responsibility for crime might emerge; in others, it might not. The system is not set up to enable comprehensive planning and organisation at local level to take place systematically.

In most local areas, there are little or no corporate information systems on crime or responses. Monitoring is largely confined to particular organisations. Evaluation and assessment of operational effectiveness is largely restricted to organisations and is seldom applied to systems or functions that run across several organisations. Since there is little collective policy and planning, there is little policy analysis or collective planning of responses as a whole. Response systems require management, since they need to be effectively organised but the fragmentary nature of the system does not enable corporate management approaches to be systematically developed.

Organisational and functional fragmentation is grounded in the lack of area response planning units. Responsibilities for the police, social services, education and probation services rests with county councils; district and borough councils are more likely to be centrally involved in housing and employment. Several police forces and probation services, such as those in London, the West Midlands and the North East, cut across a number of local authorities. Now that the Metropolitan Counties have been abolished they have no single local government structure to relate to. Thus, the task of policy coordination between criminal justice agencies and local authorities is hampered by the absence of common planning frames. There is little in the way of regional coordination and this level of planning has been largely abandoned over the last ten years. Children's Regional Planning Committees, which once had some responsibility for the coordination of services relating to child care and for intermediate treatment as part of this, have been abolished. Regionalisation in the probation services is limited to the coordination of training services. Petty sessional divisions, police divisions, probation areas and local authority planning boundaries rarely coincide. The problem of noncoterminous boundaries militates against the development of interagency planning.

Political fragmentation

Political parties have policies on crime, justice and policing but few of these policies deal comprehensively with the problem of crime or how we should respond to it. Public policy is fragmented into the mosaic of fears, panics, anxieties and concerns that reflect people's experience as a collective victim of crime. The political process tends to deal in particular issues even within broad policy subjects but without also offering a policy framework that brings all these issues together. The formation of an effective public policy for responding to crime is hampered by the compartmentalisation of central government departments and local authorities and by the way that political parties tend to follow this pattern in the way that they formulate their manifestos. This network of policy subjects and issues fails to add up to a comprehensive and integrated public policy framework for dealing with crime. The Home Office policy on criminal justice [Home Office, 1986 and 1989c] is a rare example of a policy statement that attempts to draw together all the threads of crime and justice systems. It is not reflected at local authority level, since there is no duty for local authorities to review their policy and operations in relation to crime and responses to it, even where their own service departments are concerned, let alone for the courts service and centrally run agencies.

The task of formulating integrated public policies on crime and justice is therefore hampered by the fragmentary structures of local government and the lack of coterminous boundaries of the various criminal justice organisations. This feeds through into the compartmentalisation of political party policy and to the confused and ill-defined processes of accountability of criminal justice institutions to public authorities. This weakness of public policy results in a lack of clear mandate and mission for criminal justice organisations and works against the ability to relate other areas of social policy to policies that affect crime and justice. The network of national interest and pressure groups, whilst being justified in a democracy, makes the task of policy analysis and formulation extremely complex. Lack of coordination in the network of voluntary agencies (some of which are listed in **Figure 1.2**) means that their capacity for influencing public policy is reduced.

Geographical fragmentation

There are considerable variations between local areas in the way crime is responded to. Some of these variations can be explained by differences in crime patterns and communities, levels of public expenditure and political characteristics. There is no reason why response systems should be identical in all areas. Some organisations have national standards but others do not; in some cases there are inspectorates that can manage the implementation of standards but some organisations do not (as yet) have such inspectorates (the courts service, for example).

Area variations in cautioning of offenders have been widely noted, despite the efforts of the government and other organisations to promote a consistent policy and practice in diverting appropriate offenders from prosecution. Similar variations in sentencing have long been studied and argued over. Some of these variations can be accepted as legitimate but in many debates one can witness sentencers blaming probation or social services for these variations and vice versa. There are considerable variations in the quality and quantity of services for offenders. For example, the number of probation officers is often not proportionate to the number of offenders who have been placed on probation orders. Expenditure levels on probation services have been found to be very variable, ranging between £230 and £870 per indictable offence [Audit Commission, 1989]. The Home Office scrutiny of magistrates' courts found similar patterns of variation in expenditure on courts [Home Office, 1989a].

Fragmentation of functions

The functions performed by the various organisations that respond to crime are fragmented. They lack coherence of purpose and coordination. Justice systems are oriented to individuals in that they are primarily concerned with responding to individual offenders, processing them through the various subsystems of arrest, prosecution, trial, sentencing and post-sentence penalties. The individualisation of these processes is of course necessary to the maintenance of standards of justice and the protection of the individual's rights. Thousands of decisions about offenders are made in a local law enforcement system each year. These thousands of individual decisions and events add up to the performance of the system as a whole, whether in policing, prosecution or sentencing. But the process of managing the interrelations between these functions, although complex and difficult, has not reached the level of sophistication that, it could be argued, is required by the interdependence of such functions.

When we look at how responses to crime are organised, we find that insufficient regard is paid to patterns of crime, both over geographical areas and over time. There is insufficient overview of how the various systems of response work across the boundaries of organisations. If we are to increase the effectiveness of each of the law enforcement and justice organisations then we must be able to evaluate their impact both individually and collectively. To increase the effectiveness of the police, prosecution service, courts or probation, we must be able to integrate their functions so that they support each other in a coordinated system.

The response systems are insufficiently coordinated and integrated with respect to the main functions of prevention, diversion, sentencing and rehabilitation and other services to offenders. Each of these functions is seen as being an element of the justice system in its own right. In fact each is interdependent in the way that it operates and in the consequences that successes or failures will have for other aspects of the response system. There is also a lack of coherence between crime and justice policies and other social policies, such as those related to unemployment, welfare benefits, mental health and housing. Probation and social services, the Prison Service and voluntary agencies strive to coordinate their operations with other social welfare agencies but this is often a fragmentary and ad hoc task which is not always fully supported by agency policy and planning.

Functions are delivered to offenders according to age, the main bands now being juveniles (10–16), young adults (17–21) and adults (21 and over). Whilst these divisions are undoubtedly necessary and positive, there is not a great deal of integration between them, particularly between services provided for juveniles and those aimed at the relatively new category of young adults. Some of these age differences are related to beliefs about the balance between justice and welfare or care and control that is required. The current debate about Family Courts and the long standing comparisons between the approach to juveniles in England and Wales and Scotland raises questions about whether too rigid a separation of approaches at the sixteenth birthday is in the best interests of either the individual young person or of society.

The consequences of fragmentation

The fragmentation of the criminal justice system and the functions that it performs can be analysed in a number of ways. This fragmentation of responses to crime suggests a number of consequences: firstly, because responses to crime lack a coherent approach, there is insufficient organisation to make an effective impact on the problem of crime. Secondly, because responses are organised through a variety of autonomous bodies the formation of a comprehensive strategy is confronted with insuperable problems. Thirdly, because response functions have developed in relative isolation (e.g. prevention, diversion, justice and rehabilitation) they are unable to reinforce each other. The impacts of each of these functions is reduced because of this lack of systematic integration. Fourthly, although the criminal law has been, quite rightly, concerned with justice, it has failed to develop a coherent approach to crime reduction; its focus has been on dispensing individual rather than social justice. Legislation has developed incrementally; lost in the minutiae of legal details, it has been unable to address the broader ends of social and penological policies. The machinery of criminal law lacks a clear sense of purpose and strategy as far as responses to crime are concerned. There is a lack of coherence between the criminal law and systems of law enforcement and this further reduces its effectiveness. Fifthly, the roles and remits of law enforcement and justice agencies are fragmentary and this manifests itself in overlapping responsibilities (e.g. between education and social services in responses to certain juvenile problems, such as truancy) or confusions about which agency is responsible for what. Where boundaries between agencies are confused, the result is duplication of resources and disputes about roles and professional territories. The end result of the fragmentation of responses is that the problem of crime cannot be strategically controlled. Whilst the custodians of justice have been divided the villains have won the game.

Are there any advantages to fragmentation?

It can be argued that there are positive aspects to fragmentation. A totally unified system of criminal justice might present society with an oppressive bureaucracy, a sinister centrally controlled arm of the state with rights of access into every corner of our lives. Fears about police states, political control of the courts and the spread of corruption in public agencies are legitimated by what we can see in other countries and by our knowledge of history. The autonomy of justice organisations provides barriers to the spread of corruption and prevents political interference in their policies and workings. Similar arguments are also used in discussing the case against planning in the chapter on this subject later on in this book. Whilst the disadvantages of fragmentation can be pointed to, the advantages must also be weighed.

Integration

The alternative to fragmentation is integration. What we are considering here is not simply that fragmentation is the problem and integration the solution. These are analytical concepts, to be used where appropriate. Each has its advantages and disadvantages; each offers threats and opportunities. We can analyse the various functions performed in criminal justice systems according to the degree to which we view them as fragmented or integrated. Policy makers and planners may decide whether to increase the advantages or decrease the disadvantages of either of these.

The issue of integration presents itself in other areas of social policy. Dick Stockford's book on *Integrating care systems* offers much to any consideration of integration in crime responses [Stockford, 1988]. He offers an analysis of the fragmentation/integration problem in the field of social care systems: care for the elderly, disabled, sick, mentally ill, etc. Many agencies exist to meet the needs of those in need of care: they are autonomous bodies and many have overlapping purposes. They are all response agencies, responding to the needs and problems of their 'client groups'. Recognising the problems of fragmentation of the service delivery network, Stockford argues the case for integration:

> 'The business of integration, of collaboration, of joint planning has become an industry of its own: with multidisciplinary teams, joint care planning teams, joint consultative committees, joint development offices and a whole plethora of coordinators. That is because of the importance attached to the issues – both in terms of the services offered and in terms of their value for money' [op cit, p xi].

Thus the concepts of fragmentation/integration, autonomy/ interdependence and coordination/independence are available to analyse a range of social policy and public systems, crime and justice included.

The autonomy thesis

Any discussion of the autonomy of law enforcement and justice organisations must include two themes: firstly, that autonomy can be defined in a number of ways and secondly, that there is a balance between the degree to which an organisation asserts its independence and yet operates within a system that is broader than itself. Agencies within the criminal justice system are interdependent rather than independent as far as their operations are concerned. In England and Wales, criminal justice systems are composed of at least half a dozen separate agencies, depending on what one chooses to include or exclude (these are included in **Figures 1.1** to **1.3**). Most of these organisations have formal autonomy in the sense that they are capable of exercising self-regulation without always seeking permission from a higher authority when making day to day operational decisions and they cannot be compelled to operate in a certain way other than by the authority of Parliament. This independence, it is often claimed, protects the rights of the individual and the process of justice from interference from the political system and from other unjustified sources of pressure.

The concept of the 'separation of powers' has long been regarded as being one of the keystones of the British justice system. The rights of individuals are protected and the impartiality of justice is maintained by having independent sentencers who cannot be controlled by either the legislature or the executive. Against this concept of independence a number of considerations must be weighed. Firstly, the highest ranking officials in the justice system are political appointees: the Lord Chancellor, the Attorney General, and the Solicitor General. The Home Secretary, whose powers relate centrally to criminal justice policy, is a member of the cabinet and more often than not a member of the House of Commons. Judges and magistrates are appointed on the advice of the Lord Chancellor. The independence of those who sentence offenders is a principle that is upheld by the current Government:

> 'The principles of judicial and magisterial independence and the operational independence of the police and the probation service are well established, both constitutionally and as a matter of sensible administration' [Home Office, 1986].

Secondly, all justice agencies are either wholly funded by or receive some degree of funding from central government, although for police forces and probation forces this is mostly channelled through local authorities. Where funding is dependent on an external authority, autonomy cannot be regarded as being absolute.

Accountability

Thirdly, although these organisations can be regarded as being autonomous, they are nevertheless accountable for their actions to the public and to various public committees. Sometimes however accountability appears to be rather distant and remote, a rather ritualised formality. National accountability is maintained through ministerial responsibility and, in the prison, probation and police services, through an inspectorate that is in principle at least independent of Government. The scrutiny of the magistrates' courts service recommended the establishment of a Magistrates' Courts Agency, managed by a Director-General who would be appointed by an accountable to the Home Secretary 'in whom ultimate control would be vested'. The agency would operate as a *separate organisation* but with a

> '*national framework agreement* between the Home Secretary and the Director-General, setting out the policy, objectives, priorities, performance targets, overall budget and extent of discretion in the way resources are used ...' [Home Office, 1989a, para 9].

This model, the report suggests, would ensure that overall responsibility for *administration* of the courts rests clearly with Government but that magistrates would be shielded from an '*excessive* degree of Government influence in *judicial policy*' [loc cit para 8]. The national framework agreement, the report continues, would place 'restrictions on the issuing of advice through the Agency on sentencing' and other judicial matters. Such arrangements might or might not secure a more effective, efficient and economic service from the courts. But one is bound to think whether administrative and managerial policies and processes can in practice be so readily divorced from those concerning the judicial duties of the benches. Can the professional and administrative functions of the courts be segregated any more than those of say the probation service? The view expressed in this book is that policy, management and practice in any organisation operate in a cycle of interdependence. This is clearly the case for the Probation Service, as a careful reading of the Audit Commission's report would suggest. Why then should this be less so for the magistrates' courts service?

Professional autonomy

Nearly all the organisations of law enforcement and justice have associated professional bodies (see **Figure 1.2**). These have policy formulation and promotional functions that provide inputs to the network of opinion, influence, decision making and operations of the system. Within each of the organisations, professional associations of one kind or another voice the views of their members and contribute to policy and practice in a variety of ways. Probation officers often guard their professional autonomy, sometimes viewing themselves as officers of the court and regarding themselves as being individually responsible for the decisions they make about their clients. This is beginning to decline as probation officers realise the need to cooperate together in their work and to base their individual actions on the collective policy of the service. The professional associations in the criminal justice system are autonomous but formulate policy and seek to influence government (and on occasions each other) thus forming a complex policy network. Some of the voluntary agencies that provide services for offenders receive a considerable proportion of their income from government grants (NACRO being a prime example of this). Their status as charities and their dependency on the public 'purse' is an issue which has been addressed by the voluntary sector for a long time, particularly in terms of the compromises that this imposes on their entry into policy formulation and their need to pronounce on political issues that affect their work. Similarly, the government at times seeks to influence these bodies, promoting its own policies and encouraging them to engage in new practices, modify existing practices and move in a certain direction. Influence can also include resistance and opposition.

The depth of autonomy

We have considered the network of influences and decision making within the system itself and inputs from external sources such as professional associations, reform bodies and service providing agencies. This view of the criminal justice system suggests that autonomy is rather more ideological than actual; it is autonomy in the last resort. Although certain criminal justice agencies can be seen as being self regulating, locally accountable and as having only indirect links with central government, it is clear that individuals working within this system are all prone to a diversity of influences. This discussion is germane to the issue of whether or not there can be or in fact is a collective response to crime. If, as this book argues, crime can be reduced by a comprehensive response strategy, then the character of autonomy of these organisations is of central concern. The concepts of cooperation and interdependence provide an alternative analysis of this issue.

Having independent agencies is not a necessary impediment to the development of a corporate approach. The advantages of organisational autonomy can be retained and the disadvantages ameliorated through cooperation at the level of policy and planning. A similar argument is found in the issue of Europe: the advantage of the European Community can be secured without individual countries having to abandon their sovereignty. They cooperate to their mutual advantage from within the boundaries of their autonomy. Issues of autonomy and accountability of criminal justice agencies therefore need to address both the functional and dysfunctional aspects of self-regulation and the depth of that autonomy – the degree to which it is actual or ideological.

How autonomous are the courts?

The concept of autonomy may be explored by considering the degree to which the courts are autonomous. The independence of sentencers has been widely discussed, for example by Ashworth [1983a]. In this analysis autonomy is considered largely in the context of functional interdependence. The courts are dependent on the police and the crown prosecution service for their 'business'. The number of charges and the choice of charges is often a matter for police discretion. The conduct of the case, the strength and quality of both prosecution and defence, is a factor in determining findings of guilt and sentence outcome. Likewise, the role of the probation services or the social services departments (in the case of juveniles) in presenting social inquiry reports to the courts is a factor in sentencing out-turns. In magistrates' courts, the lay bench relies on the expertise of the justices' clerk. Magistrates (not being full time officials) are open to the pressures of public opinion and the policies of their professional associations just as are doctors or accountants. Judges sometimes refer to public opinion in their sentencing speeches, indicating that they are influenced by what they deduce such opinion to be.

The courts do not function in a vacuum but are at the centre of a web of influences that are channelled and mediated in a variety of ways. They can be affected by variations in other parts of the system, as for example by the rate of cautioning. If cautioning increases and more offenders are diverted away from the court, then there is less business for the court and more time is available for each case. It has been suggested that this affects the rate of custodial sentencing (either increasing or decreasing it according to which theory one favours).

There is a close interdependence between magistrates, and crown courts. Some studies have looked at the efficiency of committing cases to crown courts for sentence. Judges train magistrates and there are established procedures whereby judges exercise supervision over their lay benches in the lower courts. There are therefore a variety of processes at work with the courts' system which influence sentencing policy and discretion. The outward appearance of autonomy can hide deep currents of influence which operate less publicly and beyond the reach of official accountability.

Magistrates, like judges, often defend their independence from outside pressures. On the one hand they must dispense justice to the individual offender and on the other they have a duty to protect the public from crime. They are limited to what the law allows them to do but the law allows them considerable scope for discretion. They may also find themselves faced with the dilemma of wishing to dispense punishment and a desire to help offenders to stop offending by addressing their welfare. In many cases, the sentencing decision must balance the need to impose punishment and control with a desire to enable rehabilitation. Very often, a sentencer is not confronted with having to choose between punishment and welfare but with the more challenging problem of how to practice both at once, or at least, how to temper punishment with welfare. Probation officers and social workers contribute to the sentencing decision through their reports, and they too often find themselves challenged by the desire to help the offender to avoid offending in the future but realising that this might only be achieved through effecting intervention and control. Sentencing therefore can be seen to reflect prevailing social values and wider policy trends, some of which appear to be contradictory or at least difficult to accommodate.

Magistrates and judges quite rightly assert their independence in the sentencing decision; but many would, I suspect, admit that they are not and need not be independent in terms of policy. There is interdependence between the policies of the courts and those of the other criminal justice agencies. The same is true of the relationship between the juvenile court and the social services department. It is common practice for social workers and probation officers to address groups of magistrates on matters relating to policy and practice and there are many opportunities for them to discuss issues with each other, both directly and through books and journals.

The quality of sentencing relies on magistrates and judges having a working knowledge of the policy and practice of probation and social services with regard to particular schemes such as community service or intermediate treatment. Magistrates sit on a range of bodies including the police authorities and probation committees. Judges however are less participatory partly because the Crown Court has a wide catchment area. The courts are dependent on probation and social services making available day centres, community service schemes, intermediate treatment programmes and so on and thus to provide them with a sufficient range of places to enable them to make noncustodial orders.

Judges maintain that they must be free of influences or external pressures to sentence in a particular way. This is understandable where individual offenders are concerned. Where the formulation of sentencing policy is concerned it is less understandable. Magistrates are sometimes prevented from sitting on advisory committees of those schemes and projects that offer noncustodial penalties. Other magistrates are encouraged by their clerks to attend such committees and to pay personal visits to the schemes to talk with those who work there. What is permissible and what is prohibited seems to vary according to the idiosyncrasies or prejudices of individual clerks.

There is a need for consultation between the courts and the agencies that provide the courts with noncustodial penalties. It is here that independence and cooperation are of considerable importance. Where schemes receive no direct feedback and guidance from the courts as to the relevance and credibility of their work (other than through sentencing outcomes), it is difficult for them to know precisely how they can develop and improve their services. It can of course be argued that the credibility of the schemes will be reflected in sentencing. But if schemes are not being used, it is difficult to assess why and what improvements should be made that would result in the court's greater use of the schemes. Many juvenile projects offering alternatives to custody for the under seventeens have benefited greatly from the advice of and consultation with magistrates. The same is often true for schemes of community service for adults.

The Government's Green Paper [Home Office, 1988b] suggested that magistrates could be given a formal oversight of noncustodial penalties, along the lines of some European jurisdictions. This might result in a closer working relationship between the courts and the schemes that provide noncustodial programmes. Some have argued against this proposal. The probation committees, on which magistrates sit, provide a formal channel of discussion about policy and planning and not only within probation. Since probation offers a service to the courts, it is sensible that magistrates should be involved in the management of this service. The same is true of police authorities on which magistrates also sit. But what is important to the effectiveness of such committees and authorities is the processes that they need to employ if they are to assess the coherence of the various functions of criminal justice (as for example policing and sentencing). The effectiveness of various response systems may be improved in so far as the task of strategic planning is approached overtly and systematically.

Pros and cons of autonomy

Having a justice system made up of autonomous agencies has its advantages and disadvantages and these are much the same as those we considered in regard to fragmentation. Autonomy guards against the unhappy consequences often associated with monolithic state organisations which develop their own cultures, often to the detriment of those they are supposed to serve. One critical analyst has gone so far as to claim that total integration of criminal justice activities is one of the hallmarks of the totalitarian state and that the centralisation of criminal justice and even some forms of consultation and liaison may threaten to undermine the values of a free society [Chapman, 1980].

Where autonomy is emphasised we would expect to see agencies competing against each other in the process of resource allocation and this is likely to lead to duplication and waste. A preoccupation with autonomy can obscure the interrelatedness of policies and operations and deny advantages that can be gained from collaborative working. Some of these disadvantages can be avoided through voluntary collaboration. The advantages of autonomy rest largely on the need to provide barriers against the intrusion of unjustifiable interests into the workings of an agency. Agencies, the police and the courts in particular, must be free to make decisions about individuals without interference, particularly from politicians. But decision making must be based on clearly established policies and on accountability for the quality of performance in making decisions if standards of justice are to be maintained.

The interdependence of crime responses

The various systems of response to crime affect each other; changes made to one system will have consequences and impacts on other systems. If we increase the impact of cautioning schemes fewer offenders will appear before the courts. If the courts increase the numbers of probation or community service orders then there will be workload implications for the probation service. Increased custodial sentencing has well understood implications for the prison service. The police play a prominent role in the management of immediate responses to crime, both through detection and arrest as well as through cautioning and crime prevention. Changes to the policy and practice of cautioning will affect the numbers going into the courts and will, indirectly affect custodial sentencing. The establishment of the independent Crown Prosecution Service in 1985-6 created another link in the chain of interdependence in the criminal justice system. Police forces now depend on the Crown Prosecution Service to bring suitable cases to court. The courts depend on the probation and social services to supply them with reports and with projects and programmes for offenders. The courts rely on the legal profession to defend their clients in court and the Crown Prosecution Service relies heavily on the legal profession, to which a lot of its work is subcontracted. Probation and social services rely, in many areas, on the voluntary sector to provide specialised services and programmes.

One of the most significant contributions to the study of the interdependence of the criminal justice system is the collection of papers edited by David Moxon [Moxon, 1985]. In an opening chapter, the fragmentation thesis is questioned by Feeney; criminal justice organisations, it is argued, do in fact constitute a 'system' of sorts, principally in their operational inter-connectedness. Those who first applied a systems approach to criminal justice emphasised its fragmentation. Thinking about criminal justice as a system has therefore become conversant with both interdependence and with fragmentation. These concepts offer apparently divergent perspectives on the structure and functioning of responses to crime. The systems approach, Feeney argues, emphasises the interdependence of parts within a system.

It is perhaps significant that the 'theoretical' introduction to the Home Office's collection of papers was written by an American. Few British authors have made contributions to the criminal justice debate along these lines. And yet, as Feeney points out, British research has illustrated in some detail how the various elements of the justice system interrelate, at operational level, and has investigated the day to day workings of this connectivity in some degree of detail. Feeney offers a few ideas for oiling the machinery of such collaboration, such as an incentive fund for interagency projects, but does not address the substantive issues of how to approach corporate strategy or how to create the infrastructure on which effective policy and planning will depend.

The interdependence of criminal justice agencies is sometimes seen in the notion of inter or multi agency schemes. The notion of multiagency policing has been discussed by Kinsey et al [1986] and others. They argue that the multiagency approach has involved a shift in emphasis from crime detection and deterrence to prevention and a shift of responsibility from unilateral to a cooperative approach involving other agencies and the community. They regard multiagency policing with considerable pessimism:

> '... the institutionalisation of multiagency policing, through the 'back door' of administrative planning within police (and Home Office) organisation, will develop forms of cooperation between the police and other agencies which will both undermine some of the remaining democratic features of our society and fail to contain crime' [op cit].

Police juvenile bureaux involve cooperation between police and social workers in the cautioning of juveniles. In crime prevention, the police work alongside a variety of community groups, voluntary bodies and businesses. There is also a degree of cooperation between the police and a range of local authority departments. Community liaison committees were established following the Scarman Report of 1981 [Scarman, 1981]. In his Report, Lord Scarman argued that local communities should be involved in the planning and provision of local services and in the management and financing of specific projects. Consultative groups were set up under the Police and Criminal Evidence Act of 1984.

Another view of interdependence is seen in discussions of cooperation in crime response measures. Government has laid much stress on community involvement in crime prevention. As Sir Brian Cubbon, Permanent Under-Secretary of State at the Home Office, declared 'crime control is the responsibility of everyone' [quoted in Home Office, 1986]. The circular issued in 1984 [Home Office et al, 1984] on crime prevention argued that the prevention of crime should be contributed to by 'every individual citizen and all those agencies whose policies and practices can influence the extent of crime.' It stated that 'crime prevention schemes are more successful where the police and local agencies work together in a co-ordinated way towards particular aims'. The Report of an Interdepartmental Group on crime, argued that

> 'efforts must be made to mobilise local services, voluntary bodies and community associations so that they co-operate together in identifying opportunities for crime reduction and in taking action on their own initiative' [Home Office, 1983a].

That interdependence of crime responses exists is already clearly established. Some would go further to say that it is right and proper that it should exist; for example an article in the *Justice of the Peace* [1989c] commented that 'The Government insists that the component parts of the criminal justice system should be interdependent.' The same article went on to state that 'The move towards greater interdependence and better management needs to be acknowledged' [ibid.]. This viewpoint therefore suggests that interdependence and effective management of the justice system are related concepts. The interdependence of criminal justice agencies and functions is understood not only in this country but also in Europe. In a Council of Europe report, Professor Andrew Rutherford, of Southampton University, explains that

> 'interaction within criminal justice, if it is to be fully understood, requires a full appreciation of the interdependence of the various stages and of the different agencies involved. Poor coordination between these agencies and from one stage to another threatens both to impair effectiveness and efficiency and to create injustices' [Council of Europe, 1987 p 7].

He went on to argue that total integration carries its own dangers, such as undermining of the essential independence of key areas of decision making. This recognition of procedural and operational interdependencies contrasts with the organisational fragmentation of the system. In another Council of Europe report it was observed that

> 'in countries where researchers and policy makers have undertaken a critical examination of the structure of their criminal justice systems, they have found that there are few common aims, that there is considerable diffusion of duties and responsibilities and little or no co-ordination between the subsystems and that there are often differing views regarding the role of each part of the system' [Council of Europe, 1980, p 10].

Problems of coordination and cooperation between different criminal justice agencies are a feature of their daily practice. In discussing this theme, Dr. D. W. Steenhuis, Advocate General in the Dutch Court of Appeal, has pointed out that

> 'in the Netherlands, consultation procedures have been organised between the prosecutor, the chief of police and the burgomaster (who, in the Netherlands, has part of the authority over the police). Yet it may be doubted whether, in the long run, this type of formal coordination may be sufficient to solve the criminal justice system's coordination problems' [Council of Europe, 1987].

Interdependencies between criminal justice agencies reflect those that exist between the criminal justice system and other systems and institutions of social control. The 1986 Council of Europe conference on interactions within criminal justice systems concluded that interactions within the system need to take account of the boundaries between the criminal law and other forms of social control. It was suggested that

> 'excessive reliance on criminal law not only overburdens the apparatus of criminal justice and undermines public confidence in the criminal justice network but also weakens other forms of control which may in many instances be more appropriate' [Council of Europe, 1987 p 127].

It also concluded that 'functional fragmentation is the essential context for the identification of strategies to improve the working relationships between criminal justice agencies' [op cit, p 128].

This brief discussion has done little justice to what is a complex subject. The implications for the planning of criminal justice systems are however far reaching. Fragmentation, autonomy and interdependence imposes on criminal justice agencies and those working in them the need to cooperate with each other as much as it sometimes engenders conflicts and resistance.

The concept of collaboration

So far I have been using the term 'cooperation' when discussing relationships between agencies and I have done this because that is the term which has been used and still is widely used to denote any form of mutual activity between organisations. But, as the following analysis will I hope reveal, we need a broader term to cover all kinds of positive interaction between organisations. We must of course acknowledge that organisations also exhibit other interactions, such as conflict. From now on I shall use the term *collaboration* to signify any form of positive interaction between or among organisations in the systems that respond to crime. I appreciate that the term has taken on somewhat negative overtones but its definition is 'working in combination' and that expresses the concept we are to use.

Why is collaboration necessary?

Those who are not keen to pursue collaboration between organisations will argue that it is a time-consuming business, that it slows down decision making or that it adds to the bureaucracy that hinders action. These criticisms are not deserved by the concept of collaboration, only by badly run collaboration. It is true that collaboration is time-consuming; but so are the problems that result from failure to collaborate and so are the inefficiencies that result from working in isolation. It may well be more time-consuming not to collaborate. Well planned collaboration should not slow down the internal decision making processes within an organisation; if anything it should speed them up by providing a common framework of reference for making decisions which will obviate the necessity for continual consultation on matters of detail. Collaboration is not about bureaucracy; if bureaucracy results then that is the fault of those who are planning the collaboration and not of the principle of collaboration itself. The case for collaboration rests on the interdependence of functions and systems that criminal justice agencies share; realising that interdependence exists and desiring to manage it to the mutual advantage of all the organisations in the system is what stimulates collaboration. A collaborative strategy, in a multidisciplinary system, achieves more than could be achieved by each of the agencies operating unilaterally.

There are general arguments in favour of collaboration. Some arguments in favour of specific aspects do, however, require closer examination. There are certain tasks that need to be undertaken which are shared by all the criminal justice agencies. One such task is that of promoting public confidence in criminal justice policies. Common principles of justice require collective advocacy. The principle of minimal intervention, for instance, is widely shared by social work and probation agencies (though not necessarily universally). If a united view in favour of such principles can be communicated by the criminal justice agencies, then it is more likely to be accepted by the public.

A cooperative approach to operations is now becoming accepted within many criminal justice agencies. One of the strategic goals of the Crown Prosecution Service, for example, is to 'build relationships with other institutions within the criminal justice system' [Crown Prosecution Service, 1989 p 27]. The 1988/89 annual report states that

> 'It has been a major objective of all members of the Service right from the start to establish constructive relationships with other institutions responsible for the efficient and effective administration of criminal justice. Co-operation and liaison were and are vital ... because we have recognised our potential for giving new impetus to the changes and developments occurring within the criminal justice system as a whole' [loc cit para 2.1.1].

The paragraph continues by saying that the Service has been able to contribute to multilateral discussions and plans for the future form of the criminal justice system. Later it states that this has enabled the Service to play a major role in identifying and working towards agreed 'strategic objectives both at local and national level' [para 2.1.5]. At national level 'senior liaison committee meetings includes representatives from the Association of Chief Police Officers, the Home Office, the Justices' Clerks Society, the Magistrates' Association, Her Majesty's Inspectorate of Constabulary, the Legal Secretariat to the Law Officers' and the Metropolitan Police and the Lord Chancellor's Department has recently been invited to send a representative [loc cit para 2.1.6]. The Service's participation in trilateral meetings with the Lord Chancellor's Department and the Home Office was mentioned in chapter one. Patterns of local liaison have also been established with the police, the magistrates' courts and the Crown Court. Liaison with the courts has in some areas taken the form of participation in Court User Groups (although in some areas Clerks are still resisting their establishment).

Collaboration in policy is of prime importance to achieving an effective corporate response to crime. Having the machinery of interagency consultation in place is a prerequisite to developing a comprehensive and consistent policy framework. Individual agencies will be able to develop their internal policies where they have been able to share policy issues with other agencies that might be affected by them. Having a forum for policy development is likely to reduce confusions and disputes about policy issues.

Drawing on previous comments, collaborative approaches also allow a rational approach to resource development, particularly the avoidance of duplication and waste. There can be increased opportunities for sharing resources. Collaboration can ensure that resources are equally distributed. Agencies might be more successful in acquiring the resources they need if they collaborated rather than competed in seeking them.

Interagency approaches can also enable the development of harmonised standards. For example, where a social services department, a probation service and an education department are involved in the delivery of a scheme of juvenile work, the formulation of common standards of procedure and practice will ensure that there is consistency and integration. Variations in the quality of services and in procedure and practice is widely observed in juvenile work and is due, in part, to there being no agreed standards.

A collaborative approach will also involve the development of a common system on information. Each agency requires statistical information on the performance of the criminal justice system as a whole. Joint monitoring systems are essential where a group of agencies are tackling a common problem. The joint commissioning of research would also ensure that information needs are met more effectively than where several agencies try to investigate a common problem independently of each other (and very often not being willing to share their results). Tackling racial discrimination provides an example of a problem that requires a group of agencies to work together in monitoring and evaluating current practice.

Finally, if a comprehensive response to crime is to be achieved, collaboration will be required. Collaborative approaches rest on the need to integrate individual responses to crime into a comprehensive strategy. This is likely to ensure that collective impact is maximised. The pursuit of a comprehensive and integrated strategy requires collaboration between the criminal justice agencies and local government, voluntary sector agencies and community groups.

Why do agencies not collaborate?

If collaboration is such a good idea, why is it that organisations in the system of responses to crime do not cooperate with each other more than they do? The processes by which resources are allocated sometimes lead organisations to compete with each other rather than to share them cooperatively. Organisations with overlapping or adjacent responsibilities, however marginal those might be, fear that they might loose part of their 'territory' and consequently part of their resources and power. There are vested interests that militate against sharing in a collective response. Sometimes these are of a personal nature; some chief officers, senior managers and indeed some groups within organisations mistrust collaborative approaches, since these are regarded as threatening to personal status or to individuals' careers. Fear of external influences is another negative factor. Many sentencers claim that cooperative forums and groupings compromise their independence and have on occasions shown themselves to be very reluctant to join interagency bodies. Fear of criticism is another barrier to cooperation; people in an organisation might feel that working too closely alongside another organisation will reveal their lack of professionalism, weaknesses, shortcomings and so forth. Organisations in which people are working under pressure generate an attitude that cooperation is a luxury that cannot be afforded. People will insist that they simply do not have the time to participate in what they deem to be interagency 'talking shops'.

Despite being encouraged to cooperate, many magistrates and judges still refuse to sit on certain kinds of interagency committees or to participate in events alongside other professionals. Such refusals appear to be based on the grounds that sentencers would be placed under undue influence that might compromise their impartiality in dealing with individual offenders. Police officers have also spurned interagency initiatives on similar grounds. The interagency groups and events being considered here are those that are concerned, not with individual offenders, but with policy and planning. It would seem therefore that either certain sentencers have misunderstood the nature of the invitations they have received or are being unduly cautious about being influenced in any way by other professionals working with them in the same system!

Interagency and interprofessional collaboration appears at times to be fraught with a range of problems and difficulties. Blagg, Smith and their colleagues have been researching interagency cooperation in criminal justice and have claimed that 'multiagency work is not an unproblematic, conflict-free solution to the problems of modern society' [Blagg and Smith, 1989 p 40]. Studies of the arenas of interagency or multiagency encounters, usually in crime prevention, community policing or juvenile justice, highlight the nature and extent of these problems. Some of the mistrust and conflict that can be observed in these arenas can be traced to inequalities of power, according to Blagg and Smith, and as they note, to the police 'further extending their power by colonising other agencies and thereby increasing their power over communities' (referring to the view of Gordon [1984] and others). Critical views of the police and their alleged manipulation of interagency agendas suggests a conspiracy model which Blagg and Smith admit 'undervalues the impact which pressure from society has had on state agencies and the capacity for reforms within these agencies' [op cit p 41].

Generalising from these observations, these authors state that 'relationships between agencies generally are marked by conflict and tension rather than by consensus and unity' and they add that 'this may not be altogether a bad thing' [op cit p 41]. This rather stark generalisation clashes somewhat with their concept of the 'complexities of multiagency work' and with their conclusion that 'inter-agency bodies seem to work best when they have a clear purpose in mind and are focusing upon a specific task ... ' [op cit, p 43]. Do agencies interact more than the aggregated sum of the interactions of individuals within them? The analysis that follows suggests collaborative interactions between individuals are conditioned by the policies of the agencies in which they work.

Other problems encountered in collaborative working stem from professionalism. Some antagonism is rooted in differential pay scales and some in differences of values and styles of working. Police officers, social workers and youth workers have been seen to clash over how particular incidents should be handled and what such incidents represent. Critical examination of collaboration in criminal justice points to some of the disadvantages of agencies working across their professional boundaries. The sharing of information about individuals is one instance of this as was recognised some time ago (for example by Vincent [1980]) and again more recently by Blagg and Smith. Illustrations are offered, in several accounts of interagency groups, of the police seeking information about individuals or families from social workers or community representatives. This was believed to be part of the police officer's intelligence gathering either generally or with respect to particular suspects. Information sharing has always been seen to be an important part of collaborative working but this is mostly assumed to involve aggregate data and information of a general kind rather than information about suspects, a point emphasised by Birley and Bright in their study of crime prevention policy [Birley and Bright, 1985]. They go on to note that critics on the left argue that multiagency approaches result in increasing police powers at the expense of individual liberties and rights [op cit para 47]. The notion that crossing agency boundaries represents an intrusion by the police, serves to underline the need for organised and policy grounded approaches rather than collaboration by individuals acting with little accountability and without agreed standards of practice.

Where there is mistrust of the intentions of people from other agencies, then there is likely to be resistance to collaboration. Without a firmly developed policy framework and set of practice guidelines in which collaborative working can be set, individuals are open to the temptation to abuse cooperative arenas. In one sense it is not organisations but individuals that collaborate but in another sense, collaboration is more soundly based where it is *organisations* rather than individuals that set the remit, structures and protocols for collaboration.

There are therefore many barriers to cooperation and many forms in which resistance to it can be manufactured. Some of these are built on myths, some on vested interests and some on 'needed' anxieties. Resistance to multiagency approaches often rests on the anxiety that autonomy will be eroded by a move towards a multilateral corporatism. More broadly, we live in a society that is placing increasing value on competition rather than cooperation and on individualism rather than collective responsibilities. Chief officers are sometimes reluctant to collaborate across agency boundaries because they feel that the status of their organisation and consequently their own personal status will be diminished.

Those who wish to advocate the benefits of a corporate and collaborate approach to responses to crime will face such resistance. The value of collaborative working must accentuate the positive gains that can be achieved and the interdependent relationships that exist between those agencies. Autonomy is not of such great value when the interdependence of justice agencies is understood. To develop cooperative responses, it is necessary to identify these resistances and to address them openly. Interagency meetings and dealings are often thwarted by an individual's covert agendas; representatives can appear to behave cooperatively but are in fact only using the machinery of collaboration to pursue their own objectives. Sometimes this goes so far as attempting to 'kill it with kindness'. Instead of being openly antagonistic, initiatives can be undermined with feigned good will. Above all cooperation must be pursued for the right reasons and not to further any hidden agendas. A badly run initiative in collaboration could do immeasurable damage and make such work impossible for years ahead.

Factors in collaboration

When we begin to analyse collaboration, a variety of factors can be observed that tell us something about what is going on. These factors can be grouped under the headings 'factors in collaboration' and 'levels of collaboration'.

Subject boundaries

Organisations that collaborate together usually do so around a subject or task. This signifies the focus of what they are collaborating about. For example, in the field of juvenile crime, an interorganisational (or as it is usually called, an interagency) group might meet together to consider intermediate treatment or juvenile justice (the organisational context), children in trouble (the problem context) or child care (service delivery context) or even youth policy (broad policy context).

Some subjects are related to the group of people (children, youth, young adults, adults, men or women) that are the focus of the set of concerns or issues the group is to consider; alternatively the subject might be focused on operational systems as for example child care or juvenile crime or crime prevention. The focus could be on the problem, the target group, the system of provision or operation or on the justice, social work or youth work dimensions of the problem. Sometimes groups are formed with an unclear definition of what their subject boundary is. If the target group is juvenile offenders, the subject could be offenders who have entered the justice system, those at risk of entering the system, those at risk of entering care or custody, those with school-related problems or those with personal or family problem problems. These are target groups which have specified characteristics; the subject focus could be narrowly defined or very general. Policies can be related to very specific groups of people or to the population as a whole.

Out of the possible options or possible boundaries, the subject should be made clear. If a subject is chosen, there are then considerations about how it relates to other subjects. If the subject of a collaborative exercise is juvenile justice, then how does that relate to child care or education? The more specific the subject, the more context there is around it. This is similar, as we shall see later, to the problem of defining boundaries around policy issues. The subject focus of a collaborative exercise is of fundamental importance as many lower-order definitions will depend upon it.

Geographic boundaries

In many cases, the spatial extent of collaboration must be defined. A collaborative initiative could be required at the level of the local authority, a division within that area or at the level of a neighbourhood. One of the fundamental problems in the organisation of collaborative exercises is that of differential (or noncoterminous) boundaries. One researcher has noted that

> 'The difficulties of obtaining collaboration relate to differences in geographical areas, communication between different levels of the service hierarchy and working together as professionals' [Vincent, 1980].

Less frequently, regional collaborations can be set up involving a number of local authorities. The issue of whether a boundary is too large or too small can be set against a number of other factors: the subject scope, the depth of detail required, the organisations to be involved and so forth. The administrative boundaries of police forces and their divisions, petty sessional divisions, probation and social services, education authorities, health authorities and other bodies do not always coincide; even within a local authority, the subdivisions within the police, probation, social services and magistrates' courts are often different. These administrative boundaries often do not relate either to real communities or neighbourhoods or to the electoral framework of constituencies or districts. One of the fundamental problems of public administration is that there is no universal system of spatial reference. Each organisation has chosen its own unique system of spatial planning for its own distinct purposes. This is another symptom of the fragmentary approach to local government.

Boundaries around functions

Collaboration can take place in order to achieve a variety of goals but generally these fall into those related to policy, those related to planning and those related to subobjectives within these such as operational coordination, information sharing or joint management of resources. Some collaboration could well be multifunctional but the more functions that are included, then either the less generalised other definitions can be or the less effective the exercise will become. If a collaborative committee is set up at local authority level, then it is likely to be more concerned with policy and broad and long term planning. The smaller the spatial boundary, the less likely the collaboration will be around policy and the more it will be concerned with operational planning.

Localised, operationally orientated collaboration will be dependent on larger policy and planning inputs. It is usually at the level of the local authority or at the level of the organisation as a whole that policy and planning decisions are made. If a local group wishes to make fundamental changes to an operating system, it might have to seek approval from 'higher up'. The appropriate spatial level for collaboration might therefore need to be related to the nature of the collaboration. Collaboration related to policy might need to be set at the local authority level; operational collaboration might be best suited to fairly small areas.

Constituent agencies

The choice of constituent organisations reflects other more fundamental choices about the subject, geographical and functional definitions of the exercise. Additionally, some choices concerning which organisations are to collaborate might be reflected in whether they should all be in the statutory sector or whether the voluntary sector, community groups or businesses are to be included. The list of potential organisations that have been or could be included in collaborative structures relating to juvenile crime is very large, for example: social service department, probation service, education department, youth service, education welfare service, juvenile court, voluntary groups, recreation and leisure services, etc. A similar list could be drawn up of bodies that are involved in crime prevention.

There is a tendency for 'interagency' groupings to be comprised of anyone who might have any interest in a subject, however remote. Constituting committees in this way is often a mistake and leads to meetings that are too big to work effectively. An alternative approach is to select the key organisations that all have about the same level of interest in the subject; this provides a core group, or working party, which then calls in representatives from other organisations or departments as and when the business on the agenda requires their assistance. In the field of juvenile crime, it was widely assumed that the education departments should be included in any interagency committee that was set up; it was also widely found that education department representatives seldom attended the meetings. The problem here was that only a small proportion of the business at these meetings was of immediate concern to education departments. It would have worked more effectively, if education representatives were invited to attend on those occasions when education related matters formed a substantive item on the agenda. General meetings of all and sundry are generally less effective than small closely knit and task focused groups.

The choice of which organisations should be included in a core group can be a sensitive issue particularly where the group is believed to be capable of exerting a degree of power or influence. Political considerations can be important in circumstances where the choice of organisations to form a core group could be thought to have a bearing on the outcome of the exercise. Should elected members be included? Should voluntary sector bodies be included? The composition and balance of collaborative groups is often a key factor in determining their success or failure.

Level of representation

Many of the organisations involved in the criminal justice system are hierarchical structures. The level at which the organisation is represented, from chief officer to basic grade practitioners, is therefore a key factor in the composition of collaborative bodies. As a report about community policing in Exeter observed

> 'Whether groups work well has as much to do with personalities as with status; however, many professionals seem to find it less inhibiting to work with their peers in other agencies, than with people who are either senior or junior to them' [Blaber, 1979].

The ability of a group to carry out its chosen or delegated functions will depend on its having an appropriate level of representation. Groups with an agency policy focus are generally speaking composed of chief officers or their immediate subordinates. Groups of people from other levels in organisations can of course work on policy and formulation processes often require specialised groups of people to analyse issues and operations and to make recommendations for authorisation at a higher level.

The level at which agencies are represented in a collaborative group depends on the type of task involved. It also depends on the degree to which the group can exercise any decision making powers, or whether it is solely concerned with coordination and the exchange of information. Some of the interagency groups set up in the juvenile crime field, for example, were ineffective because the level of representation was insufficiently senior in relation to the functions they were expected to fulfil.

Levels of collaboration

Having described, in somewhat bald terms, the factors involved in defining collaborative exercises, the second set of factors to consider are those related to the level, or degree, of collaboration. If we consider the degree to which two or more organisations engage in collaborative action, we can analyse the following levels of collaboration:

Liaison
Coordination
Cooperation
Partnership
Consortium
Corporation

This represents a continuum of collaboration in which organisations become increasingly coengaged. The level at which collaboration takes place can be related to four key factors: policy, planning, resources and information. These factors also allow an analysis to be made of the degree of collaboration taking place in an area or system.

Liaison

In liaison each agency operates autonomously, with little or no reference to other organisations. Policy formulation is therefore almost completely unilateral. There is little or no sharing of planning with outside bodies; consultation is confined to those issues where other agencies are immediately concerned. Resources are isolated and used only internally. There might be some minimal sharing of information. There are wide demarcations between professional practices and standards.

Coordination

In coordination, relationships with other agencies are developed.

There might be a degree of consultation between chief officers prior to the formulation of internal policies. There might be some generalised concordance of views about common policy issues. Planning is coordinated in the sense that operational systems of one agency are modified to fit with those of another, on a selective basis. The general picture is one in which two organisations conduct independent activities but where some activities are selected so that one set of autonomous procedures are modified according to procedures in another agency. There is a desire to reduce unnecessary duplication of resources and some attempt to settle the worst aspects of demarcation disputes. There might be some joint action, for example a joint conference to promote a mutual concern. There is an enhanced readiness to consult other agencies on matters of overlapping concern. Each agency operates independently with regard to professional standards but there is some internal modification on the basis of other agency's standards. Sharing of information might take place where this seems to confer mutual benefits.

Cooperation

Each agency shares in early discussions about key policy issues. Some attempt is made to provide coherence between one agency's policy and others. There might be agreement over fundamental policy goals and a greater degree of shared planning. Each organisation develops its own role in relation to others that are relatively close in terms of operation or professional orientation (such as probation and social services where juveniles are concerned). There might be a willingness to share commonly used resources or mutual financing of third party projects. There could be a move towards common training programmes, some selective agreement on common standards and procedures and greater consent as to what constitutes good practice. There is a move towards conjoint standards of professional practice. Some joint information systems might be established with some cooperation in monitoring and sharing the results of research.

Partnership

Whilst partnership is usually seen as involving two organisations, the same principles could apply to two or more bodies. Partnership usually involves a high degree of cooperation but over a fairly small range. For example, a social services department and an education department might form a partnership to provide a project for truants. Partnerships between social services departments and voluntary bodies are fairly common. Such bilateral collaborations might involve an agreed joint policy, mutual engagement in planning, the creation of joint provision and sharing of staff, buildings or services. It is because the scale of the exercise is usually limited (for example, the creation and running of one particular scheme) that the level of cooperation can be relatively high. Partnerships have worked well where the scope of the collaboration was fairly narrow, enabling a pair of organisations to develop joint policies, plans and resources. This has, in a few cases, lead to broader patterns of collaboration.

Consortium

In some areas, several organisations have banded together to provide a scheme of resources or projects. A few examples of this have been seen in work with juvenile offenders and in community crime prevention. Schemes have been set up involving a consortium of projects and programmes provided by local authority departments and a variety of community groups or voluntary bodies. Again, the scope of the exercise was relatively narrow, though broader than that found in partnerships.

Corporation

Although there are almost no examples to be found in the field of responses to crime in this country, a final mode of collaboration might be postulated. Here there is maximum integration of policy, planning, resources and information among the organisations involved. The scope would extend over a wide range of common organisational functions and boundaries. Each agency would agree to a corporate policy and would formulate its own internal policies with reference to it. There would be a framework of multilateral planning, each organisation seeking to integrate its operations fully into a corporate planning system. Each organisation would have a clear role and remit with a corporate planning strategy. Whilst each body would have its own finances and resources, there could be opportunities for pooled resources and finances where this achieves strategic corporate objectives. There would be relatively easy secondment of staff from one member body to another and a commitment to interdisciplinary teamwork approaches where this would achieve the best results. There might be collaborative management of operational systems. There would be a corporate strategic information system, giving each agency access to common information services or appropriate access to each other's aggregate data (within the limits of legal or professional confidentiality). There could be multilateral agreement on standards of practice and common training programmes for commonly exercised skills. Professional standards could be set by corporate groups.

This is a hypothetical mode of collaboration but it does serve the purpose of setting into relief the other less collectivised modes of collaboration. You might ask: why bother having different agencies at all? Why not just have one organisation? The resulting monolithic body might be unmanageably large. Just as most big organisations have different departments with different roles and functions within the whole body, so a corporate crime and justice strategy would have 'departments' that are autonomous agencies (police force, courts, probation, etc.) but where that autonomy is exercised within the framework of a corporate strategy. The existence of separate organisations is and still would be based on the need to engage in specialised operations and practices.

Models of collaboration

Using the analytical devices offered above – factors in collaboration, levels of collaboration and their relevance to policy, planning, resources and information – it is possible to devise various models of collaboration. These can be used in the development of local collaborative networks and to analyse and evaluate the problems, threats and opportunities that are inherent in fragmentation, autonomy and interdependence. This can contribute to the process of strategic planning and, in particular, the integration of local crime responses.

Some would of course prefer to use conflict models and these can be equally valid. The purpose of collaborative modelling is to enhance collaboration and integration and conflict models might be less useful for this reason. The corporate level of collaboration assumes that each of the agencies shares an equal level of interrelatedness. It might however be impractical to develop equal relationships between all agencies involved in a collaborative network. What might be better is to work on bilateral relationships as these might be easier to manage. **Figure 2.1** depicts a group of agencies connected with each other in a web of mutual relationships. This assumes that a corporate approach has been established without the mediation of a central coordinative structure. An alternative model is shown in **Figure 2.2** where a central body, in this example a coordinating *commission* of the kind suggested in the final chapter, mediates the relationships between each agency. Both models can achieve a corporate approach but the management of that approach is different in each case. In **Figure 2.1** there are ten relationships whereas in the model shown in **Figure 2.2** there are only five. The most significant difference between the two models is that the centralised model could confer a large amount of power on the mediating body as well as, of course, a considerable degree of responsibility. The model shown in **Figure 2.2** may be easier to manage than that shown in **Figure 2.1** where the number and complexity of relationships make the process of corporate planning very much more difficult.

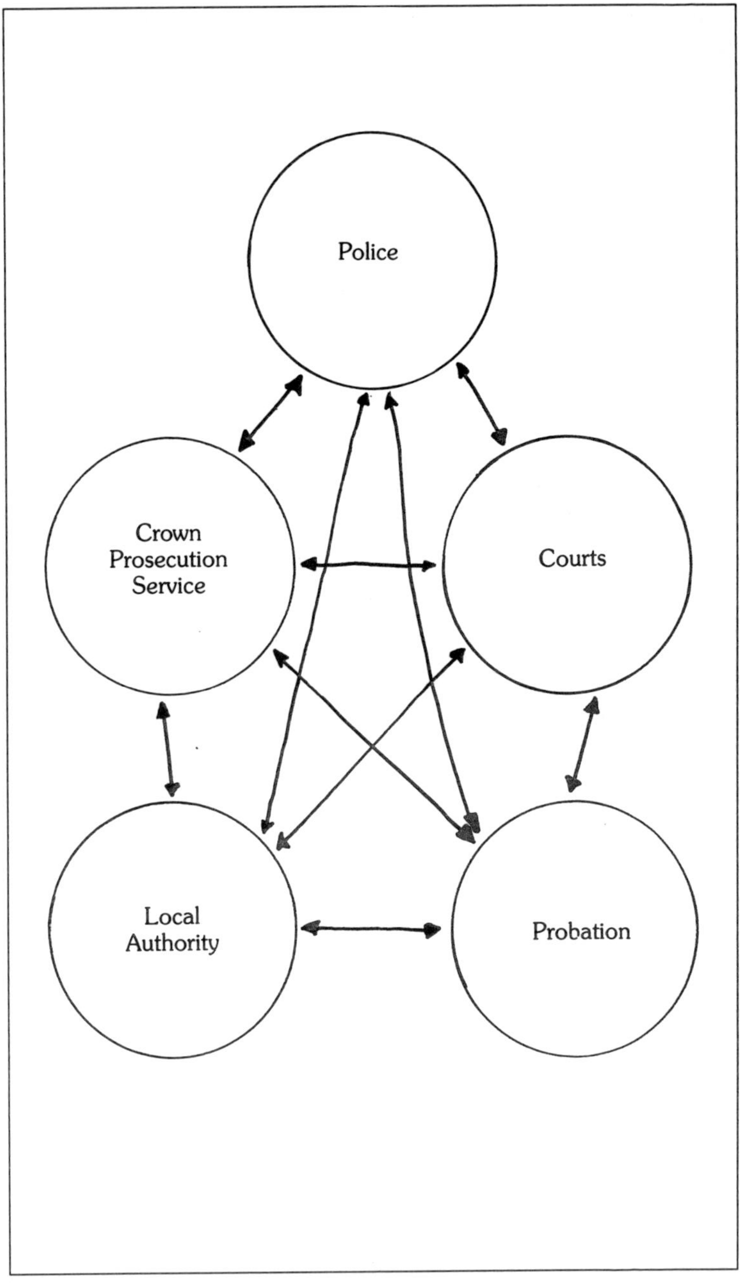

Figure 2.1 Network of corporate relationships in strategic planning (model 1)

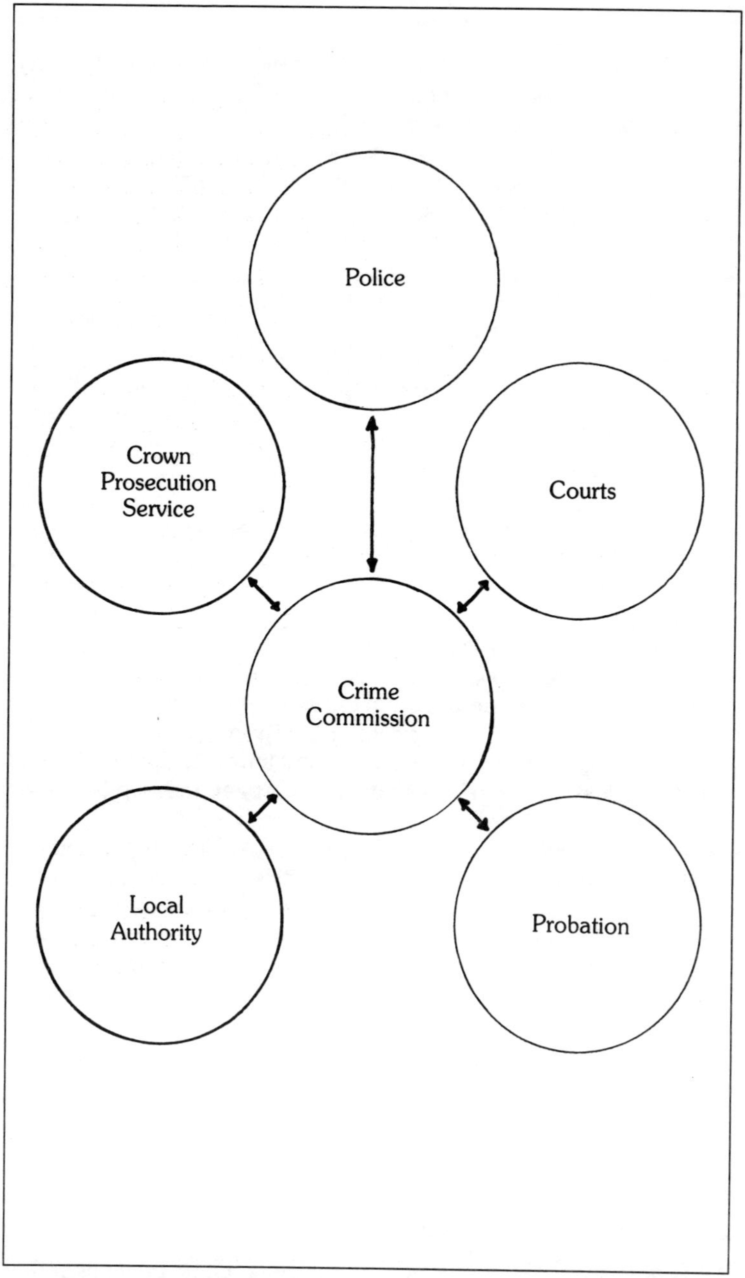

Figure 2.2 Network of corporate relationships in strategic planning (model 2)

Structures for collaboration

Much of the day to day work of collaboration takes place between individuals in informal contact [Vincent, 1980]. There are times however when people must meet together in a formal setting to discuss policy issues, to make decisions, to evaluate their work and to make collective plans. Not everyone agrees that formal structures are useful in interagency working; there are limits to collaboration and informal links are sometimes more likely to be fruitful than formal structures [Smith, 1988].

The creation of structures such as committees, forums or working parties is sometimes necessary to ensure that certain collaborative functions are fulfilled in a manner which is open and accountable. Arrangements that depend on personal contact between individuals in different agencies can be jeopardised by staff turnover [Magistrates' Association et al, 1978 p 16]. Formal committees can perpetuate themselves beyond the participation of individuals [Vincent, 1980 p 81]. Where practitioners or middle managers have not been given a clear mandate to pursue collaboration with other agencies, confusions and conflicts can arise. Where collaboration is to be pursued routinely, a clear agency policy is required to support this. The formalisation of certain types of collaboration is also necessary if it is important that such groups are to be held accountable for the decisions they make. The maintenance of open records of a committee's proceedings confers a greater degree of commitment than would be the case in informal, off the record agreements. Against this, it must be acknowledged that committees are sometimes the public face of private business, decisions perhaps having been made prior to the meetings.

Not all interagency meetings involve or need to involve decision making. There are numerous opportunities in the criminal justice system for people to meet each other in conferences, seminars and on various informal occasions. Many local justice systems are composed of a fairly small network of people, most of whom know each other well and meet fairly frequently. The establishment and development of collaboration might require the creation of an *infrastructure* that will enable collaboration to happen in an organised manner that is related to policy. In the final chapter we will look at proposals for establishing such infrastructures in local criminal justice strategies.

Cooperation in juvenile justice

It has been in the fields of juvenile justice and crime prevention that encouragement to cooperate has been most noticeable. This analysis offers material that adds to the more theoretical consideration above.

At national level cooperation takes place between central government departments and between the government and voluntary organisations. There is of course also conflict, resistance and opposition just as there is at local level. What governments have not done is to legislate for the creation of mechanisms that would allow local cooperation to flourish in the juvenile field, despite a number of recommendations that this should happen.

In one case, cooperation was given an incentive through the provision of funding. The DHSS offered, in 1983, grants for the development of intermediate treatment projects under its 'Circular LAC(83)3' on the condition that there was a partnership between the local authority and the recipient voluntary body. The circular made it clear that interagency management committees for the projects were desirable. By and large this was successful in bringing various organisations together and, through this collaboration, of considerably reducing the use of custody for juvenile offenders.

Interagency cooperation in the field of intermediate treatment has been advocated by a succession of governmental agencies over many years. The White Paper of 1968, on which the Children and Young Persons Act of 1969 and subsequent provision of intermediate treatment was based, stated:

> 'One major effect of the proposals described in this part will be to encourage and strengthen consultation and cooperation between juvenile court magistrates, the police, the local authority services concerned – including the schools – and the probation service. ... it will be suggested ... that they should arrange periodic meetings at which each are represented, to review the operation of the new procedures in their areas and to discuss how each can make the most effective contribution ...' [Home Office, 1968].

In the booklet issued by the DHSS in 1972, advising local authorities on how to develop and plan their intermediate treatment schemes, the point was further emphasised:

> 'To deploy effectively the resources available within the community for suitable forms of treatment, there will have to be early consultation and the fullest cooperation between the various local authority services and between statutory and voluntary agencies' [DHSS, 1972].

Three years later the House of Commons Expenditure Committee gave the 1969 Act a thorough going over and came up with this recommendation:

> 'We recommend that liaison committees – representing magistrates, teachers, social workers and probation officers should be set up in every local authority in respect of children and young people to discuss not only the progress of individual children in care or under supervision, but also

more general matters such as the development of intermediate treatment' [House of Commons, 1975].

In response to the Expenditure Committee, the Government issued a White Paper in 1976 in which they said that they:

> 'wholly share the committee's view of the importance of the closest cooperation at local level among all those who share responsibility for the care and control of young people who get into trouble ...' [Home Office et al, 1976b].

In the following year, the DHSS issued a circular to the local authorities in which they acknowledged the importance of coordination: ' ... general planning and coordination of different agencies are essential' [DHSS, 1977]. They did not however go on to advise the implementation of the White Paper's recommendation that local consultative machinery should be set up to bring together the wide range of agencies that share responsibility for young people in trouble. A Home Office circular, issued jointly with the DHSS, DES and the Welsh Office, addressed primarily to the police, stated that the primary rationale for cooperation was as follows: 'The prevention of juvenile delinquency is not the prerogative of any single agency' [Home Office, 1978] and it went on to state that:

> 'Although activities are (and often need to be) undertaken independently and there are often differences of approach, cooperation between all agencies is essential. A concerted approach can avoid misunderstandings, apparent clashes of interest, and wasteful duplication of effort. It can also lead to a constructive awareness of the respective roles and contributions of the different agencies and of the drawbacks to any of them acting in isolation'.

A group of MPs produced a report in 1981 which argued that

> 'the Government should consider whether a statutory duty should be imposed on local authorities to establish interagency committees and coordinate policies concerning juvenile delinquency' [Kilroy-Silk, 1981].

In the White Paper on young offenders the Government affirmed that it 'cannot emphasise too strongly the importance it attaches to such local co-operation' [Home Office et al, 1980a para 36] and went on to say how much it believed that increased consultation and coordination would help to effect reductions in juvenile crime. But it did not take the view that 'this can best be achieved by legislation'. Making people cooperate by act of parliament has not had a good track record in the annals of history. The Government therefore intended to 'continue to do everything possible to encourage interagency co-operation at a local level without imposing any centralised formula' [op cit].

The Government was not the only body to have thought along

these lines. In 1977 a group set up under the Personal Social Services Council concluded that:

> 'such a committee, positioned centrally, provides the framework within which the officers of different agencies, elected members and magistrates can establish an overview of the development of intermediate treatment facilities within the authority, assess their effectiveness and initiate steps to fill any gaps in the range of provision' [Personal Social Services Council, 1977].

In a report resulting from a project to involve voluntary agencies in intermediate treatment, Phil Hope, then working for the National Council of Voluntary Organisations, argued that

> 'The third major obstacle to the development of intermediate treatment is the present fragmentary nature of services for young people in trouble. In order to improve services, greater co-ordination between statutory agencies and between statutory and voluntary sectors at both national and local level is necessary' [Hope, 1981].

Thus there were several strands to the reasoning behind this emphasis on interagency approaches to the problem of juvenile crime. Several agencies were responsible for the operation of the various systems that responded to juvenile crime; thus responsibility was fragmentary and this led to clashes of interest between agencies. The system of response could not therefore perform coherently to achieve an overall set of goals and its development was slow and blocked by a variety of obstructions. Collaboration offered a means of making the contribution of any one agency more effective, avoided duplication of resources and parallel developments in response mechanisms, could fill gaps in provision and allow for the development of policy and planning. The rationale was conveniently summarised in a United States report:

> 'Experience has shown that good planning can result in better understanding of crime and criminal justice problems; greater co-operation among agencies and units of government; clearer objectives and priorities; more effective resource allocation; and better quality criminal justice programmes and personnel. Taken together, these results can increase public confidence in and support for criminal justice processes, thus enhancing system performance and, ultimately, the integrity of the law' [Cushman, 1980].

Our own government has expressed a similar view in the following terms:

> 'The increasing demands on all the criminal justice services from rising crime and pressure on resources make it all the more necessary both to preserve the services' independence and to develop the closest possible cooperation between them, both nationally and locally' [Home Office, 1986].

In its latest strategy statement, the Home Office continues to press for cooperation in tackling crime: 'co-operation and co-ordination are vital to the smooth working of the system' it says, in the last chapter entitled *Tackling crime together* [Home Office, 1989c, p 70].

Discussion: the lessons of history

What the above analysis demonstrates is that it has for a long time been the policy of central government to encourage and promote greater cooperation between and among the various agencies of criminal justice. This has been particularly true in the field of juvenile justice and crime prevention. Despite the rhetoric of such policy, few initiatives have been taken by the Government to provide any solid infrastructure through which such collaborative efforts might be channelled. One reason for this is that the Government has rightly understood that it cannot legislate that collaboration must happen among a network of autonomous bodies. There are some specific instances where consultation is required between agencies concerned with a particular problem (e.g. child abuse or mental health). But, the only example of government providing a legislative basis for collaboration was the Police and Criminal Evidence Act of 1984. Short of legislation, the only other method available to government is to provide funding for local initiatives on the basis that two or more bodies must work together in order to secure funding and this happened with the DHSS intermediate treatment initiative of 1983. That however only offered such funding to those who applied for it and the exact nature of local collaborative arrangements varied greatly amongst the 110 recipients of the grant-aid.

Policies favouring collaboration in juvenile justice seem to have poured fourth from government and other national bodies over the past twenty years but similar policy initiatives seem to have been comparatively lacking where the adult system is concerned. More recently, the increasing appreciation of interdependence is leading to a more accurate understanding of why collaboration is necessary in the criminal justice system and how exactly it needs to take place. The 1989 Home Office strategy statement on crime argues that 'independence does not mean isolation' and goes on to claim that many of the issues it describes are receiving a collective approach [Home Office, 1989c p 70]. The Home Office also acknowledges that the community must also be involved in patterns of local collaboration in responses to crime and this view has been expressed for some years now. The community is of course a broad term and some thought has gone into deciding which parts of the community need to be involved in what aspects of responses. One term used in the statement, rather incidentally, in fact deserves closer attention: *shared commitment.* Our discussion has pointed to a variety of ways in which agencies and groups can combine their efforts. What makes collaboration happen, and happen effectively, is the sharing of a commitment to a common goal or concern. It is this idea – the sharing of commitment – that will become highlighted when we begin to consider a strategic approach to crime responses.

Conclusions: towards an integrated response

Our discussion of responses to crime has covered much ground. Three sets of concepts have been considered:

fragmentation/integration
autonomy/interdependence
Independence/collaboration.

We have looked at the view that individual criminal justice organisations can make only a marginal impact on the crime problem. Yet, in their day to day operations and in terms of their effects on each other, these organisations present a network of policies, plans, operations and activities that produce a wide range of out-turns. The concept of an integrated response to crime assumes considerable importance if we accept that fragmentation is one of the key factors in reducing the effectiveness of the agencies of criminal justice in particular and of the wider patterns of response in general. But the concept of integration is not without its problems, not least that of ensuring that it does not lead to injustice and corruption or to the oppressive use of power. The very independence of the police, courts, lawyers and prosecutors is a check on the spread of corruption and malpractice, ensuring that the rights and liberties of citizens are maintained.

Each agency performs a specific set of functions that require knowledge and expertise of particular kinds. Criminal justice agencies, in common with most other networks, are grounded in a division of professional labour. Fragmentation and autonomy are, in this respect, functional. Organisational and professional autonomy has its advantages and disadvantages. On the one hand it protects rights of the individual and on the other it fragments the policy and planning functions that are necessary to the effective response of the various services involved. Feeney [1985] argues, correctly in my view, that fragmentation can be overcome through interagency coordination, consultation and liaison. Setting a clear purpose for that collaboration is equally if not more important.

It is justified that we conceive the criminal justice system as being composed of a set of autonomous agencies. The degree to which those agencies are autonomous depends on what characteristics or functions we choose to consider. If we take a systems view of criminal justice, then the conception relies less on autonomy and more on the interdependence of one agency with another, one set of functions with another and one role with another. Since this interdependence exists, each organisation can consider the degree to which collaboration with other organisations assists it in achieving its objectives or performing its duties effectively. The task of setting up and running collaborative exercises involves managing interrelationships between a variety of factors that define the boundaries of the exercise. The degree to which collaboration will be effective will be a function of the choices made concerning these interrelationships.

Collaboration, as we have noted, can be viewed in terms of multiagency approaches to particular issues or operations. If the development of multiagency responses is to be effective, there must be an infrastructure to enable this to happen. Multiagency approaches have been tried in many areas over a long period of time. These experiences have been recorded and can be used to reach a theory of multiagency collaboration. The discussion in this chapter on levels of collaboration suggests a theoretical framework in which agency's collective policy and planning processes can be examined and developed. Such theory will contribute much where there is to be a collective strategy of responding to crime, particularly in local areas. In weighing up the pros and cons we must try to assess the consequences for society of an integrated response to crime. Corporate approaches could be seen as achieving a highly integrated response to crime, but there are dangers in corporatism which must be recognised before we move in that direction. There are also, I would argue, dangers in allowing the present weak and fragmentary response to crime to continue.

The lack of integration in responses that we see in the current picture is a consequence of there being no overall authority responsible for the strategic planning of responses at local level. In the final chapter I offer an approach to dealing with the problems of fragmentary responses to crime by coordinating and integrating into a coherent strategy the various influences, policies and services that can be shown to affect the rate of crime in a local area and, more widely, at national level.

3 The strategic approach

Introduction

The previous chapters attempted to show that the way in which society has responded to crime has been ineffective. The failure of responses to crime was explained by the fragmentary systems of crime control and the lack of coordination amongst criminal justice agencies. The systems of response are composed of autonomous yet interdependent organisations that cannot individually make any great impact on crime and cannot function effectively without the cooperation of the other parts of the system.

Strategic planning offers the means by which to increase the effectiveness of responses to crime. For such an increase to be achieved, the problems inherent in fragmentation need to be solved. This is most likely to happen through the management of interdependence and by building on the opportunities offered by a collaborative approach. A comprehensive and integrated approach to the planning of responses to crime is the alternative to fragmentation. These ideas can be summarised in the concept of a crime response and criminal justice strategy. Improvements in responses to crime can be achieved through the development of a strategic approach, applied comprehensively to a local area and supported by a complementary national strategy. Before moving to considering what a strategic response to crime might look like, the concept of strategy is discussed; this is a necessary exercise because the term 'strategy' is used more widely than it is clearly defined.

What is strategy?

The term 'strategy' is being used with increasing frequency in the field of crime and justice. The authors of the Home Office policy statement *Criminal Justice* [Home Office, 1986] use the phrase 'the

Government's strategy for tackling crime.' The same terminology can be found in the 1989 statement, in which chapter one is called *A strategy to tackle crime* [Home Office, 1989c]. It is clear that there has been something of a shift in recent years from using the term 'policy' in referring to a body of ideas, beliefs or proposed actions relating to an issue towards using the term 'strategy' to refer to much the same thing. That is not to say that use of the term 'policy' has declined, only that some of its previous usage has been replaced. It is not terribly clear, however, whether the Home Office writers are using the term 'strategy' as a generalised concept, as a synonym for policy and planning or as a technical term derived from operational management. There is not a great deal of talk about 'strategic planning' in the Home Office's public outputs on crime and justice. Other government departments, however, have latched onto strategic planning and some have officers or departments responsible for this aspect of their organisation. In central government an *Efficiency Strategy* was inaugurated by Sir Derek (now Lord) Rayner in 1979 to improvement management and efficiency [Metcalfe and Richards, 1987 p2]. This and various other aspects of central government administration have brought significant changes to the services concerned with criminal justice, as is evidenced by the scrutinies now taking place and the reports being produced by such bodies as the Audit Commission.

The term 'strategy' has also lodged itself in the criminal justice field generally. During the 1980s it became fashionable, in the field of juvenile justice, to talk about 'strategies for dealing with young offenders'. More recently, those in the field of crime prevention have begun to think in terms of preventive strategies. The term 'strategic planning' has not caught on in criminal justice circles in this country to the same extent that it has in the United States where it appeared in several studies during the 1970s. It has however appeared in other aspects of public life: in the health service, in the energy industry, in unemployment services and in certain sections of the voluntary sector. This country has produced little evidence of the application of a strategic planning approach to responses to crime, other than somewhat vague references to various 'strategies'.

A strategy is a coherent approach to achieving a *vision*, undertaking a *mission* and fulfilling a *purpose*. This is true for an individual, an organisation and for a system of organisations. A strategy is concerned with bringing about change, with making things happen and with increasing effectiveness. A crime response strategy will be concerned with making an effective impact on the problem of crime, with bringing about change in the crime that is committed and with changing the effectiveness of response systems. If we are to be effective in a task, then we must be able to identify those factors that are critical to our success: factors that are strategically important in determining the degree to which we will be successful in fulfilling our purpose. A strategy specifies what is critical to effectiveness and relates together the critical elements of goals, priorities, plans, methods, resources and information.

Strategy combines together the functions of policy, planning, information and operation. A strategy translates goals, priorities and principles into plans, operations and practices. In so far as strategy is about change, then it is about ordered change, the direction, rate and extent of change. The term change, as used here, can refer to a variety of things: to increasing the effectiveness of achievement, to making more impact on a problem (such as crime), to responding to external demands or variations and so on. In devising a strategy some definition of timescale is usually made: sometimes people refer to a 'long term strategy' or to a 'short term strategy'. Sometimes a single organisation will have a variety of strategies, reflecting the various functions performed within that organisation; a sales strategy, research and product development strategy, a growth strategy and so on. These sub-strategies are part of an overall business strategy from which they draw their objectives. When we refer to a 'crime response strategy' it is very likely that a series of sub-strategies will be implied.

The same approach can be applied to any criminal justice organisation; we can, for example, look at strategic policing, a strategic plan for a police force or we could devise a strategy for a probation service and indeed some probation services do now have corporate strategy statements. There is a statement of the Crown Prosecution Services's strategy [Green, 1987]. The same set of processes apply equally well to a system of organisations, depending on there being a group of people who equate to the senior management in an organisation.

One of the central arguments of this book is that responses to crime should be based on a *comprehensive* strategy. A crime response strategy will not work effectively if it is confined to only one segment of the whole problem or to one or two criminal justice agencies. Crime strategies pose some very fundamental choices and priorities: do we give priority to prevention or to criminal justice? Do we put increased funds into the probation service or the prison service? Should we increase the number of police officers or the number of judges? These are by no means unusual choices: politicians have to make such choices across a vast range of social and economic policies. Such choices will depend on the management capacity of those in the organisations that will implement strategy since there is no point in devising a large-scale strategy that is beyond the capacity of those whose task is to develop and manage it. Part of the strategy might, however, be about increasing management capacity and effectiveness.

Strategies can be developed through intentional processes and we will be looking at these later. But, strategies emerge in other ways. Some organisations realise that they have a strategy without having intentionally developed it. Others might claim to have a strategy and can articulate it but there is no evidence of it being put into practice [Johnson and Scholes, 1988, p 27].

Most organisations or systems (such as the criminal justice system) depend on decisions. Decision making is the core function which drives an organisation. People who want an organisation to be successful, to achieve results, want to make the right decisions. They also want to make the right decisions about those things that are most important. This is what strategy is all about: achieving success, knowing what choices are most important and being able to make the right decisions about those aspects that are critical to success.

Strategic thinking

At several points in this book reference will be made to 'strategic thinking' rather than to strategy. We might refer to 'being able to think strategically about crime prevention' or to 'applying strategic thinking to the problem of imprisonment'. Strategy, in this sense, is not an activity but a way of thinking about problems or needs and what should be done. Strategic planning is, however, an activity in that planning is something that is done, although of course it must be thought about in order to be done. Strategic thinking is the capacity to think clearly about why something needs to be done, what needs to be done and how to do it effectively. If we think strategically about a task, then we will be clear about the goals to be achieved, clear about what are the most effective elements of the task that will contribute to its achievement and clear about the methods that should be employed in order to achieve maximum success. This requires thinking about the task, organisation and system *as a whole*. Strategic thinking about crime 'looks at all the components in the system and the causes of broad trends' [Falkin, 1979 p 5]. Strategic thinking about responses to crime looks at preventive responses, all parts of the criminal justice system, social services, probation services and social and economic policies that influence the rate of crime. What I hope this chapter will achieve is to set out *clearly what strategy* is and what 'thinking strategically' amounts to. This, I hope, will help those concerned with or working in the criminal justice system to apply the techniques involved in strategy development and strategic planning and move them away from using the term 'strategic' as a cosmetic adjective.

Vision

Mission

Goals

Why does the system exist?

Principles

What are the root values?

Priorities

Which aspects of the system are crucial to its success?

Resources

How is the system to operate?

Figure 3.1 Components of strategy

Components of strategy

Strategic thinking requires that we concentrate on four essential elements of organisation: *goals* (the purposes of the system), *principles* (values, concepts, guidelines), *priorities* (relative values) and *resources* (with which goals are to be achieved). These components are listed in **Figure 3.1.** Thinking about these components requires four questions to be answered: (1) *Why does the system exist?* This calls for a statement of purposes, goals, aims and objectives. (2) *What are the root values involved in the system?* This requires a statement of the fundamental ideas on which the development and operation of the system will be based. (3) *Which aspects of the system are crucial to its success?* This requires clarity of direction, definition of progress and a grasp of the relative importance of various aspects of the system. (4) *How is the system to operate?* This requires a specification of the physical, financial, personal and conceptual resources that will be required and how these will be deployed.

These basic questions can be applied to a system as a whole (such as a criminal justice system), to individual organisations (for example, a probation service) or to a particular function (such as sentencing).

Each of these questions interrelate, except that the question about *why* relates only downwards, since it provides the irreducible foundation for the system (as far as the strategy internally is concerned). Questions about *why* and *what* are policy components; questions about *which* and *how* are primarily planning components, though this distinction is not wholly watertight.

The scope of a strategy

A strategy sets the scope and rate of change: the *scope* of change determines how much change should take place and the *rate* of change determines the speed at which changes need to be made in order to achieve optimal impact. The appropriate scale of the change must relate to the ability of the organisation or group of organisations to manage that change. Setting the right rate of change is important since there are dangers in attempting to bring about change either too quickly or too slowly.

Strategies must also have *boundaries*; a strategy to reduce crime in a local area is both bounded by the area and by the limits of what can be included in the strategy. Deciding what the scope of a strategy should be is often one of the hardest functions of formulation. The problem of crime can be traced out beyond offending to wider and yet wider social and economic circumstances. A crime response strategy can be seen as being composed of a variety of more specific strategies: of crime prevention, of law enforcement, of justice, of social and rehabilitative programmes and so on. There is no rule which can be applied to defining the scope of a strategy; it is a matter of judgement. In an organisation, judgements about the scope of its strategy relate to the boundaries of its duties and responsibilities, what activities it can (or should) and cannot (or should not) undertake. These judgements also involve relating strategic scope to an organisation's resources or powers. It would be unwise to set a scope that is beyond the organisation's capacity.

Vision and mission

Two terms are often used in discussions about strategy: 'vision' and 'mission'. These are everyday terms but in planning they have a technical definition. A strategic *vision* is an expression of what is to be achieved through mission; it defines what the state of affairs will be if the goals of the strategy are achieved. A strategic vision, for an organisation, is a clear idea about an organisation's purpose – why it exists, what are its aims and goals, what it wishes to achieve and by when and its strategies – how it will go about getting there [Beck, 1988 p 1]. Vision was one of the headings used by the Audit Commission in their report on local government in 1983. In this report, they asked local authorities if there was a summary statement of the aims of the council's major services. They also asked if there was any statement of the most significant changes that the council expected.

Change is more likely to occur successfully if there is a clear vision of what is desired and what constitutes success in achieving it. A *mission* is the authority to pursue a vision, the giving of a 'go ahead' to get on with the work. The mission of the criminal justice system is partly conferred by Parliament and government agencies and partly by local authorities. In certain respects the courts system is an exception to this in that it sets its own mission to the extent that the 'separation of powers' principle operates. The missions for most criminal justice organisations derive from public policy processes. It has been suggested that a national framework agreement should be created for magistrates courts (for the first time) that would set out clear overall objectives and priorities for the service [Home Office, 1989 para 9.5]. Would this represent a formulation of vision and mission? The Home Office scrutiny team, in its work on magistrates courts, believed that 'it is vital to maintain a distinction between the agency's management functions and wider criminal justice policy objectives.' This would not seem to accord with current theories of effective strategic planning. To achieve effectiveness ends and means must be related strategically. A mission to fulfil a purpose cannot therefore be separated from the management mission to put that purpose into practice.

In some respects, a mission is that part of a policy which states goals (aims, objectives, targets) and specifies the role of an organisation. A mission is therefore the definition and authorisation of the purpose and role of an organisation or system of organisations. We can define a mission for a system of organisations, such as the criminal justice system, as well as for individual agencies, such as a police force or the Crown Prosecution Service. Having a strategic vision and a clear mission is what contributes to effective action. A probation service that has a clear vision of its purpose and a mission to achieve that purpose is far more likely to be successful than a service where there is no clear idea of what is to be done and no sense of mission to get on and do it.

These two terms have been used in business to express the purpose of an enterprise. They can be found in discussions of strategic planning where they have been used to indicate the thrust and direction of a strategy. The vision of a company that sells, for example, computers is to achieve a certain level of profit, a specific place in the ranking of computer retailing companies, a percentage of the computer sales market and a desired return to its investors. This vision is translated into a corporate mission for the business as a whole (the authority being conferred by the shareholders), a mission for the sales department (e.g. to achieve its sales targets), a mission for the research and information department (e.g. to provide effective marketing services) and to the administration department (e.g. to support the work of other departments). Vision and mission provide the core of the strategy; they define why something is to be done, how it is to be done and what indicators will show when it has been done. If a clear vision and mission can be expressed and communicated to those who work in the organisation, then there is more chance that the organisation will be effective. Vision and mission need to be shared by all who work in an organisation or system, not only the senior managers. The communication of clear messages about what the vision and mission are enables people to share in them; but motivation to share in them is also important. Responses to crime depend on people who produce them having a common purpose.

Finally vision and mission should not be assumed or taken for granted; neither are they abstract 'states of consciousness'. An organisation or a system should have a written statement of its vision and a statement of its mission, which has been carefully and systematically formulated and exactly worded so as to provide a reference for those who engage in policy and planning.

All systems and operations that are organised will have three elements: policy, planning and information. These are closely related and must be carefully integrated if a strategy is to be successful. Policy and strategy have similar characteristics and for this reason they are sometimes confused. Some policies are strategic but not all policy is strategic. We will be considering these in detail in the next three chapters but for the moment as brief introduction to these concepts is offered

Policy

A policy, as we shall see in the next chapter, includes a statement of the goals of the organisation or system. A policy also states the definitions, boundaries, principles and requirements that are used to set up and to operate a system. We could assume that the primary goal of responding to crime is to reduce it; this is perhaps more realistic than assuming that we can eliminate it. If crime reduction is our keystone goal then other strategic goals and objectives should be related to it. Other goals might of course be of value in themselves, such as fairness or equality. Because response to crime is necessarily a large and complex field, a variety of goals will be found within the responsive systems (prevention, diversion, justice, etc.). Each of the organisations involved in the law enforcement and criminal justice systems will have its own set of goals. A *strategic* choice is deciding which, if any, of these goals deserves to be given priority over others. A policy therefore is what defines the purpose of the strategy; it is the foundation on which planning is built. It sets out the characteristics of the strategy and acts as a reference for those who are to be involved in it. It reflects the vision of what is to be achieved and the mission to achieve it.

Planning

Planning is a process through which policy is put into practice. It is about organising what is to be done in the future. It is the process of bringing about desired out-turns. I have used the terms 'organisation' and 'management' to indicate very broad and general ideas; policy, planning and strategy are the major functions that are employed in management in order to produce organisation.

Once a strategy has been devised and formulated it must be put into operation and that is a process that involves planning. If we accept the idea that responses to crime should involve a variety of organisations, then we must ask who will be responsible for planning at the corporate level. This question is considered in the final chapter. I realise that the term 'corporate' has particular connotations; it is often associated with single organisations but can also suggest a collective and collaborative association of organisations and services.

Planning is a task carried out by people and if we are to devise effective systems of planning then we must be clear with whom responsibility for planning is to be located at least as far as corporate planning is concerned. This is currently one of the missing links in the system of organisation and management of local criminal justice systems. An essential preparation for planning is to get a clear idea of what it involves. Planning should be based on clearly understood ideas and concepts; it is a complex task and common sense is insufficient as a foundation for pursuing it. The practice of effective planning requires techniques and methods rather than intuition; it is a practice that requires a degree of discipline. To practice planning we must 'tool up' our minds with a set of concepts and equip ourselves with skills and knowledge. Planning is a craft and its quality is dependent on the 'tools' available for its practice and on the skill with which those tools are applied.

The following two chapters of this book consider policy and planning in some detail and will, I hope, make the distinction between them clear. Even though it might seem from this discussion that policy and planning are quite distinct functions or activities, in practice they are often indistinguishable. The aim of separating them conceptually is to examine them and to improve the way in which they are practised.

Information

Information, in a variety of forms, is gathered, analysed and used throughout all the processes involved in strategic planning and plays a central role in policy formulation, providing feedback to managers and others to show how planning is working or failing to work. Information provides indicators of the operational performance of a system. Information about the critical success factors of an organisation or system will indicate the extent to which a strategy is or is not effective. This process of gathering and using information in an organisation is often referred to as a 'strategic information system'. As we shall see in chapter six, information takes a variety of forms: data, statistics, maps, diagrams, descriptions, lists and so on. Information is of vital importance because strategy relies so heavily on making informed decisions, on making the best choice between options and alternatives and on knowing what is happening within an operational system. Information is a fundamental process of organisation and management.

Falkin's approach to strategic planning relies very much on information [Falkin, 1979]. Falkin developed a computer simulation of California's juvenile justice system and used this as a tool for informing policy and planning decisions. Information about the operation of the system and about key variables in crime rates, was introduced to a simulation model. This then provided a mechanism for deriving conclusions about the relative merits of policy options and for making decisions about the cost-effectiveness of various programs.

Strategic planning

Strategic planning has been developed in a variety of disciplines, most notably in management science. It is often employed to signify a specific approach to planning. The term 'strategic planning' became fashionable in the 1960s and some would even say this was its 'golden age' [Brehny and Hall, 1984]. It was used in military operations, civil engineering, business, town planning, local and regional government and energy systems. Often it was associated with long term planning. Its heyday was however short-lived, probably not more than a decade. It went out of fashion when people failed to make it deliver the results its proponents claimed for it. In the rapid social, economic and political change that characterised the 1970s it became increasingly difficult to make long term plans. Recession, inflation, the cold war, the arms race and various other uncertainties about the future brought about a retreat from planning into pragmatism. People (such as Peter Hall) began to write about 'great planning disasters' and 'planning blight'. In local government, subjected to strictures, restrictions, cutbacks and increasing control by central government, planning gave way to day to day struggle for survival. In an environment of increasing uncertainty, long term planning was abandoned as being impractical.

Whilst academics and practitioners (in various fields) alike supported the need for a systematic and theoretically founded methodology for planning, the onslaught of the Conservative Party on the fabric of local government and its centres for planning (such as the

GLC) led to a retreat from the ground that had been gained. There was also a retreat from theory:

> 'Professional and academic attitudes have changed just as dramatically. There is now a yawning gulf between theorists and practitioners, with the former showing very little interest in practice and the latter often displaying anti-intellectual hostility towards academics' [Brehny and Hall, 1984 p 96].

Strategic planning is now enjoying a renaissance, particularly in the world of business. Planners have learned to work with shorter timescales, to adapt the notion of strategy to the environment of the 1980s, to work with uncertainty and to face up to change rather than being flummoxed by it. Strategic planning has, to some extent, become a method of managing the present rather than the future. What has contributed to this revival of strategic planning has been, in part, a redefinition of its task and also the development of the theoretical foundation on which the practice can be based.

Strategic planning is currently becoming very widespread in business and management, both in the private and public sectors. In this country it is often referred to as corporate planning (especially in business circles), though corporate and strategic planning are not always one and the same thing. It is also referred to as 'strategic management' though some degree of definitional fuzziness often creeps into such permutations of terms. Some writers suggest that we can distinguish between strategic and operational planning (concentrating on changes in structure, capabilities and capacities), long range and short range planning (defined by timescale) and corporate and partial planning (defined by organisational scope) [Baynes, 1973 based on the work of Adler]. This distinction between corporate and strategic planning seems to be based simply on the setting in which such planning is conducted.

The importance of strategic planning to public and voluntary sector organisations has been stressed in the following terms:

> 'strategic thought and action are increasingly important to the continued viability and effectiveness of governments, public agencies and non-profit organisations of all sorts. Without strategic planning it is unlikely that these organisations will be able to meet successfully the numerous challenges that face them' [Bryson, 1988 p 74].

A bold claim but one that is very pertinent in the contemporary political climate where the public sector is on the defensive against policies seeking to emphasize free market enterprise rather than state provided services. What strategic planning offers is a set of conceptual tools with which politicians, chief executives, managers and research and development staff can steer their organisations in a determined direction. Steering and controlling organisations requires thinking, decision making and action. To move forward and to keep to a determined route, these three factors must be applied coherently, not only at the 'top' but throughout the organisation.

The revolution in new technology and information systems has also provided planners with more powerful conceptual and analytical equipment than was available in the 1960s. This has led to increases in the credibility of strategic planning as well as to its effectiveness. The difference between a strategy and a strategic plan is perhaps academic. Both have to be devised, formulated or designed. A criminal justice strategy is concerned to identify the key variables on which crime rates depend and the most important components in the system of responses to crime. Falkin [1979] emphasises a policy oriented approach to strategic planning. When I began to read Falkin's book, I was very impressed by this emphasis on policy; although still impressed, I have shifted away from seeing policy as being of prime importance in strategic planning to giving both policy and planning about the same degree of importance. This is because, even if a very good policy has been formulated, it still remains to be put into effect.

Without equally good planning, good policy remains inert, unable to realise its full potential. In reaching this position, I have had to think about the difference between policy and planning and have done this more widely than in the context of criminal justice. My view is that strategic planning is a discipline in so far as it has a theoretical framework and a body of practice. It is however a discipline that is practised more without the conscious attachment of the label 'strategic planning' than with. People in central government departments, local authorities, statutory and voluntary bodies and businesses engage in strategic planning but often do so without attaching a specific label to such activities. It is not important what we call it; but what is important is applying sets of theories and methods to this task in order to make it effective.

If the task of strategic planning is to be improved then it must be subjected to the same interplay of theory and practice that is central to all complex professional processes. It has long been possible to identify and to develop theories that relate to management; we can say that there is a set of disciplines called 'management science' and, more recently, people have talked of 'policy science'. In the same way, a set of theoretical foundations to strategic planning can be identified and articulated.

Strategic planning is undertaken in criminal justice but often without being referred to as such. Those whose task it is to undertake strategic planning of responses to crime can improve their performance and effectiveness by increasing their knowledge of these theoretical foundations. There is probably not a single theory of strategic planning but sets of theoretical formulations that allow it to be developed. Some of these theories relate to policy, some to information, some to systems analysis and others to operational research, organisational studies and so on. Whilst we currently see some criminal justice organisations practising strategic planning some of the time, my hope for the future is that all these organisations will come to practice it all of the time.

The process of strategic planning.

Strategic planning involves activity; as with most activities, it can be conducted effectively if those who are pursuing it have access to the theoretical foundations of what they are doing. Whilst strategic planning does have well established foundations in theory, there is no one 'theory of strategic planning' and, consequently, there is no absolutely 'correct' way of doing it. In this respect, strategic planning is an art rather than a science. There are however certain aspects of the process of strategic planning that are widely accepted as being of fundamental importance. To show how a process might be devised, let us consider the example offered by Bryson. He argues that 'usually key decision makers need a reasonably structured process to help them identify and resolve the most important issues their organisations face' [Bryson, 1988 p 74]. He outlines one such process which, he maintains, has proved to be effective in practice. The process consists of eight steps; these can be very briefly summarised as follows. (1) '*Development of an initial agreement concerning the strategic planning effort*'. Bryson quite rightly regards the starting point as being getting agreement on who should coordinate the strategic planning process, designing a process and marshalling the resources to undertake it. A strategy is not something that can be formulated effectively on a trial and error basis.

(2) '*Identification and classification of mandates*'. Bryson's article is concerned with public and non-profit organisations (such as charities) and he sees these as being given mandates from higher authorities such as legislation, government departments or trustees. These mandates stem from public policies and, as we shall see in the next chapter, stress is laid on the factor of public policy in determining what criminal justice agencies should be doing in their responses to crime. These mandates determine what the organisation must do and allows planners to decide what they can or cannot do.

(3) '*Development and clarification of mission and values*'. A mission is articulated in a 'mission statement'. This proclaims the organisation's reason for existence. Bryson says that a stakeholder must exist (that is, a group or body of people that has a stake in the organisation) to provide the organisation with the mission. In police forces, for example, the stakeholder would be the police authority as a representative of the rate payers. The mission of the police force might be to protect the public from crime, to maintain the enforcement of law and to keep order on the streets.

(4) '*External environmental assessment*'. All organisations exist in a 'political, economic, social and technological' environment in which there are trends, events, changes and values. Bryson argues that this external environment must be analysed in order to identify the 'opportunities and threats the organisation faces'. The process of environmental scanning will be discussed later.

(5) '*Internal organisation assessment*'. Bryson's next step requires an analysis of the strengths and weaknesses of the organisation. Three assessment categories are suggested: resources, present strategy (or process) and performance. Since he is discussing strategic planning within organisations, these make good sense. A more developed model of organisation analysis is that offered by Meltzner and Bellavita in their work on policy and organisations [see Chapter 7 of Meltzner and Bellavita, 1983]. We shall be looking later at the significance of strategic planning for organisation and management. So far, Bryson's process follows familiar principles of analysing external and internal environments and assumes conventional concepts of input and output systems. This approach is reflected in Falkin's view of strategic planning in criminal justice [Falkin, 1979] and in many of the writings on policy formulation. Some readers might find these initial steps rather basic and somewhat obvious and be uncertain as to their value or relevance. It is often because fundamental issues of this kind are not included in such processes that planners lose their way in subsequent and more complex stages of their work. In strategic planning it is desirable, if not necessary, to state the obvious and to do so in simple terms. If the purpose and mission of an organisation are in fact known and clearly understood then these steps can be completed rapidly. It is surprising however how difficult it can be to make these fundamental statements.

(6) '*Strategic issue identification*'. Bryson defines strategic issues as 'fundamental policy questions affecting the organisation's mandates, mission and values, product or service level and mix, clients, users or payers, cost, financing, management or organisational designs'. He goes on to explain that strategic issues embody conflicts (or, I would argue, choices) and these may be over (or about) ends, means, philosophy, location, timing and who might be helped or hurt by different ways of resolving the issue. Although Bryson does not make sufficiently clear how we can identify those issues that are intrinsically *strategic*, the general thrust of his discussion leads to the conclusion that *strategic* issues are those that will determine the success or failure of the organisation's mission.

(7) '*Strategy development*'. In discussing this step, Bryson offers a definition of strategy: 'a *strategy* is a *pattern* of purposes, policies, programmes, actions, decisions and/or resource allocations that define what an organisation is, what it does and why it does it' [Bryson, 1988 p 77]. Whilst this definition is understandable, it fails to pull out

and explain the significance of the term *pattern*. Bryson is correct to stress the word *pattern* because all of the components that follow do conform to a pattern when they are strategic. But what is *strategic* about them is their fundamental importance to the achievement of outcomes, their contribution to the organisation's successes, or to its effective performance. Bryson goes on to discuss a process of strategy development; this is fairly conventional so it need not be annotated here other than to mention that it includes identifying practical alternatives (a concept to which we shall return in the following chapters on policy and planning) and also the idea of 'vision'. Strategy development requires the formulation of action planning and work programmes.

Bryson concludes his discussion of this step with a very useful comment:

> 'An effective strategy must meet several criteria. It must be technically workable, politically acceptable to key stakeholders, and must accord with the organisation's philosophy and core values. It must also be ethical, moral and legal!' [Bryson, 1988 p 77].

(8) '*Description of the organisation in the future*'. The final step in Bryson's process is the description of the organisation's 'vision of success'. To formulate this part of the process, planners might ask 'What will be the best possible results if this strategy is successfully implemented?' Bryson points out, quite rightly, that these steps do not necessarily happen sequentially; planning groups might have to go back a couple of steps and review their work and then jump forward a few steps before they are satisfied that they have completed the process. A strategic planning process is not undertaken on a one-off basis but is a periodic activity; most commonly it is an annual cycle. Not all steps need to be repeated annually; reassessment of mandate, mission and vision may remain constant over long periods but external and internal environment assessments are, to some extent or other, necessarily conducted annually.

What Bryson offers is not a 'correct' way of organising a strategic planning process but one model of such a process. Similarities will be found between this process and those contained in the subsequent chapters where we discuss policy formulation and the process of planning. Bryson has helped us to recognise that strategic planning is an organised activity that should itself be planned and that the success of the whole operation depends upon the quality of the process adopted. In order to practice strategic planning it is necessary to understand what it is, what it is designed to produce (its out-turn) and what conceptual tools can be employed in such practice. Strategic planning processes can be used by police forces, probation services, the Prison Service, by interagency groups concerned with crime prevention or diversion and so on. In our final chapter, the argument is set down that strategic planning should be used by local interagency groups to comprehensively organise all responses to crime in a local area.

Strategy and decision making

Policy formulation and planning can be viewed as processes of decision making. Such decisions are fitted together using the framework of strategy. Various levels of decision making can be identified: firstly, definitional and fundamental decisions, such as deciding on the goals of a system or organisation, articulating basic principles on which action can be based, defining boundaries of responsibility and so on. Here we may be concerned with the corporate strategy of a group of organisations, or the strategy of a single organisation. These decisions characterise policy formulation, as will be seen in the next chapter. Secondly, we can identify a range of decisions related to operational planning. These are decisions about how to implement policy, how to translate objectives into methods of operation, how to apply principles to practice, what performance indicators to select that will indicate success or failure or identify blockages and problems in operation. These decisions will have a fundamental affect on the performance of the system or organisation and often they will require choices to be made between alternative possibilities.

In formulating a strategy a large number of decisions will be made; many of these will interrelate and it is necessary therefore that each of them is made in the knowledge of how other decisions will be affected. A decision network could be prepared that will show the connections between decisions. Key decisions are those which affect many other dependent decisions and these are likely to be the most strategic. Friend and Hickling [1987] emphasise the importance of making these fundamental decisions, which they regard as being *strategic* choices. In particular, they look at how decisions are linked and offer a number of techniques for clarifying the decision making process such as defining decisions areas, drawing decision trees and so forth.

Strategic choice

In responding to social problems there is seldom a set of absolutely correct solutions; it is often necessary to make choices between various options, possibilities or opportunities. Some things are more *possible* or feasible than others. The advantages and disadvantages associated with any particular criminal justice option need to be analysed [Bishop, 1988]. The making of strategic choices is based on strategic analysis; this is 'concerned with understanding the strategic position of the organisation' [Johnson and Scholes, 1988, p 10]. This requires several questions to be asked: what changes are taking place in the outside world? How will such changes affect the organisation or system? What impact will such changes have on resources and how are they being deployed? Are resources being used effectively? Will changes taking place now or in the future require fundamental shifts in priorities? Questions such as these characterise a strategic analysis within an organisation. The aim of '*strategic analysis* is to form a view of the key influences on the present and future well-being of the organisation and therefore on the choice of strategy' [Johnson and Scholes, 1988, p 12].

If something is thought to be possible, it is necessary to determine under what conditions it is possible. If we are tackling a problem, then what are the possible solutions and how do we choose between them? What factors are thought to be of central importance in choosing one option or solution from others? Making strategic choices depends on how opportunities and constraints are evaluated, on what options are considered to be feasible and desirable and on priorities. Strategic choices in responding to crime are dependent on, for example, how crime problems are defined or perceived, the availability of resources, the importance that is attached to maintaining ethical practices in work with offenders, and so on [Bishop, 1988, p 57]. We might need to analyse the pros and cons in both the short-term and in the long-term. Some options might be expensive but more reliable in achieving results. Other options might be cheaper but have undesirable consequences.

Part of our analysis of options might involve an assessment of how effective they might be and what conditions their effectiveness will depend on. To assess the likely effectiveness of particular options we should relate them back to the relevant aims and objectives. To what extent does an option fit with the goals of the system or organisation? It is these processes that lie at the heart of the development of a *strategic* approach. Strategic choice is about the connectedness of one decision with another and involves a readiness to look for patterns of connectedness between decisions in a manner that is judgemental and selective [Friend and Hickling, 1987 pp 27–33]. They also explain that there are various modes in the process of making strategic choices: a *shaping* mode which takes a variety of inputs from a problem, a *designing* mode in which possible courses of action are thought up, a *comparing* mode in which their consequences are assessed and a *choosing mode* in which commitments are made to proposals. These interconnect and form a cyclical process (op cit, pages 19 and 22].

Another dimension of strategic choice is the question of methods. We looked at the question of how to relate options for action to goals. Part of this is about the relationship between ends and means. We need criteria for choosing between available methods, criteria that will indicate which methods are the best. When we come to make a strategic choice we must be able to estimate the consequences of that choice. Consequences rely on the degree of certainty that the outcome will be achieved; if we can estimate only a low degree of certainty of being successful then we might decide that this is not a good option to choose. This issue is discussed by Pepinsky [1980]. He looks at how we can evaluate the chances of controlling particular crime rates. Information can be gathered and analysed to assess the value of a proposed strategy. Once the strategy has been implemented, monitoring data assists us to evaluate the degree to which the out-turn was achieved and how it compared to the desired outcomes. Pepinsky claims that the best laid plans to change crime rates can consist of no more than some educated guesses. This approach gives rise to a number of difficulties. Crime control planners, he argues, can make two types of error in their predictions: a 'type I error' or 'false positive' in which something is done but unnecessarily and a 'type II error' or 'false negative' in which something is not done or is insufficiently done to improve a situation or keep it from getting worse. He also argues that errors tend to compound each other; two small errors can contribute to create a great big one. We can choose to avoid 'type I errors' or 'type II errors' but not both, he argues.

Another aspect of prediction is that the bigger the problem, the greater the degree of uncertainty that there will be a solution. Rates of burglary for several million people can be predicted more reliably than for a small housing estate. Rare crimes are almost impossible to predict compared to frequently committed offences. Pepinsky argues that some crime control strategies have been abandoned before they have begun to work because planners wrongly predicted the expected rate of change. This was partly due to errors in modelling and partly due to failure to use correct measures in monitoring implementation and outcome. In discussing what crime planners should control, Pepinsky lists the following:

Measures of crime
- Convictions
- Police data (e.g. arrests)
- Victimisation

Measures of criminality (i.e. criminals)
- Incarcerations
- Self-report studies
- Recidivism

Measures of costs
- Cost-benefit analysis

Though insufficiently thorough, Pepinsky's analysis does illustrate two well established measures: the number of crimes and the number of offenders. It is possible that the crime rate will increase if the same number of offenders commit crimes more frequently. You can work out other permutations of this principle yourself. There are pointers here for strategic planning. If we are to control crime then we must decide what it is that we are to control; that decision will reflect, among other things, the controllability of factors relative to available resources. Pepinsky's approach to planning relies on setting out to change various rates; this is a positivist approach but one that is generally closely related to the use of data in the monitoring of criminal justice systems. In his view, we can only know if a strategy has been successful if we can measure its impact, that is, detect changes in rates. For that to be valid we must be sure that there is a direct relationship between the implementation of the strategy and the rates we are using to measure such impact. This is fine in principle but poses considerable difficulties in practice.

Effectiveness, efficiency and economy in strategic planning

These initial stages of constructing a strategy lead on to issues about how effective it will be, the opportunities and constraints surrounding strategic choices and those relating to availability of resources and how resources are best deployed. These are topical issues in the public sector. The government is currently engaged in a campaign to promote or to inflict 'efficiency, economy and effectiveness' in or on public sector organisations. On the face of it this sounds sensible and rational, though, for some critics, this represents an agenda of 'rolling back the boundaries of the state' to allow the growth of private enterprise. To the more cynical critic, it represents an undue preoccupation with doing things on the cheap. What on the face of it represents a sensible approach to management in any setting has become a political issue: 'the connotation of efficiency as a politically neutral, no-nonsense way of improving performance is a useful weapon in political debate' [Metcalfe and Richards, 1987, p 29].

Nearly all the agencies of criminal justice have been scrutinised for the 'three Es'. The scrutiny process was designed to pose basic questions about the costs and results of the operations of government departments and produce recommendations about how their effectiveness could be improved [Metcalfe and Richards, 1987]. This originated from the Financial Management Initiative, as part of the efficiency strategy mentioned above, launched by the Prime Minister in May 1982, in an attempt to gain 'value–for–money' from public services and to reduce public expenditure. From this Initiative, three key principles of effective and efficient management have been defined:

' – there must be clear definition of who runs the organisation, and to

whom they are accountable, and a clear statement of objectives and priorities;
– resource planning processes must require managers to account for what past expenditure has achieved and the efficiency with which existing resources are used, and relate future resource plans to defined and where possible quantified targets for output and performance; and central processes must keep actual spending within agreed limits;
– managers must have the control over resources which they require to achieve optimum performance, backed by adequate training and information about costs' [Home Office, 1989a, para 7.2].

The background to and development of the FMI, as well as the broader trend towards improvements in public service management are ably discussed by Metcalfe and Richards [1987].

I have, throughout this book, made liberal use of the term 'effectiveness'. My concern in this book is with improving the effectiveness of the various responses that are made to the problem of crime. Strategy and strategic planning are put forward as being the means by which enhanced effectiveness can be achieved. In order to be effective in anything, a clear sense of purpose is required. It is impossible to measure effectiveness in the absence of clear and specific goals and objectives. We must be able to make things happen in the way that we want them to happen. We must also have the resources to pursue our purpose: we must have the requisite financial, physical, personal and informational means to achieve our desired or given ends. Effectiveness therefore requires a good fit between ends and means. Measuring or evaluating effectiveness requires an analysis of how resources have been used and how they could be used in the future.

We could consider the effectiveness of a system of responses to crime, or of a criminal justice system, of a particular organisation or of a set of resources within an organisation. Effectiveness will depend on the degree to which those elements that are critical to success, such as finance, equipment, people or information, are deployed strategically. This requires that each of these elements works in a way that is integrated. In evaluating effectiveness, a system of measurement is required.

Johnson and Scholes [1988 pp 95–96] suggest six measures of effectiveness for commercial organisations. These can be translated into the public service domain in the following terms:

(1) *use of people.* Criminal justice organisations depend more on people than on physical resources. The quality of performance or practice of those working in crime response agencies is one of the most critical factors in success.

(2) *Use of capital.* The 'capital' used by criminal justice agencies includes financial resources, buildings and equipment. These affect the effectiveness of the people who work with and in them.

(3) *Use of marketing and distribution resources.* Crime responses require the confidence of the public and of public representatives. Crime responses are, so to speak, 'sold' to public consumers; they are distributed to everyone but how equitably are they distributed? Are they distributed to those who 'need' them most? What are the social, political and economic costs and benefits of the way that responses are distributed? How effectively are responses 'marketed' and distributed?

(4) *Use of knowledge.* Research, information and knowledge are important and critical factors in the success of crime response strategies. If crime is to be reduced, then we must have reliable knowledge about the influences on rates of crime. We must know how much crime is being committed in any area. These issues are addressed in chapter six.

(5) *Use of production systems.* We can measure the effectiveness of the production of policing, sentencing, probation, imprisonment and so on. We should also be able to measure the effectiveness of the production of systems of crime response in local areas. Our concern here will be for the planning, provision, practice and operation of response systems.

(6) *Exploitation of intangible assets.* Responses to crime depend on many intangibles – public awareness of crime, fear of crime, willingness to cooperate with the police, social values and morals, etc. These are often difficult to measure at all, let alone reliably, and yet all contribute to the effectiveness of systems of crime response.

Effectiveness is being able to do things – about achieving objectives. This is a rationalist idea and as such has its limitations; 'in government, objectives are notoriously difficult to define, are frequently in conflict and are often subject to change' [Metcalfe and Richards, 1979, p 33]. By contrast, efficiency and economy are concerned with the means of achieving ends, though the distinction is by no means absolute and these concepts interact with each other. 'Efficiency is concerned with how "well" resources have been utilised irrespective of the purpose for which they have been deployed' [Johnson and Scholes, 1988, p 93].

Efficiency is often linked with productivity and generally is regarded as being an equation between inputs and outputs. Efficiency can be improved by increasing outputs relative to inputs. It is often associated with the amount of energy or resources required to achieve a task. Economy is often associated with pursuing a task without wasting resources.

Economy is concerned with achieving objectives with the minimum (or, some would say, optimum) use of resources. This is frequently confused with doing things as cheaply as possible. Value-for-money is not the same as cheapness or least cost. Economy is about balancing effectiveness with efficiency. Too great a preoccupation with efficiency can sometimes reduce effectiveness. It is seldom the case that effectiveness is desirable at any cost. Efficiency is affected by the choice of methods for undertaking a task. A task may be carried out efficiently but might not be the most effective method of doing that activity. Sometimes the most effective way of doing something is not the most efficient, unless one of the objectives of the task is achievement with minimal use of resources.

Strategically we might, on some occasions, have to choose to prioritise effectiveness or efficiency or economy. Ideally, we might like to have a combination of all three but this must depend on the values, goals and principles that drive the strategy. Effectiveness, efficiency and economy are involved in a constellation of functions: policy, organisation, management, production and so on. Strategic choices are involved in all these functions. It can also be argued that time is one of the most valuable resources, although its supply is always a constant. Doing things in time may be more important than doing them efficiently or in the most economic way. Value cannot always be measured only in monetary units, despite the adage that 'time is money'.

I wish to suggest that effectiveness is the *strategic* concept; efficiency and economy are secondary to this. Without a clear concept and definition of effectiveness, it is impossible to decide how to do things efficiently or economically.

Does strategic planning work?

At various points I have suggested that strategic planning will increase the effectiveness of responses to crime. We must of course examine the validity of that suggestion. One way of doing so would be to evaluate the contribution that strategic planning has made to responses to crime. However, such an evaluation can only be undertaken if there are examples of it being applied in this field. Several references are made in this discussion to strategic planning in the United States criminal justice system. I have heard that it is employed in the Dutch system. Falkin [1979] and Cushman [1980] have suggested that strategic planning is a necessary function of the organisation of effective criminal justice systems. In this country strategic planning is being applied by various criminal justice agencies to their organisational processes but that is different from applying it more generally to the task of organising responses to crime on a multiagency basis.

The problem of evaluating the outcome of strategic planning, as far as the criminal justice system is concerned, is finding examples of it being applied comprehensively and consistently over a sufficient period of time in order that its contribution to effective crime responses can be measured. The difficulty in doing this lies in being able to accurately define what strategic planning is, such that we can identify that it has been applied. Unfortunately, what we tend to find is that some of it has been applied some of the time. There are plenty of examples of the application of policy or planning processes but these do not necessarily represent a strategic approach. We can find instances of management or organisational practices that resemble strategic planning but, without a carefully defined concept of such planning, we cannot confidently identify these as being valid examples of such practice.

We would encounter the same problem if we were to attempt to evaluate management. We would be bound to define what management is, identify styles or methods of management and have a clear idea of what management practice would look like before we would begin to measure its contribution to the impact of an organisation. There is a problem here with the level of generality. Evaluation methods usually require specific and measurable processes; the greater the degree of generality and hence the higher the degree of complexity, the less feasible it becomes to identify quantifiable factors that can be measured in outcomes evaluations. If the practical impacts of strategic planning are to be evaluated, then we must be sure that what we are looking at is a fully practised strategic planning approach. Evaluation at that level of generality would be difficult.

I wish to argue however that, firstly, the strategic planning of crime responses have been insufficiently defined and has conceptualised and secondly, that it has not been sufficiently, comprehensively and consistently applied over a sufficient period of time, in a criminal justice system, to enable a thorough evaluation to take place. An alternative approach to evaluation is to look at other fields in which strategic planning has been applied, such as local government or business. An examination of effectiveness in improving company performance, for example, has been attempted by Greenley [1986]. In his article, the methodological problems of this kind of inquiry are established. Problems are identified in defining exactly what strategic planning is (such that it can be studied in evaluative research). Similar problems are found in being able to define and measure company performance. Even if these definitional and measurement problems could be resolved, we would still be left with the problem of determining the relationship between planning and performance (or effectiveness). Greenley's review of research studies into the effectiveness of strategic planning in manufacturing companies concludes that the results are far from conclusive in establishing this relationship. This lack of conclusive results can be explained by methodological weaknesses in the research, by a lack of common parameters across the various studies that we reviewed and by subjective bias on the part of the researchers. Greenley concludes that 'although there is a strong *a priori* case that strategic planning provides a range of both advantages and intrinsic values, empirical evidence is lacking to substantiate these' [Greenley, 1986, p 108]. Similar issues of evaluating effectiveness are discussed by King [1988] in his article on information systems planning. This suggests that assessment of the impact of complex processes, such as strategic planning or the design of organisational information systems, requires the development of appropriate assessment methodologies and their systematic application.

Greenley's study fails to address the issue of the link between the definitional clarity and the standard of practice involved in strategic planning. It is not clear whether the companies studied had formalised strategic planning processes or simply strategies that have emerged through experience. Were the strategies fully implemented? Researching impacts such as this is always fraught with difficulties. What I have set out to do in this book is to describe strategic planning, not as a technique, but as an approach to fundamental functions of organisation, such as policy and planning. Strategic planning is often not a method of doing something but a way of thinking about something that is to be done. It nevertheless remains valid that we should wish to find evidence that strategic planning does have observable benefits where it has been practised.

Strategy, policy and planning

The extent to which the concept of strategy is understood is central to its being applied effectively; this also assumes that it can be clearly distinguished from adjacent terms such as 'policy', 'planning' or 'information'. If we talk about 'strategic policy' or 'strategic information' then we should be clear about how these are distinguished from policy or information that is not strategic. The term 'strategy' therefore is often used loosely, sometimes as meaning 'policy' or 'planning'. Whilst this usage is not illegitimate, the concept of strategy becomes more powerful if it is given a precise meaning.

What characterises strategy is its orientation to choice of objectives, the selection of certain options from those that are generally available, the identification of central components in operational systems and the extent to which all of these are pivoted around the achievement of goals. Strategic decisions are those that will make the largest impact on achievement and performance. Strategic resources are those that will contribute most to the performance of the system or organisation. Strategy is therefore a concept that applies to a selection of components in organisation and management.

Because the terms 'policy', 'planning' and 'strategy' are frequently confused it is necessary to disentangle them; this is by no means an

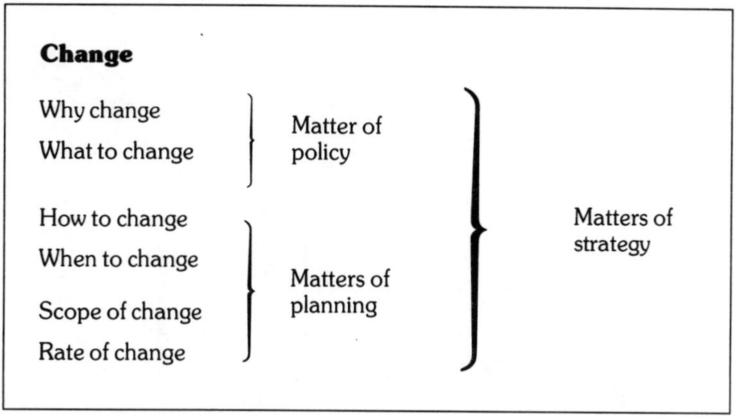

Figure 3.2 Policy and planning in strategy

easy task but the device illustrated in **Figure 3.2** begins to suggest the nature of the differences. Not all policies or all plans are strategic; not all components of policies or plans are strategic. Those components that are strategic are those that are most crucial to success, to the achievement of purpose. In policy and planning there are often wide varieties of options and alternatives. The criteria used to decide between options and to set priorities are strategic – they provide the framework of reference to which subsequent decisions and designs can be related. A strategy therefore has essential components. **Figure 3.3** builds on our previous diagram and some of the details in this figure will become clear in due course.

Strategy and the management of change

Strategic planning can be viewed as relating both to the operation of existing systems and to the development of new systems. In both respects strategy is about change: it can be about creating change or it can be about responding to it. Strategies for creating change rely on knowing *how* to make things happen. Strategies for reacting to change rely on knowing *what* will happen and what the consequences will be. Crime response strategies can set out to change, for example, the rate at which certain types of crime are committed; they also have to respond to changes – in population, in the criminal law, to political trends and so forth. It has been argued that change in strategy and change resulting from strategy tends to be incremental and continual rather than taking place in one 'big bang'. Fundamental change in an organisation's strategy is relatively rare. This process of gradual

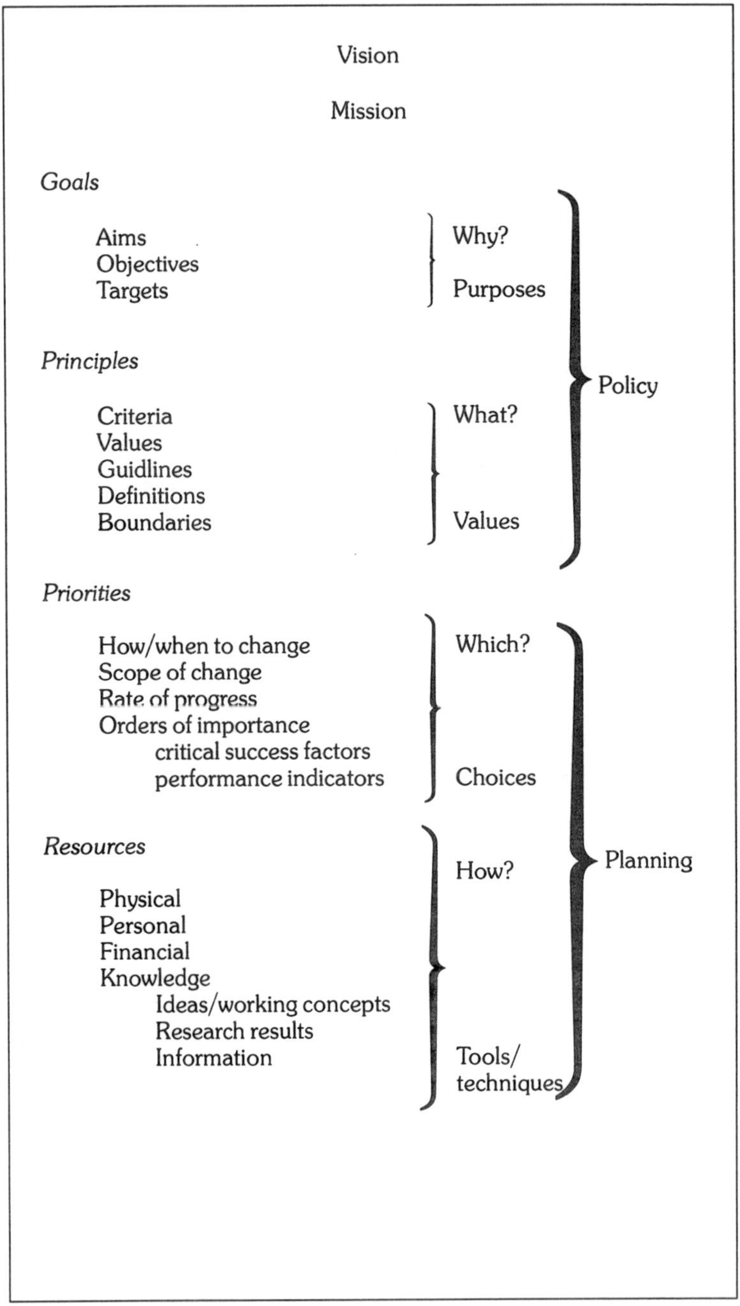

Figure 3.3 Components of strategy

change makes sense, it is argued, since organisations could not function efficiently if they were to undergo frequent major revisions of strategy. Incremental change might be viewed as a process of adaptation to changes in environment, except where the environment itself undergoes rapid or large-scale change that organisations cannot keep up with [Johnson and Scholes, 1988 p 25].

Change is however a complex concept and a varied phenomenon. Various types of organised change can be identified: firstly, *innovatory* change in which something new is introduced, either as a small scale modification of the existing system or as a large scale restructuring of it; secondly, *incremental* change in which an existing activity is increased and thirdly, *decremental* change in which an existing activity is reduced. Change might involve the addition of new resources; it could equally well involve redeployment of existing resources. We could seek to make existing resources more effective within the confines of existing constraints and within the framework of existing opportunities. This could mean increasing the efficiency with which existing resources are deployed or decreasing the load on resources to make them more effectively targeted. We might look at how widely resources are spread and try to decide if such resources could be made more effective if strategically targeted. In deciding the value of proposed changes we should cost not only the changes themselves but also the cost of not making those changes. The value of change is not just about what might be achieved but what disadvantages or losses might be entailed if change fails to occur.

In planning change, concern must be shown for effective management of the processes through which change is achieved. Where action is required to achieve change, planning attempts to ensure that such actions are effective in achieving intended results and in avoiding unintended consequences. This involves prediction; some changes can be predicted as almost certainly resulting when action is undertaken. In other cases, the relationship between action and result might be less certain. Planning attempts to work out in advance the sequence of actions and the interrelation between actions; this might involve defining what actions must take place before subsequent and dependent actions can occur. Planning might well require detailed scheduling of actions, events or operations before final results can be achieved.

In order to plan a schedule of change, some degree of modelling might be required. The model should indicate which variables in the system are independent and which are dependent, which can be easily controlled and which can be controlled only with difficulty or not at all. The model should also represent the relationships between variables, in other words, the dynamics of the system. Planning sets out to achieve ordered change. Change will be ordered to the extent that the processes or events that constitute the operations of the system can be controlled or managed. Most organisations can be modelled in terms of systems and subsystems. To achieve change in a major system, change in subsystems might need to occur and vice versa. A variety of processes can be involved in strategic planning of change: policy development, training of staff, monitoring of operations, resource redeployment, research projects, redesign of management procedures and so on. Many of these processes are interrelated and, in planning, these connections must be identified and analysed. In planning for change, the overriding task is to ensure that objectives are achieved. Planning needs to be goal oriented.

Putting strategy into an organisation or system is a process of change. Being able to create change requires information, control, regulation, culture and political organisation [Johnson and Scholes, 1988, p 292]. Change is, however, often met with resistance and inflexibility, especially by those who feel it is being imposed on them. Some resistance is due to uncertainty or confusion. Planners ideally foster commitment to change rather than having to impose it on people and prefer to motivate people to change rather than compelling them to alter their practice. Such motivation is generated from involvement in the decision making processes of formulating strategy and defining what change is required. Resistance to change in organisations derives largely from the culture of the status quo. Johnson and Scholes [1988] see cultural change as involving changes to current beliefs and assumptions and ways of doing things. This requires a change in the way that people see their organisational world replacing existing concepts and values with new ones.

The Johnson and Scholes analysis argues that the process of culture change involves *unfreezing* the status quo; this might be triggered by something (in criminal justice this might be a major change in government policy, a sharp change in crime rates or the introduction of new technology). The process might involve a deliberate challenge to the status quo, exposing its shortcomings or inadequacies. They also say that 'it is likely that there will be a need for the reconfiguration of *power structures* in the organisation' [op cit p 309]. Processes of organisational change often involve upsetting existing roles, responsibilities and commitments. New modes of practice might need to be introduced. There might be increased legitimisation of dissent from those who are in favour of such changes. Outsiders can play a crucial role in enabling change. Much of NACRO's work in fostering change in criminal justice agencies has utilised the strength of outsiders in assisting people to advocate and implement change (an issue that will be discussed again in the final chapter when we look at development work in strategic planning).

Johnson and Scholes see *unfreezing* as being followed by the adoption of a new *recipe* – the 'set of beliefs and assumptions held relatively commonly throughout the organisation, taken for granted in that organisation, but discernable to the outside observer in the stories of organisational history and explanations of events' and they add that 'the recipe makes sense of the situation managers find themselves in and provides a basis for formulating strategy' [op cit, pp 39–40]. The introduction of a new strategy involves a mechanism of demonstration that the innovation will produce tangible and visible improvements. *Symbolic activity* may also play an important role in achieving the acceptance of change and they go on to discuss in some detail the part played by such symbolic action in achieving strategic change [op cit p 310].

Review and evaluation are of central importance to the management of change. Change frequently involves stages and each stage should be reviewed to see what the out-turn has been. Processes of change generate a great deal of detailed information and it is necessary to stand back at times and try to see the 'wood' rather than the 'trees'. The strengths and weaknesses of what has been achieved need to be evaluated, successes and failures need to be analysed and performance and impact measured. Where things have gone wrong, lessons need to be learned; where successes have been achieved, there is a need to know why and how. None of these things happen spontaneously; these are functions that should be planned to happen.

Planning in a changing environment

Those responsible for the development of an organisation's strategic plan need to know what changes are happening or are likely to happen in the 'outside world'. What changes are likely to happen that will affect the organisation? How will the organisation have to respond to those changes? These are questions that decision makers and planners in police forces, probation services, the courts and all the other agencies have to tackle if they are to manage effectively (or even if they are to survive at all in some cases!). Organisations exist in an environment of political, social and economic forces that are constantly changing – a situation that has been called 'environmental turbulence' [Narchal et al, 1987 p 96]. Police forces, for example, have to respond to considerable changes in their political and social environment. They have to adapt to the introduction of new legislation, respond to issues that are being heightened by the media, to changing demands from local authorities, or organise their operations to take account of changes in crime rates and patterns.

The process of looking at and for current and future change in the environment of organisations is referred to in the literature on planning as *environmental scanning*. This involves scanning the environment at various levels (for example, nationally and locally) and using a variety of sources (statistics, news, published reports, verbal contacts, etc.). These changes call for consequential changes in an organisation, by planned reorganisation, by adaptation of practices, grasping opportunities, defences against threats and so forth. This is as true for criminal justice organisations as it is for other types of public bodies and for businesses. Just as individual organisations have to respond to change, so too does the criminal justice system as a whole.

If decision makers are to be able to decide how their organisation is to respond to environmental changes, then they must know what changes are happening or are likely to happen. This requires that they receive information about their organisation's environment and thus scanning is undertaken to indicate impending changes that might be relevant. Information about the environment provides input to the processes of strategic planning. If the scanning process is to be effective it must be integrated with the organisation's policy and planning processes. It must also be focused on those issues or indicators that are of the greatest significance to the organisation (as well as including a *penumbra* of peripheral issues). It has been argued that environmental scanning must look at the outside world as a whole, must be sufficiently sensitive to it and must be able to make forecasts based on detected evidence of impending change [Murphy, 1989, p 101].

Environmental scanning would appear to be a highly complex task and a very sizeable undertaking. The environment of any one organisation in the criminal justice system, or of the system as a whole, could well be the whole of the outside world. How can the task of scanning be made manageable? Clearly, each organisation needs to define its environment and structure its understanding of it. This process requires selection of those indicators of change that are important to planning and operation. In order to select appropriate indicators, there needs to be some analysis of *how* the organisation relates to the outside world. Scanning provides the signals about impending or current changes or events that will affect these relationships. The manager's task is to interpret how those changes will affect the organisation. This can be achieved through the use of 'influence diagrams' that depict how the environment impacts on the organisation or system [Narchal et al, 1987, p 99] (see **Figure 3.4**).

Some changes happen continuously (for example, changes in the rates of patterns of crime), some happen more or less periodically (such as changes to legislation) and some happen at prescribed intervals (general elections). Current changes can be monitored with relative ease; the prediction of probable changes in the future is less easy but of no less importance. The significance of predicting environmental changes relates to the ability of an organisation to make pre-emptive plans.

Scanning therefore requires techniques of prediction, forecasting and probability. Connections between trends or events can be included in the analysis. For example, if we have an event A and an

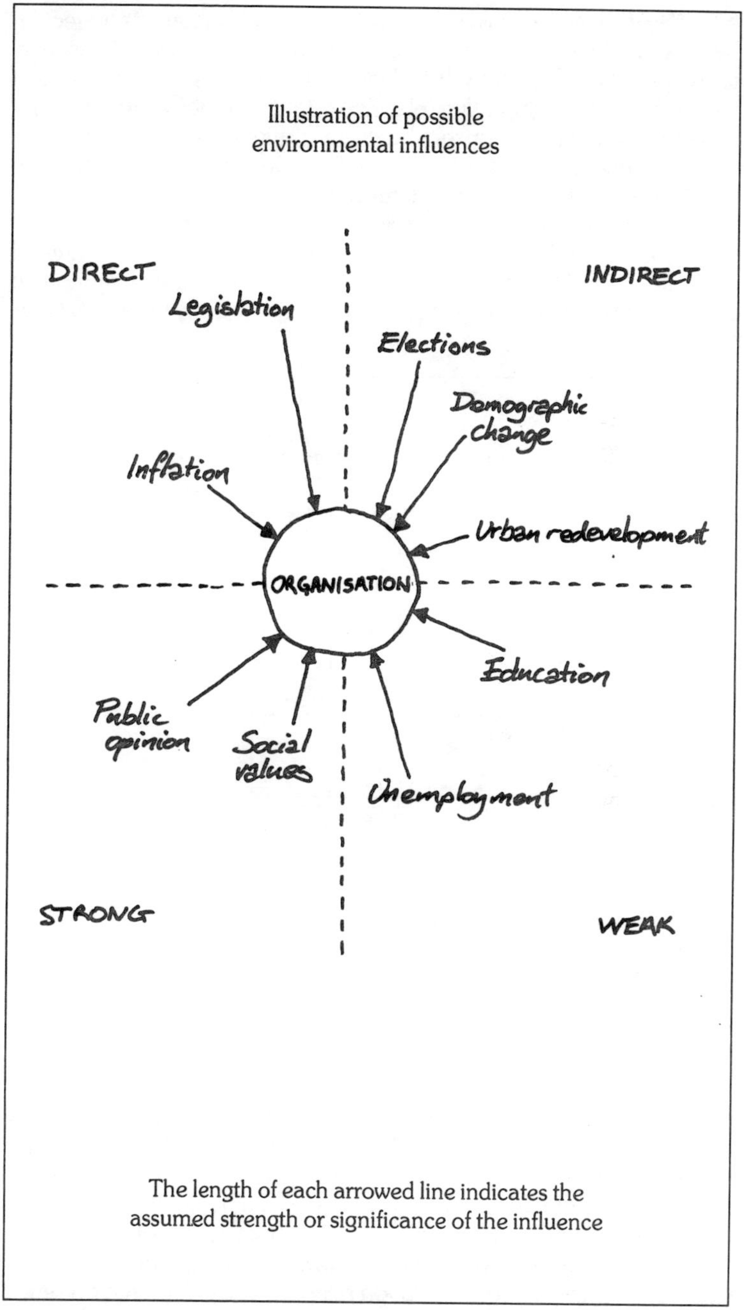

Figure 3.4 Influence diagram

event B, we need to know if there will be a direct or indirect connection between them. Are the conditions that will give rise to event A essential to the occurrence of event B? What will be the strength and speed at which the relationship takes place? To take another example, if we have postulated a relationship between cautioning and custody, such that an increase in cautioning will bring about a decrease in imprisonment, are we able to determine how this process takes place, under what conditions it will or might take place and at what rate it will take place? If we are scanning the conditions surrounding rates of custody, will we be able to detect increases in the rate of cautioning and then be able to reliably predict the level of custody that will follow?

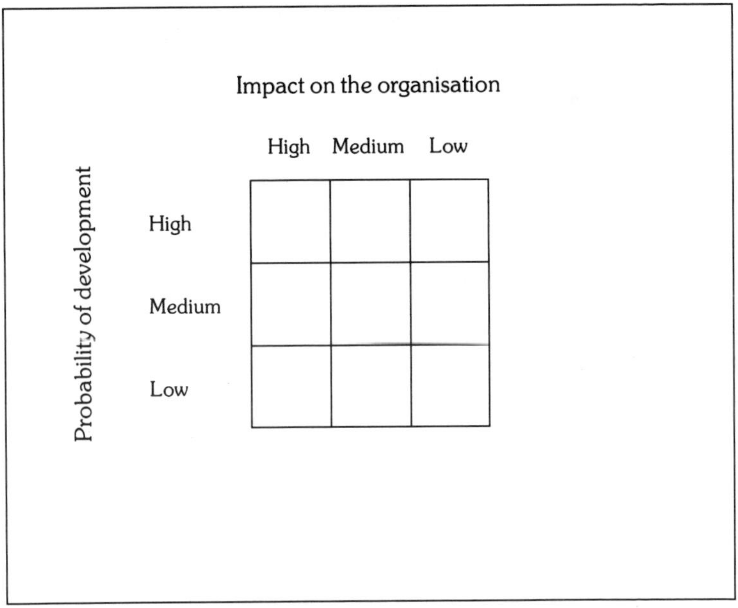

Source: Based on Murphy [1989]

Figure 3.5 Probability of change matrix

Murphy [1989] has suggested a method of relating the probability that future changes in the environment will impact on an organisation (see **Figure 3.5**). The matrix illustrated suggests that high, medium and low probabilities of developments can be related to high, medium and low levels of impact. Clearly, highly probable developments that will have high levels of impact on the organisation are of the greatest significance. Results from scanning can be used in deciding what strategic responses the organisation needs to make. If we have a series of indicators of change, then we need to measure not only the indicators themselves but also the conditions surrounding them that influence the direction and speed of such change. We also need to model the way that these changes impact on an organisation [Narchal et al, 1987, p 99].

This line of thinking raises questions about how far ahead it is feasible to look for possible changes. Given the uncertainties that exist in the environment, reliable predictions are generally unlikely or impossible beyond about five years. The length of time we might look ahead needs to be related to the strategic planning functions of the organisation. Murphy suggests that 'as a rule of thumb, we now establish a time horizon twice that of the strategic plan' [Murphy, 1989, p 102]. Moving backwards in time, evaluations can be made of successful predictions in the past and of the usefulness of certain indicators. Such evaluations will allow the scanning system to be improved.

Developing an environment scanning process

The development of a process for environment scanning can commence with a series of questions:

Who will use the information produced?
What information will be needed?
How will that information be used?
When will it be needed?

Understanding how environment scanning can contribute to planning requires conclusions to be reached about how the organisation must, could or might respond to external changes. This will begin to define what information will be needed. That definition can be further enhanced if the users of information are asked to define what elements of the environment they consider to be important. This kind of enquiry and analysis could generate long lists of information headings; what needs to be drawn out and prioritised is *strategically* important information.

Which aspects of the environment need to be scanned? Types of environmental aspects can include: issues, trends, forces and events. Policy *issues* are of particular relevance to criminal justice. The policy environment contains many issues that are relevant to crime response agencies, such as privatisation of public services, introduction of electronic monitoring of offenders, reduction of the prison population, impact on offenders of social security changes, changes in insurance practices, increase of the proportion of violent crime, etc.

Criminal justice agencies already monitor *trends* in the population (particularly the proportion of young people), in crime, in policing (e.g. clear-up rates), in sentencing (e.g. proportionate use of custody), in probation (e.g. reoffending) and so forth. A wide variety of *forces* or influences impact on these issues: pressures from campaigning organisations, the media, professional bodies, politicians etc. Current and future *events* represent concentrations of such forces; elections, trade union disputes, demonstrations, deaths or riots in prisons, major conferences, speeches launching policy initiatives, the publication of influential books or articles are but a few examples. Some of these will represent easily recognisable and well established processes of change; some might be identified as being indicators of new trends or developments.

These horizon events require an 'early warning system' to detect them and to alert policy makers and managers to impending changes in the environment well before they become an active force on the organisation. The process of developing a scanning system is outlined in **Figure 3.6**. Once the environment has been defined, key indicators have been selected and their influence on the organisation has been determined, the process then moves on to deciding what the responses will or might be. Scenarios of possible changes and responses can then be constructed. The scenarios might need to draw on a range of indicators and part of the task is to decide how these indicators interrelate. The end results of this process are then applied to strategic planning.

Environmental scanning systems require considerable bodies of information. Narchal [1987] discusses the development of an 'environmental database' comprising various sets of information. One database assembles information about the responses and performance of the organisation (strategic information systems) and another contains information about the organisations' environment. If we extend this thinking to crime response systems, it will become clear that databases relating to crime and justice processes will be required.

Using the results of environment scanning

Mention has already been made of the need to integrate environment scanning with strategic planning. Central to this idea is the identification of strategic options and issues. Murphy states that it is during this phase of the process 'that all the variables of the strategic jigsaw are assembled' [Murphy, 1989, p105]. Opportunities and threats recognised by the scanning system are related to the strengths and weaknesses of the organisation (see **Figure 3.7**). This allows critical success factors to be selected and alternative strategies to be developed. Results from scanning can be fed into the formulation of the organisation's strategic plan. Planners can use the results in setting performance indicators, in monitoring change within the organisation and in the development of training and operational resources.

Environment scanning techniques were developed by businesses where competition was the order of the day. Competitive businesses needed to respond to changes in market forces. In the crime response

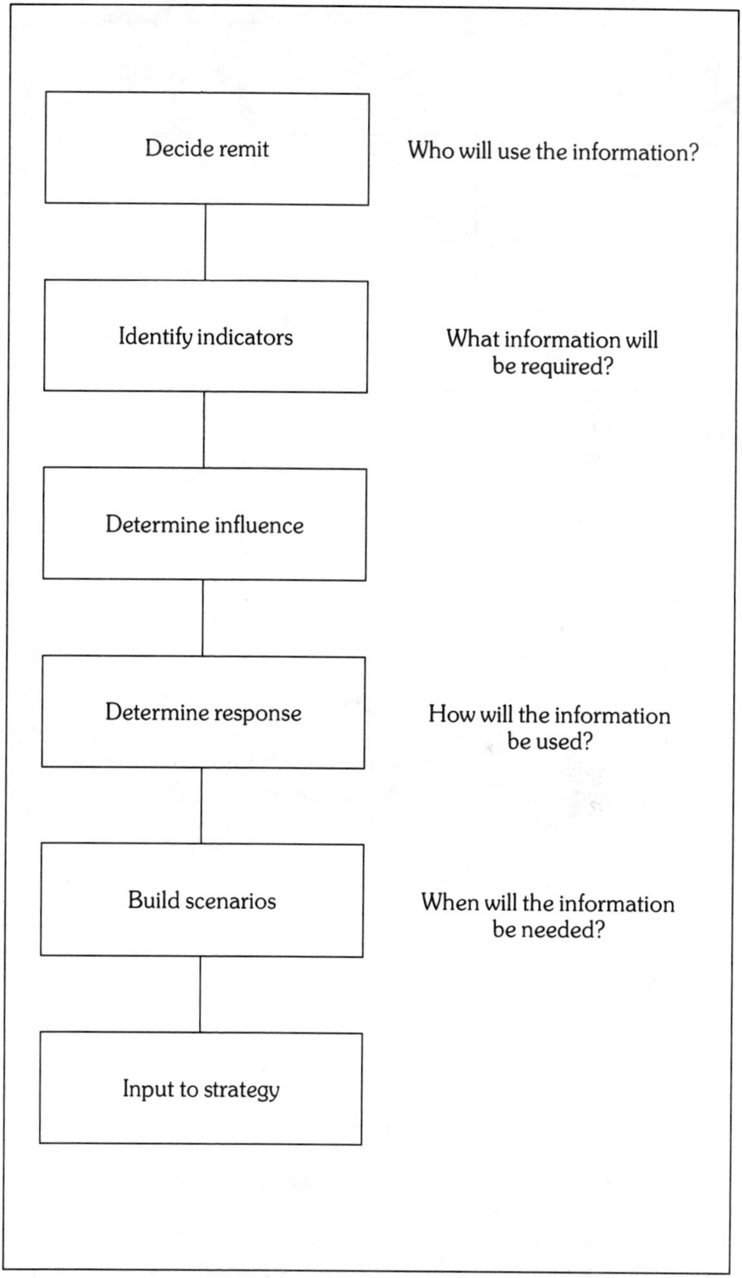

Figure 3.6 The process of developing an environmental scanning system

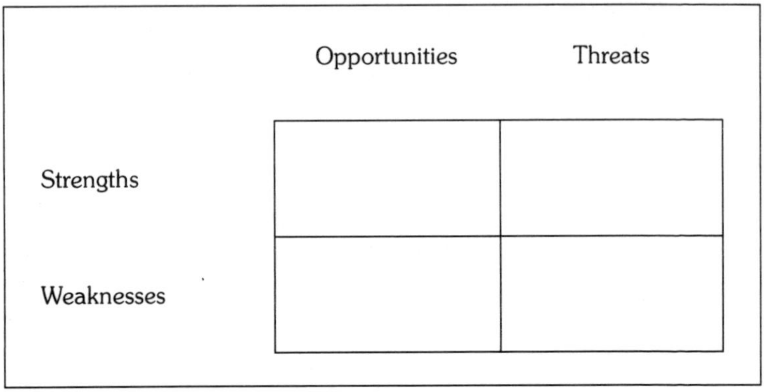

Source: Based on Murphy [1989]

Figure 3.7 Using environmental scanning. Implications for the organisation.

system, it is cooperation that is required rather than competition. Criminal justice agencies could cooperate in the provision of a common environment scanning service. Since each organisation has all the other organisations in its environment, the exchanging of details of proposed changes from one organisation to another will contribute to the process.

Those who have written about scanning acknowledge the practical difficulties of making it work. There is no doubt that criminal justice organisations already practice scanning in some way; it is the daily routine of chief officers and the bread and butter of their professional associations. This discussion points to two central issues: firstly the need to integrate scanning with planning and secondly, the need for this to be applied to the crime response system as a whole.

Organisation and management

The criminal justice system is an organised collection of activities; more pertinently it is an organisation of people. Several thousand people are employed to work in it and many more come into contact with it occasionally. The degree to which the criminal justice system is effective depends on the degree to which it is organised. The system can be viewed as a decision making system and one that relies on information in making decisions.

Police forces, the probation, courts and crown prosecution services are all organisations in which strategic decisions are made about resources (the number and types of staff required, the number of vehicles and buildings) and about operational systems and procedures (e.g. method of arrest, sentencing, procedure in court, monitoring reports). In the last analysis, it is people who make any organisation work; but it is people that need to be organised in order to achieve their goals.

We noted earlier that what enables people to work effectively is a clear understanding of what their task is, motivation to pursue that task and having the resources to do their job effectively. What inhibits and obstructs effectiveness is confusion and uncertainty about what the task is, how it should be done and what the result is supposed to be. Having a clear sense of vision and mission is necessary at all levels of the organisation. Strategic planning is therefore not only about resources, goals, priorities and systems; it is fundamentally about people and ensuring that an environment is created in which people can work effectively. Good policy and planning will enable people to maximise their performance.

Management is the process through which organisation is maintained and improved. Managers are the people who are responsible for formulating and reformulating policy and for translating policy into planning. But policy is put into practice by everyone at all levels in an organisation. The task of management is to improve organisation. Where managers are effective there will be a high level of organisation; where their performance is poor, organisation will be poor. Whilst management might be about maintaining organisation, it can also be about change. Managers are both the recipients and initiators of change. They have to respond to orders or requests for change from above and respond to changes taking place below them. They can propose change in either direction or laterally to other managers. Success is achieved through people and in a system, such as criminal justice, people are the most strategic resource. Having resources that are strategic

> 'requires the development of managers and employees who possess a variety of skills, the ability to work flexibly, a sense of involvement in the affairs and future of the firm (or organisation) and the capacity to adapt and change. These qualities can be summed up as the three 'C's: competence, commitment and capacity for change' [McEwen, Carmichael et al, 1988, p 72].

Improvements in effectiveness are dependent on the degree of organisation. Increasing the degree of organisation is a process of change. A desire to achieve more can be generated from within an organisation or it can be imposed from outside. Some achieve change; others have change thrust upon them.

A strategic response to crime

Having discussed the theoretical foundations of strategy, we now move on to a consideration of how that theory can be applied to responses to crime. The rest of this chapter forms an introduction to the following chapters on policy, planning and information. The conceptual core of this book holds that if society is to respond effectively to the problem of crime, then it must respond to it strategically. If organisations are to devise a strategic response, then they need to have a clear vision of what they are to achieve and a clear mission to pursue that achievement both collectively and individually. In formulating a vision for crime response strategies, we must be careful not to overdo it. We could say that we would like to have a crime-free society but this is idealistic and would cost too much freedom. Also, there is the danger of engaging in over-generalisations that are impossible to utilise. If we say that our task is to minimise crime, then how do we define the minimum? If we are to formulate a vision that is practical then it needs to be realistic and achievable. It would be more practical if, instead of wanting to achieve a society without crime, we focused on our vision on crime prevention, law enforcement and criminal justice systems and clarified what we would like them to achieve. Some would call this 'crime control' and others 'crime management'.

The development of a strategy requires us to think about its overall architecture. The task of formulating a global strategy for responding to crime is enormous; it can only be undertaken by formulating at a variety of levels and by breaking the strategy down into sets of manageable sub-strategies. In doing so, we should be careful not to re-introduce fragmentation. Strategies often divide into sets of sub-strategies and tactics but in order to achieve integration between these, organisations need to ensure that all of these sub-strategies are related to a collective and comprehensive strategy. This is likely to be the strategy devised by national government on the basis of public policy. Within sub-strategies, care should be taken to ensure that chosen sets of tactics do in fact fit comfortably with the overall strategy and with other sub-strategies. This requires us to look carefully at the boundaries between sets of responses. For example, if we have three sub-strategies – diversion, prevention and sentencing – we should examine their interfaces (see **Figure 3.8**) and we might ask some analytical questions about these overlaps: are the strategies duplicating each other unnecessarily? Or are they providing useful complementary functions? Are there positive areas where objectives are being achieved for both sets by one function and should this be increased? What is the relative importance of each of these sets? (This might lead us to draw some circles in **Figure 3.8** larger than others). Are any of these sets competing with each other?

Another aspect of the architecture of a strategy is consistency. If one sub-strategy or set of tactics surges ahead in its development, then this could have kickbacks for other parts of the strategy. If we are faced with the interdependency of functions and the need to achieve

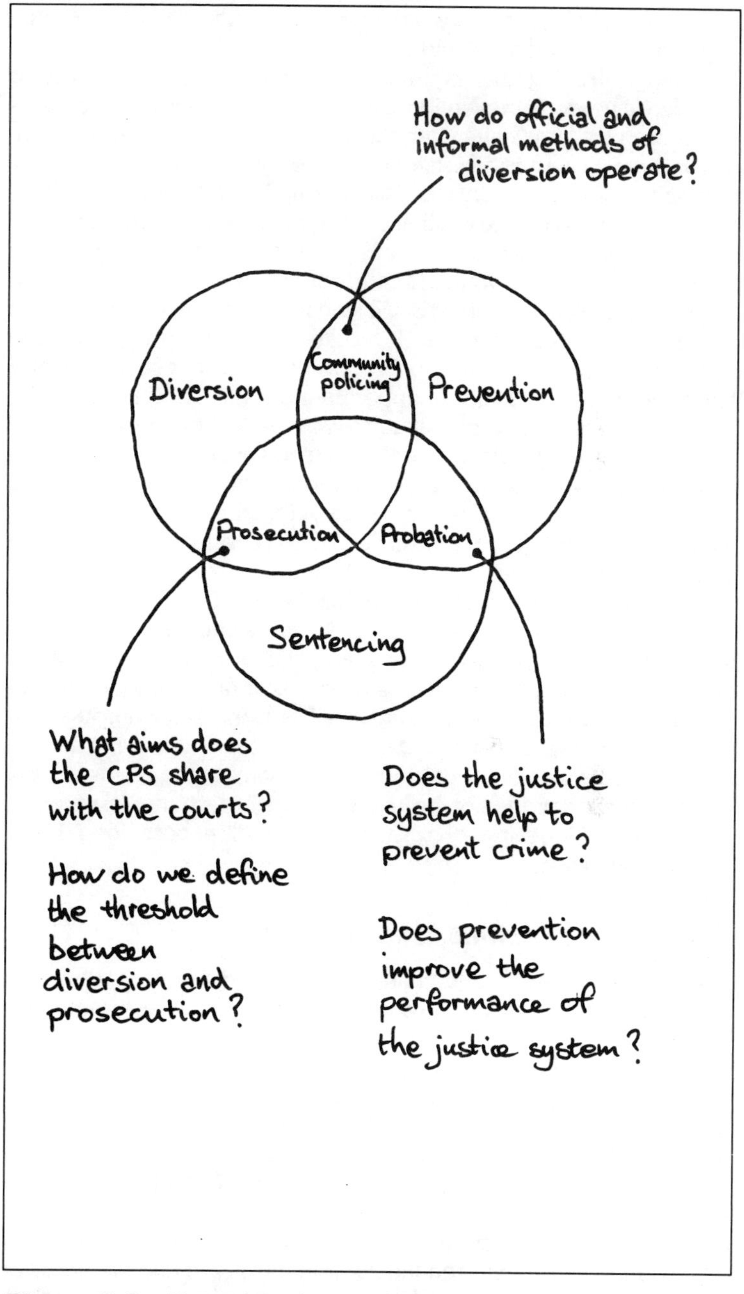

Figure 3.8 Examining the interfaces between sub-strategies

integration within a comprehensive strategy, then consistency is an important consideration. All this requires a considerable amount of knowledge. Taking the example given above – the relationships between diversion, prevention and sentencing – we might assume that these problems have interrelationships but how much is known about them? There is a certain amount of research on how each of these affects the others but little of it thoroughly explores the interfaces as a whole. We might expect that cautioning will affect the lower end of the sentencing tariff, that successful prevention schemes will reduce the numbers going through the courts or that effective sentencing will reduce recidivism and that this will feed into preventive work. But do we really have enough research results to verify such expectations? Can we construct a reliable model of how these responses interrelate? Have we worked out all the opportunities available in the interface between diversion and prevention? We can analyse these issues by looking at the way in which diversion and prevention schemes operate officially but we should also look at informal activities in order to get a complete picture of what is happening. A reliance on official statistics, without complementary information about informal processes, can lead to unreliable results.

The inadequacies in our knowledge base of the dynamics of the criminal justice system pose problems for the development of strategic responses. We might believe, for example, that cautioning should be developed or that there should be more places on community service schemes but to what extent are such beliefs founded on thorough and conclusive research results? If we lack research results, we could rely on what local monitoring schemes tell us but these require us to have well constructed models of the local system in order to make use of the information. Modelling of responses can utilise both formal and informal processes.

The concept of a criminal justice strategy

The Home Office paper 'Criminal justice' [Home Office, 1986] and the more recent 'Tackling crime' [Home Office, 1989c] are statements of the Government's policy on criminal justice and accounts of what plans are being put into operation. It conveys purposes (policy) and programmes of action (plans). The earlier paper begins with an outline of the Government's response strategy, setting out 'principles and management' in chapter one. The Government's objectives can be paraphrased as follows: (1) to sustain the rule of law, (2) to maintain and encourage public confidence in the criminal justice system, (3) to increase the system's greater efficiency and effectiveness and (4) to maintain a balance between the rights of the citizen and the needs of the community as a whole. These aims are translated into practice as follows: (1) by preventing crime, (2) by detection and conviction of offenders, (3) by effective sentencing, (4) by providing resources related to demand, (5) by strengthening the powers of the police and the courts, and (6) by providing effective support to the victims of crime.

That 'wider social policies, for example for education, housing, employment and support for the family, must also play a part' is another principle that is stated in the paper [op cit, p 3]. To back up the implementation of these policy components, the paper states that the Home Office is 'working on the design of measures of performance or output', a 'management information system' is being employed and research is being undertaken as part of the long-term planning process [ibid].

It is apparent from the earlier statement that most of the elements of strategic planning outlined in the first part of this chapter are in place: goals, principles, methods and information and management. However, in order for this to be a strategic policy (as previously defined), choices, options, emphases and priorities of a strategic kind must be reflected. Various chapters of the paper cover key elements of responses to crime: prevention, law enforcement, policing, trial and sentencing, offenders in the community, imprisonment, helping the victim and organisational collaboration. It is clear that the strategy is comprehensive in that it covers the main elements that we would expect to find in a statement of this scope. This is accentuated by what we find in chapter XIII ('The Way Ahead') about the wider context of crime. The drive to halt the rise in crime, the statement argues, depends on standards of public behaviour, parental responsibility, standards and values disseminated in schools and the images of crime presented in the media. Crime reduction is related to the strengthening of social stability and cohesion, particularly in urban areas. Thus, the Government is 'tackling the task of urban renewal' and recognises that there is a 'need to respond to the long-term changes in the economic structure of cities' and considers urban renewal as being another component of this wider context of crime reduction [op cit, p41]. These approaches are underpinned by the need for collaboration amongst the variety of agencies in the statutory, voluntary and community sectors.

Finding the key strategic options in this Home Office policy statement is more difficult; for the most part they have to be inferred since they are not clearly spelled out. We might, for example, look for the relative importance of the various components of the strategy that indicate where key strategic choices have been made. It is fairly clear that a major plank of the strategy is the emphasis placed on not seeing the criminal justice system as being the sole response to crime ('the criminal justice system does not operate in a vacuum' [op cit p 41]). Crime prevention is added but the relative weight of prevention to justice is not clear. The Home Secretary (at that time, Douglas Hurd) writes, in a forward to the paper, of the 'priority given to law and order' but does not make clear what this priority is in relation to, unless he means it is an overriding priority that carries more weight than anything else. We would have to look beyond the paper in order to determine the priority of criminal justice policy relative to other government policies, as for example, the health service, education or defence.

The statement says at its outset that the strategy has three underlying themes: public confidence in the criminal justice system, increasing efficiency and effectiveness and the balance of individual rights to community needs. These are more in the nature of principles than goals. It also states that the strategy is particularly concerned with the organisations that deliver law enforcement and the justice process, since the formal system is crucial to deterring potential offenders, protection of the public and in helping offenders. The relative importance of each of these components is not well articulated.

The later statement (of 1989) is structured along similar lines. Whereas the earlier paper began with the 'Government's programme: principles and management' the new paper kicks off with 'A strategy to tackle crime'. Both papers define the problem with a chapter detailing crime rates and patterns. The more recent paper then continues with an analysis of the costs of crime, not found in the earlier statement. A chapter on 'helping the victim' is brought forward from chapter eleven to chapter four and this might perhaps indicate an increased concern for that issue. Both papers look at policing, prevention, the courts and justice issues, imprisonment and probation work. There is also specific attention to the need for a collaborative approach and community based measures. Over the three years between the papers we can detect certain changes in emphasis in the Home Office's strategy. The five objectives now appear to be: (1) promoting action to prevent crime, (2) supporting victims, (3) providing the criminal justice services with the resources they need, (4) strengthening the powers of the police and the courts while safeguarding the rights of the individual and (5) improving the efficiency and effectiveness of the criminal justice system [Home Office, 1989c, p 8]. I think I can also detect a shift towards placing greater emphasis on the criminal justice system having the overall strategic purpose of reducing crime; this was present in the earlier paper but seems to be stated more clearly in the later one.

There is also a clearer regard, in the later paper, for collaboration and integration of services, which 'have to work together, and to support and complement one another, while at the same time retaining their identity' [op cit, p 7]. Indeed, this is the theme of the final chapter where we find such phrases as 'independence does not mean isolation', 'co-operation and co-ordination are vital' and 'collective operation of the system' [op cit, pp 70–71]. What seems to be clear is that the dual concepts of collaborative working to counteract fragmentation and the management of interdependence have been taken on board over at least the last three years.

In conclusion we can say that the Government does have a policy and a set of plans for responding to crime and that now, this constitutes a strategy, by the definition put forward in this chapter. There are however still weaknesses in the Home Office approach to strategy; this might perhaps be due to not having worked on the conceptualisation of strategy quite enough and lacking a firm theoretical basis for strategic planning of the system as a whole. There is a lack of clarity about the relative significance of key policy elements in the strategy. Another fundamental weakness is that although the contribution of wider social policies is clearly acknowledged and some indications of what is being done in this respect are given, there is less attention paid to this area then would be expected. Finally, my evaluation of the strategy also holds that insufficient weight has been attached to the importance of delivering criminal justice services at the local level and to the needs for linkage between national and local strategies, and how such linkage can be developed.

The first extensive study that I found of the application of strategic planning to criminal justice was the work of Gregory Falkin *Reducing delinquency, a strategic planning approach* [Falkin, 1979]. His task was to 'present an approach to design a strategic plan to reduce crime' [op cit, p 2] and his framework rested on three aspects of crime control: '(1) the definition and causes of crime, (2) the structure and behaviour of the criminal justice system, and (3) the impact of crime control programs on criminal justice goals' [op cit, p 3]. He argued that these must be integrated; analysing any one of them in isolation leads only to inconclusive and perhaps misleading results. Strategic planning, he argued, must treat all the components of a system comprehensively. Quoting Daniel Glaser, he explained that criminal justice planning is concerned with the explanation, projection and manipulation of those key variables on which most aspects of crime depend. In developing a strategic plan, therefore, the entire system must be studied.

Falkin took a proactive approach to strategic planning. Instead of reacting to the problem of overcrowding in prisons, resulting from custodial sentencing, a proactive strategy seeks to control or influence sentencing and correctional programs because that contributes to crime reduction and justice. Criminal justice strategy development involves three major tasks: firstly, determining the causes of the behaviours that society defines as criminal; secondly, devising policies for the allocation of resources and responsibilities among various agencies, both within and without the criminal justice system and thirdly, planning a knowledge-building apparatus to deliver feedback to key decision makers.

Falkin's work was rooted in a systems analysis of criminal justice and emphasised large-scale research and monitoring. His analytical technique was to see the criminal justice system as a policy system, with public policy as the input and crime reduction and justice as the outputs. He makes the point that strategic planning requires that policy makers establish priorities for reducing specific types of crime, since 'different crimes are caused by different factors' [op cit, p 19]. Falkin leaves us in no doubt that the principle, strategic purpose of the criminal justice system is to reduce crime. Despite this seemingly self-evident conclusion, we find that many of the functions and activities performed by criminal justice agencies fail to address this purpose and that evaluations of policy and practice often disregard this as a criteria. The mismatch between purpose and production in the system can be explained in a number of ways but if its effectiveness is to be increased, then clearly this mismatch must be of focal interest. Some explanations of it can centre on the culture of fragmented and autonomous agencies, the values and preoccupations of different professions (for example, the contrast between social worker's and police officer's values and perspectives) and on the relative lack of interprofessional collaboration. The mismatch between purpose and production is most clearly evident at present in the probation service.

There has been for a long time a tradition of social work in probation which holds that the role of the probation officer is to work with the personal problems that offenders present rather than, as a priority, their offending. The motto of the service is 'to advise, assist and befriend'. There has been a recent trend towards drawing the service more closely into the criminal justice system and this was most clearly evident in the Home Office Green Paper of 1988 [Home Office, 1988b]. Critics viewed offenders as being 'sentenced to social work', and the issue of care and control, like that of justice versus welfare in the juvenile arena, generated fierce controversy. During the 1980s the service has been subject to increasing government control and the Statement of National Objectives of Probation, issued by the Home Office in 1984, 'significantly shifted the balance of power between central government and local agencies' [Harris, 1989, p 55]. The Government's latest strategy statement holds that the 'Probation Service has a central and increasingly important position to play in any programme for dealing with offenders in the community' and that it needs to be 'recognised as an efficient, effective *criminal justice* service which can divert more offenders from custody and with the explicit task of *reducing offending*' [Home Office, 1989c p59] (my emphasis). The Home Office view of the Probation Service is that it is a criminal justice service that has its roots in social work but which also has to accommodate functions of control and, where the controversy is most marked, of punishment [Faulkner, 1989]. In essence the Home Office view of probation is that it serves to reconcile care with control, using social work in conjunction with the implementation of criminal justice measures and pursuing the explicit task of reducing reoffending [op cit, p 607]. This concept was articulated in the Green Paper of 1988 [Home Office, 1988b] and its message was that

> 'an offender must be thought of as a whole person, both at the stage of the social inquiry report and during the period of the order, and not as a collection of needs and characteristics to be fitted into whatever facilities or activities the service thinks it would like to provide' [Faulkner, 1989, p 626].

Pulling the Probation Service more closely into the criminal justice system is proving to be a less than easy task and there is a current of resistance to this, based on professional ideologies as much as on political tastes. The issues and tensions in probation exemplify the problems inherent in constructing and implementing crime response strategies. These are not confined to the probation service but can also be observed in most of the other professions in the criminal justice system – in policing, in sentencing and in law. We can say that there should be a common strategic purpose to the criminal justice system but putting that purpose into practice is by no means an easy task, not least because there is not a universal agreement as to purpose among those that work in the system. Planning therefore needs to address the mismatch between purpose and production and the cultural conflicts that arise from fragmentation.

The criminal justice system (both in this country and, it would seem, in the United States) lacks a clear, specific and purposeful remit, a mission which can inform and guide its functions and operations. Instead, it has to cope with confused, contradictory and inconsistent goals, priorities and demands. This is reflected in the allocation of resources to the various arms of the system; budget allocations are not made on the basis of the contribution of those arms to effective crime reduction but on the basis of a range of historical and political factors.

It is these problems that strategic planning addresses. Falkin took the view that the function of what he called *policy research* is to clarify and analyse the relationship between objectives so that they can be ranked, and to allow priorities to be set objectively. Falkin's stance was that of the positivist and reflected the confidence in rational, rather than, say, political solutions to social problems that was characteristic of much of the output of the United States Department of Justice in the late 1970s and early 1980s. Political, social and economic conditions have moved on since then, the era of Reagan and Thatcher brought new dimensions to public and political policy and the practice of strategic planning has had to make adjustments to these conditions. The strategy and planning theories used by Falkin and those on whom he drew was rooted in the management science of the American and European business world. Those roots continue to provide the sap of strategic thinking but much has been learnt over the past two decades that needs to be digested. Falkin's contribution was to demonstrate that there could be a strategic planning conception of crime reduction.

Applying strategic thinking to responses to crime

To think strategically about a problem and how we are to respond to it we must consider four basic questions: why, what, which and how (see **Figure 3.1**). Why do we respond to crime? What are the goals of our responses? Which aspects of the problem and our responses to it are most important? How should we respond if we are to be most effective? Our discussion has already touched on the question of whether or not the reduction and control of crime should be the principle strategic goal of the system of responses to crime. If we do choose this as our strategic goal, we must decide what rules need to be applied to criminal behaviour, which behaviours need to be defined as criminal and what are the boundaries between criminal jurisdiction and other systems of public control, such as civil law, maintaining order through military means, the distribution of constraints through the mental health or child care systems and so on. The definitional and boundary issues are crucial to the formation of public policies. What strategic thinking requires is that these issues are decided in a consistent manner and that the resulting policies provide clear missions to public agencies to carry out their work in a certain way.

On what values should crime response strategies be based? Justice involves a cluster of values and if these are not clear, injustice can be perpetrated in the pursuit of crime reduction. Freedom from crime is a value, but unprincipled pursuit of that freedom could lead to injustices (if not crimes). Nothing is more unjust than an unprincipled onslaught on criminals, including the wrongful prosecution of people who later turn out to be proved innocent. Proportionality between an offence and its mode of punishment is a value that is fundamental to sentencing policy and practice. The justice system employs considerable powers of intervention in people's lives; such power needs to be tempered by values and principles. The inclusion of principles in policy will be considered in the next chapter.

Another pivotal value of crime responses is equality. Offenders should be treated equally irrespective of their race, social class, age or gender unless, as some would hold, there are acceptable and positive reasons for discriminating in their favour. Offenders who are shown to be suffering from problems of mental health are treated differently to those who do not have such problems. Children and very old people are often treated differently from adults.

Defining the values of a strategy is therefore part of the task of developing that strategy. Being able to set goals, define principles, allocate resources and plan information systems are other components and these will be considered in subsequent chapters. The final point that needs to be made here is that strategic thinking about crime responses requires a comprehensive and integrated approach both to defining the problem and to devising responses to it. Chapter two set out to establish why this is important for criminal justice systems.

The scope of a crime response strategy

There are three fundamental dimensions to the scope of crime response strategies: the temporal, the spatial and the functional. In the temporal dimension we must make decisions about the scope of a strategy's timescale, about how far into the future our strategy can realistically be extended. In the spatial dimension we consider the area that should be covered by the strategy, whether it is primarily national or local. In the functional dimension we must make decisions about the boundaries of the systems involved; for example, we could say that our strategy will cover only criminal justice or that it will cover all conceivable responses to crime. We can define our strategy narrowly or broadly depending on what we think are the realistic limits of what can be managed. A national strategy will have different dimensions of scope to that based on a local area. A national strategy might be able to manage a wider range of social and economic factors than would be possible in a local strategy. Some components of a strategy could be shared between national and local government. These dimensions interrelate and an illustration of this is given in **Figure 3.9**.

In determining the scope of a strategy a number of strategic issues need to be addressed and we will return to discuss these in the final chapter. Not least is the issue of where the boundaries of a *crime response* strategy should lie and the related issue of the overlap between crime response strategies and those that will affect crime and offenders indirectly.

Conclusions

I have argued that if we are to improve the effectiveness of responses to crime, whether that is through the criminal justice system, prevention or broader social policies, then we should develop a comprehensive and strategic approach to that task. The piecemeal, incremental, pragmatic and fragmentary approach has not produced a satisfactory level of effectiveness in reducing or controlling crime. The main focus of crime strategies has been the impact of the criminal justice system. In order to further develop a strategic response, we need to evaluate the relative merits of each of the functions performed by criminal justice agencies and formulate policies and plans

	National	Local
Short term	Increase inter-departmental collaboration Issue policy guide lines	Increase security publicity Media campaign Public meetings
Medium term	Increase police manpower More probation officers through funding Legislation	Police recruitment Probation recrutment Demonstration projects Develop employment training schemes
Long term	Economic development Anti-poverty program Urban planning policy Reduce long term unemployment Housing strategy	Business development scheme Welfare rights campaign Urban planning practice Employment creation Housing renewel

Figure 3.9 Dimensions of strategy (example)

accordingly. That requires us to have clear and well defined overall strategic goals for responding to crime. If such goals include the reduction of crime and maintaining high standards of justice and equality, then we can begin to evaluate each of the available responses against those intentions. Within particular response systems – prevention, policing, sentencing and so forth – we need to have clearly defined policies and plans but to make these *strategic* we need to define priorities that will contribute both to the internal goals of those systems and to our overall strategic assessment. Our overall strategy should be comprehensive and integrated, for reasons argued in previous chapters. That integration must be at the level of organisations, through the development of a collaborative approach and at the level of functions, so that prevention, diversion, sentencing and so on support and complement one another. This chapter has argued that the development of a strategic approach requires a full understanding of the concept of strategy and a grasp of the theoretical foundations that assist in the application of that concept. If those working in response systems are to develop effective strategies and are to practice good strategic planning, then theory must be learnt and understood. Much benefit can be gained by those in criminal justice professions from theory and practice in other fields both in the public and private sectors.

Suggested reading

There is a very extensive range of books and periodicals on strategy, strategic and corporate planning and strategic management. The bulk of this relates to business but a few books have appeared relating to the public sector. A good general but also detailed introduction to strategic planning is Gerry Johnson and Kevan Scholes's book *Exploring corporate strategy*, 2nd edition, 1988, Prentice Hall. This relates to commercial organisations but, as the authors themselves maintain, the material is also relevant to organisations in the public sector. Reference is made in this chapter to Gregory Falkin's *Reducing delinquency, a strategic planning approach*, 1979, Lexington Books. This is worth reading, particularly for its attention to policy dimensions and for its description of the large-scale simulation model of the California juvenile justice system and how this was used in strategic planning. A very practical account of strategic planning processes is given in *Planning under pressure: the strategic choice approach* by John Friend and Allen Hickling, 1987, Pergamon Press.

Books on criminal justice strategy are rare but Norman Bishop's report on *Non-custodial alternatives in Europe*, 1988, published in Helsinki by HEUNI offers some useful insights into strategic issues. A much smaller document but one that addresses the English context is

NACRO's report *The real alternative: strategies to promote community based penalties*, 1989 from NACRO, 169 Clapham Road, London SW9 0PU. The United States Department of Justice has also published several reports and monographs that offer source material on this subject; current publications are listed in *NIJ Reports*, published bimonthly by the National Institute of Justice, Box 6000, Rockville, MD 20850, USA. A series published recently on *Perspectives in policing* includes two interesting papers of relevance here: *The evolving strategy of policing* by Kelling and Moore and *Corporate strategies for policing* by Moore and Tojanowicz (both of which are included in the bibliography at the back of this book).

The Home Office strategy statement *Tackling crime*, 1989, can be obtained from IBIS Ltd, Waterside, Lowbell Lane, London Colney, St Albans AL2 1DX. Also, the Home Office book edited by David Moxon *Managing criminal justice: a collection of papers*, 1985, available from HMSO will be of interest to some readers.

The Journal *Long Range Planning* (International Journal of Strategic Management and Corporate Planning) frequently contains articles that offer useful material to those concerned with specific aspects of strategy and some of these relate to the public sector, both directly and indirectly. It is the Journal of the Strategic Planning Society and is published by Pergamon Press, Oxford.

The Strategic Planning Society offers an extensive programme of conferences, courses, special interest groups and regional meetings. The majority of its members come from and its events are geared to the business world, but occasionally conferences are offered to those in the public and non-profit sector. The Society is located at 17 Portland Place, London W1N 3AF. Some public sector readers might however look to the Royal Institute of Public Administration as a source for general material on strategic planning; their address is 3 Birdcage Walk, London SW1H 9JH.

4 A matter of policy

Introduction : policy in responses to crime

This chapter assumes a management approach to policy. Its aim is to provide a conceptual framework (or theory) with which to understand what policy is, what functions it performs and how it can be formulated. It offers practical guidance to those in criminal justice organisations where policy is developed as part of the task of organisation and management. Just as a theory of policy can be applied within any one organisation, so too can it be applied across a system as a whole. The term 'criminal justice policy' often needs to be set in this broader context. If a corporate (or systems) response to crime is to be achieved, then a corporate criminal justice policy (or set of policies) will be required, otherwise the present situation of fragmentary policy making cannot be moved beyond. This view envisages that the criminal justice agencies in a local area will collectively develop a common framework of policy. The purpose of such policy, it can be assumed, is to reduce crime. Corporate policy might also include principles of justice that must be applied in pursuing that goal.

Policy theory allows us to define levels of policy, as for example national or local, and one of the tasks of those working with criminal justice policy is to integrate these levels. Some national policy is mandatory (i.e. criminal law) and some is permissive or expressive (e.g. certain Home Office circulars). Where policy is permissive, allowing discretion in decision making or action, how can governments ensure that the purpose of the policy will be carried out? The task of policy formulation is demanding and requires considerable skills to be exercised. Fundamental differences of values and beliefs aside, the integration of levels of policy employs techniques of policy analysis and evaluation. Some writers prefer to think in terms of policy science (e.g. Dror, Falkin) and some in terms of the 'art and craft' of policy (e.g. Wildavsky). Policy science is an academic discipline that originated in the pioneering work of Lasswell in the 1950s and developed by writers such as Dror in the 1960s. Its growth was described by Dunn; he writes that Weber and Mannheim might well be regarded as laying the foundations of policy sciences [Dunn, 1981]. According to Dror policy science is concerned with the contribution of systematic knowledge, structured rationality and organised creativity to better policy making [Dror, 1975]. These are but manifestations of the same thing: the recognition that there is a difference between good and bad policy. Such a difference is due, in part, to the skills available to those who work with policy. The practice of policy work, like any other practice, can be extended through theory. Policy theory contributes to the improvement of policy practice.

Policy, planning, management and practice are all aspects of strategy and work together as interdependent elements. Policy makers, planners, managers and practitioners involved in crime and justice systems can benefit from advancing their theoretical and conceptual grasp of policy, planning and strategy. This, I argue, will be one of the more important trends and developments in the field of criminal justice over the next few years. In this chapter an attempt is made to assemble a framework of concepts through which policy can be more clearly understood and more effectively applied.

Why policy is important

Policy and planning are essential to good organisation and management, and to increased effectiveness of the justice system and responses to crime. Too much attention has been paid to the substance of policy, to policy issues, without at the same time attending to the processes of policy formulation and to the structure or format of written policy. If the process of formulation, analysis and communication of policy could be improved then it is likely to become more effective. We should try to avoid 'knee jerk' policy formulation - cobbling policy together in a crisis.

Policy is most important in organisations and systems where people have discretion and where they must make decisions on a day to day basis. The criminal justice system provides police officers, magistrates, judges, prosecutors and many others with considerable scope for the exercise of judgement but it makes that provision within a framework of law and principles of justice. A policy is a framework of goals and principles within which decision making and action can be made in a way that is fair and consistent. Discretion and judgement should not be allocated in order to indulge in license or personal prejudices. Policies are provided to ensure that decisions are made in a consistent manner and with reference to a central set of values and purposes. A policy expresses the philosophy of an organisation or a system. It is what lays the foundations on which organisation is built.

Policy is an essential function of organisation because in order to make systems of response to crime more effective, we must make them more highly organised. Policy helps to create organisation; policy also continues to re-create organisation. Policy is also something that is produced by organisations; policy statements are made either by the organisations themselves, through a process of formulation, or by individuals who represent organisations. Within organisations, policy is a process that involves people in its formulation and implementation. Some organisations lend themselves to this process, for example, trade unions or political parties; these bodies have complex procedures for formulating and authorising policy. In other organisations the policy process may be obscure: commercial companies do not often have democratic structures, but policy making and implementation is nevertheless a fundamental aspect of their management processes.

What policy is

Sir Charles Cunningham, once Permanent Under-Secretary of State at the Home Office, said: 'policy is like the elephant – you recognise it when you see it but cannot easily define it' [Smith, 1976]. Many writers have attempted to define policy; some have drawn together and analysed collections of such definitions [for example Smith, 1976 or Heclo, 1972]. Heclo has looked at policy through those who write about it and picks out several threads. Firstly, policy is generally regarded to be about decision making activity. Secondly, policy is purposeful; it is about goals and the means by which those goals are achieved. Heclo has found that some writers consider policy to consist of a purpose (ends) whilst others regard it as including both a purpose and the behaviour through which it is realised (ends and means). Heclo argues that policy is, however, more than just a statement of purpose. Thirdly, policies often result in unintended consequences. Policy, Heclo argues, should embrace both the purpose and its results. 'One can therefore suggest that policy should be operationally identified, not by its goals, but by the actual behaviour attempting to effect the goals'. Heclo therefore views policy as a course of action (or inaction). Some writers have defined policy as resulting from a process [Pollitt et al, 1979] and some prefer to differentiate between policy and the goals that policies seek to effect [Smith, 1976]. Sometimes policy is seen as a process for solving problems or for responding to needs and opportunities [Hambleton, 1978].

Each definition leans on one particular discipline, approach or aspect of policy. Sometimes policy is allied with decision making and sometimes with administration. Some prefer to think of it in terms of action or inaction. The only conclusion we might draw from the miscellany of definitions is that policy is a very varied concept and in many ways is ill-defined. We use the term 'policy' in everyday speech, sometimes in a vernacular way and because it is familiar we are seldom inclined to consider it as having any technical definition. People and organisations are frequently not concerned with the technical dimension of policy but this casual approach leaves us with a number of problems, not least that of knowing what can legitimately be regarded as policy and what is actually something else. If failing to do something is as much a part of policy as doing something then it becomes problematic to distinguish between policy and negligence. There is little consensus about what policy is and what it is not. For most writers 'policy' is a generic term frequently qualified by other terms such as 'public', 'government', 'management' or 'social'. A policy or a particular element of a policy can be either positive or negative; a policy can either prescribe that something should happen or proscribe that it should not happen. Refraining from something is, in policy terms, as important as doing something. Some commentators regard inaction or absence of a policy to be as significant as action or having a policy. This theme will be returned to shortly.

Policy has also been defined as a 'disagreement or conflict among policy actors about an actual or potential course of government action' [Dunn, 1981 p 60]. Much policy debate is centred around issues (the subjects of policy), such as the death penalty, education, defence, taxation, and so on. Where there are conflicting views there are policy issues. The same writer has also commented that 'policy issues not only involve disagreements about actual or potential courses of action, they also reflect competing views of the nature of problems themselves (Dunn, 1981 p 101). We will return to this idea of the subject or issue of a policy when we consider the components of policy.

A clear understanding of what policy is requires us to differentiate it from those concepts that are adjacent to it. As was mentioned earlier, policy is often closely associated with administration. One writer, for example, found it difficult to distinguish between policy and administration and implementation. He defined policy as

> 'a deliberate course of action or inaction taken by those in office under the influence of values or pressures on the way resources (expenditure and coercion) are to be used in pursuit of objectives or in support of objectives or in support of other policies' [Smith, 1976].

He went on to say that public policy is:

> 'the outcomes of decisions about the political allocation of resources and is therefore characterised by the use of legal and coercive sanctions; by being of general concern; and by the application of political values to problem solving' [ibid.].

Policy and planning

Though policy and planning are closely connected and involve similar functions, they are not the same thing and it is useful to separate them conceptually. I have set out to show that policy expresses the purposes of a system and that planning is about deciding what will happen, in the future, in practical terms. Planning is therefore a process for putting policy into action, of organising a system of activities to bring about the achievement of a purpose. The relationship between policy and action is however not a unidirectional one. It has been argued that

> 'rather than treating implementation as the transmission of policy into a series of consequential actions, the policy–action relationship needs to be regarded as a process of interaction and negotiation, taking place over time, between those seeking to put policy into effect and those upon whom action depends' [Barrett and Fudge, 1981].

This view of the relationship between policy and planning (including practice) rightly accounts for the interactions between policy actors and policy subjects. My purpose has been however to distinguish between policy and planning so that the processes involved in each can be clearly understood. My purpose in distinguishing between them is not to deny that they are combined in practice, but to offer a clearer view of the functions they perform in organisational processes. Other writers have also seen fit to make such distinctions and some have distinguished between 'policy', 'plan' and 'programme' [Friend and Jessop, 1977].

Planning usually involves the acquisition and allocation of resources; this must be anticipated in policy, since one function of policy is to attribute budgets. Policy should determine what resources are required, of what quality, in what quantity and how such resources will be deployed. Once the allocation of resources has been decided by policy makers, planners set out to apply those resources in the pursuit of policy goals.

Planning is a function of strategy and tactics. Often, planning must succeed at both macro and micro levels as well as over the short and long term. But, in criminal justice and crime management, there is also the fundamental problem of 'unplannability' – the resistance of people and agencies to planning. This resistance is manifested in the defence of autonomy ('our agency is/must be independent'), in fragmentation and in competition among agencies for ownership of territories and resources. Those aspiring to plan criminal justice begin at a severe disadvantage: they are often unwelcome and unwanted.

Although policy and planning are often inseparable in practice, they can be differentiated conceptually. Policy and planning involve different sets of functions and it is for this reason that I have set out chapters on each. Some authors would not wish to make this distinction or make it so clearly, or would prefer to discuss policy planning or to use policy and planning as interchangeable concepts. Clearly, I regard this as confusing two distinct functions and processes.

What is also significant for me is that policy and planning are correctly placed in the overall framework of strategy. Some policies can be strategic or have strategically important components. But policies can contribute the key elements of strategies, where they articulate goals and principles. Policy is also frequently confused with strategy. The position of policy in the framework of strategy was discussed in chapter three and an illustration of how policy and planning relate to strategy is given in **Figure 3.2**. From this it will be seen that policy relates to the purposes of an organisation or system and planning relates to the means through which policy is implemented. As we saw in the last chapter, strategy is what qualifies policy and planning with those aspects that are critical to success.

We might also consider what policy is *not*. Policy might be generated from philosophical debate but it is clearly not a branch of philosophy. Philosophy might offer insights into values and meanings, or might deal with ethics and morality, but policy is a process of selecting (making decisions about) values and meanings. Policy making is a fundamental part of politics but there are clearly other aspects of politics that are not about policy making. A political ideology might involve policy but it is not wholly made up of policy. Policy and politics are not synonymous but simply overlap to some extent. If we can understand what policy is or what we would like it to be then we might be able to make it work more effectively for us.

What policy does

For the purposes of our present discussion, rather than dwell on definitions of policy, I would prefer to think about what policy does. As stated above, policy is an essential function of organisation. A fundamental reason for creating policy (and this is also a fundamental problem for policy makers in criminal justice) is the need to reconcile individualised decision making and action with the performance of an organisation or system. In criminal justice systems, hundreds of decisions are made every day about individual offenders and they are made by hundreds of different professionals, not to mention victims, wives, husbands and indeed the general public who read about crimes in the press or hear about them on their televisions and radios. These hundreds of individualised decisions have a cumulative effect on the performance of the justice system as a whole. But they are also made within a framework of rules, principles, guidelines and previous decisions and actions. If a policy exists and is adhered to, then this will reduce randomness, uncertainty and confusion in a system. Organisation confers order, certainty and clarity. A system of decision taking that is systematic, and policy related, will be fairer and more just (assuming that the policy itself is fair and just).

Policy provides a framework for operational decision making. If a policy provides a set of principles for decision making, decisions are more likely to be made with consistency than would be the case if such decisions were made in isolation. Rules are sometimes necessary but where decision making is complex, it may either be too complicated to formulate an effective set of rules, or so many rules might be required that they would never all be remembered. Principles, as an alternative, provide the logic behind the rules. Once the principles are understood, they can be applied to the wide variety of situations in which decisions are likely to be made. Principles embody values and where they are being applied, decision making is more likely to be consistent because each decision is being related to a common set of values. Policy provides decision makers with authority, most commonly with the authority of the organisation within which they work.

Although policy can be viewed as issues or conflicts between people with opposing views, it can also enable the resolution of conflicts or disagreements, by providing regulation of power or arbitration between opponents. It can reduce uncertainty or confusion by laying down definitions or setting limits and boundaries. Some will see policies as inducing conflict, leading to confusion or inhibiting actions. That is however more to do with the process of policy debate, or arises from badly formulated policy. A conflict model of policy views policy processes as repressive where policy is being made by the powerful and imposed on the weak.

Another function of policy is that of coordination. If a set of criminal justice organisations elect to subscribe to a common policy then they can achieve a greater degree of coordination. Policy enables coordination and reduces the fragmentation of the system. As we will see later, it provides the foundations for planning and operation.

Types of policy

Policy is by no means a monolithic phenomenon. The term policy has been applied to a very broad range of statements and sets of ideas. Four types of policy have been identified based on the functions that policy performs: (a) *distributive* policy that benefits everyone; (b) *constituent* policy that sets the 'rules of the game' (e.g. election law); (c) *regulative* policy that governs behaviour or activities and (d) *redistributive* policy that takes from one group and gives to another [Lowi quoted in Goldsmith, 1980].

This typology was based on an analysis of social policy. In organisational policy, we could consider three types of policy: (1) *general/expressive* policy; (2) *operational/programmatic* policy and (3) *authoritative/regulatory* policy. These classes are based on the kinds of functions that policy can perform. Any policy statement can contain all or some of these classes. A *general/expressive* policy is one that provides a broad conceptual statement on which further, more specific, sets of ideas can be built. It might reflect the philosophy of an organisation or a system and explain its purposes at a fundamental level. An *expressive* policy is one that seeks to communicate values, beliefs, assumptions, opinions, morals and so forth. In pure form, these expressions are not immediately practicable, other than as guidance for more specific decision making; they provide a basis on which operational policy can rest. The manifestos of political parties often contain a good deal of expressive policy, conveying the ideology of values.

An *operational/programmatic* policy is concerned with setting an agenda for action, with articulating objectives and the methods for achieving them. Legislation is a form of such policy; it prescribes what will be done or authorises what can be done. An Act of Parliament may, for example, contain clauses that allow a department to spend money; this is permissive policy, setting out what can be done. Other clauses instruct a department to act in a certain way, stating mandatorily what must be done. *Permissive* policies often set out the conditions under which action can be taken. *Programmatic* policies authorise the implementation of a system of actions. An Act of Parliament, for example, might *allow* an airport to be built in a certain place or it might *require* an airport to be built in a certain place. *Authoritative/regulatory* policies seek to govern actions that are taking place rather than to create new systems of action. Sentencing policy, for example, regulates the decision making powers of the courts. Criminal law (a form of such policy) authorises sentencers to impose certain sanctions but regulates them by setting maximum penalties or by determining the levels of fines that may be imposed.

This classification probably fails to provide for all kinds of policies that might exist; it does, hopefully, cover most of them. One other way of looking at types of policy is to say that some policies are *formal* and some *informal*. *Formal* policies are those that are documented and authorised through established procedures. *Informal* policies represent an unwritten consensus of views, a conventional wisdom, and their authority is inherent in the group within which the consensus resides.

Policy as product

Policy can be viewed as the product of policy processes. Policies can be produced by political systems, bureaucracies, organisations, groups or individuals. The outcome intended by a policy is not always the same as the results of a policy [Smith, 1976]. A policy outcome is what policy makers intend to happen; the results of policy, achieved when a policy is implemented, can be called its out-turns (or sometimes outputs). This distinction is important because, as some commentators have observed, policies can result in unintended consequences [Goldsmith, 1980]. The same distinction will be found in the chapter on planning.

As mentioned above, some outcomes are positive and some are negative; a policy can determine that something shall or shall not be done. Similarly, a decision not to do something or a decision not to decide on an issue can be as important as a positive decision. Policy can either promote change or resist it [Smith, 1976]. Being able to predict the out-turns of a policy is a problem that confronts policy makers in formulating new or revising existing policies. Prediction and forecasting are problems that also confront those who implement policy, as we shall see in the next chapter. Policy products often interact with each other: the results of one policy might form the inputs (impacts or influences on) another policy. There is a relationship between, for example, social security benefits policy and policy relating to minimum wages.

Policy can be seen as a product; some regard it as being the product of government [Burch and Wood, 1983] but policy is also made by a wide variety of other organisations and for a variety of other purposes. Government itself is influenced by policies generated by trade unions, pressure groups, professional bodies and so on. Policy can be made by political processes, can be the product of choices or decisions, result from negotiations, conflicts or from consensus. Sometimes policy results from action; at other times it produces action. One writer argues that 'policy is what governments choose to do or not to do' [Dye, 1972]. The relationship between policy and action is problematic as we shall see when we come on to the issue of evaluation.

The scope of policy

Some attempts have been made to typify policies by their extent or scope. *Macro* policies apply to the whole of a nation, organisation or system; *micro* policies cover a local area, a department or a mechanism within a larger system [Meltsner and Bellavita, 1983]. Some policies are very general, others very specific. A number of policies can be networked into a larger policy system; economic policy, for example, is a network of policies related to money supply, interest rates, overseas trade, taxation and so on. Policies that are made by national government (macro policies) interact with policies made by local governments (by comparison these can be seen as being micro policies). Some policies affect the whole of a community at the same time and others affect particular segments of the community at different times [Froman, 1970].

When we look at criminal justice or crime prevention policies, the issue of scope will be directly relevant. Making judgements about the scope of a proposed policy is difficult; if a policy is set too narrowly it can be fragmentary and fail to deal adequately with the problem. Conversely a policy that tries to deal too widely with responses to crime, that is cast too globally, can fail to be implemented or become too complex for any one person to organise or comprehend it. It is therefore necessary to break down large-scale policies into a series of specific policies, each of which can be more easily formulated or analysed.

Components of policy

In everyday terms a policy is about something, as for example defence, the environment or the economy. For most people the subject of the policy *is* the policy and, generally, policy is what policies are about. A policy on a particular subject might be part of a wider policy; for example, a policy on inflation might be part of a wider and more general economic policy. This is illustrated in **Figure 4.1** which shows that individual policies are often part of a wider policy universe of discourse. Conversely, global policies are made up of sets of lower order policies that deal with specific subjects. Dunn refers to there being a hierarchy of policy issues (major issues, secondary issues, functional issues and minor issues) and these can contain either strategic or operational decisions [Dunn, 1981 p 103]. Often policies overlap and intertwine to form policy networks. Sometimes these subsets of two or more policies might themselves represent discrete policy subjects, like policies that represent the overlap between health and social work (e.g. mental health). In some cases policies can be seen as hierarchies rather than sets [Smith, 1976].

As we shall see later, defining the boundaries around a policy can be problematical. Any particular policy subject might have a fairly fluid boundary and might easily flow out into other subjects. Some writers

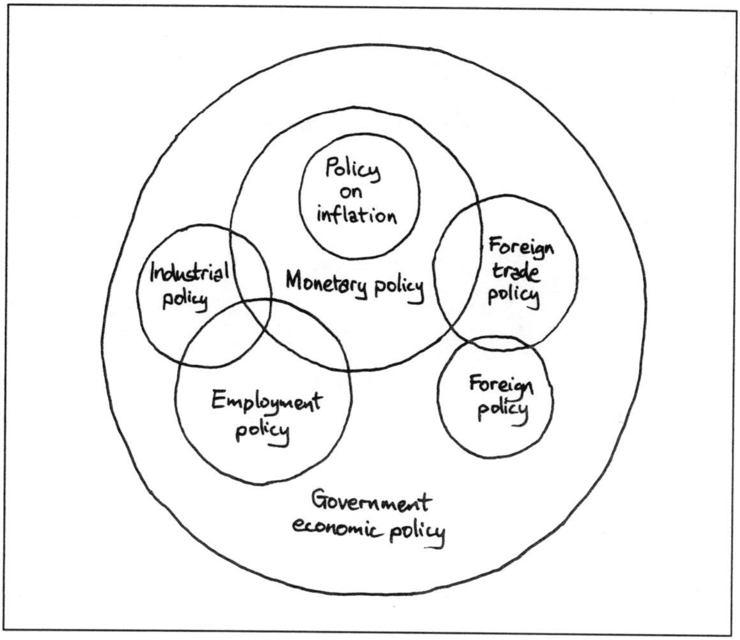

Figure 4.1 Example of policy sets

have referred to the subject of a policy as being the 'policy problem' [Dunn, 1981] and others to the 'policy area' [Smith, 1976]. Boundaries around a policy subject can be modified by those who pursue it as an issue. Changes to the boundary can result from the process of policy formulation. Setting and defining the boundary is therefore a fundamental part of policy formulation. Policy statements give only a snapshot picture of a policy since for most issues or subjects policy is in a state of constant flux. The issue of policy boundaries will be discussed again below under the heading of 'policy formulation'.

Relatively little attention has been paid, in the literature on policy theory, to the components of policy – its external structural characteristics. Some writers have attempted to define the essential elements of most policies [Smith, 1976 or Goldsmith, 1980]. Drawing on the work of Ranney, Smith identifies five components that he regards as being essential to policy: (1) a particular object or set of objects (that which is to be effected), (2) a desired sequence of events, (3) a selected line of action (set of actions to bring about a course of events), (4) a declaration of intent (statement by policy makers as to what they intended to do, how and why) and (5) implementation of intent (actions actually undertaken) [Smith, 1976].

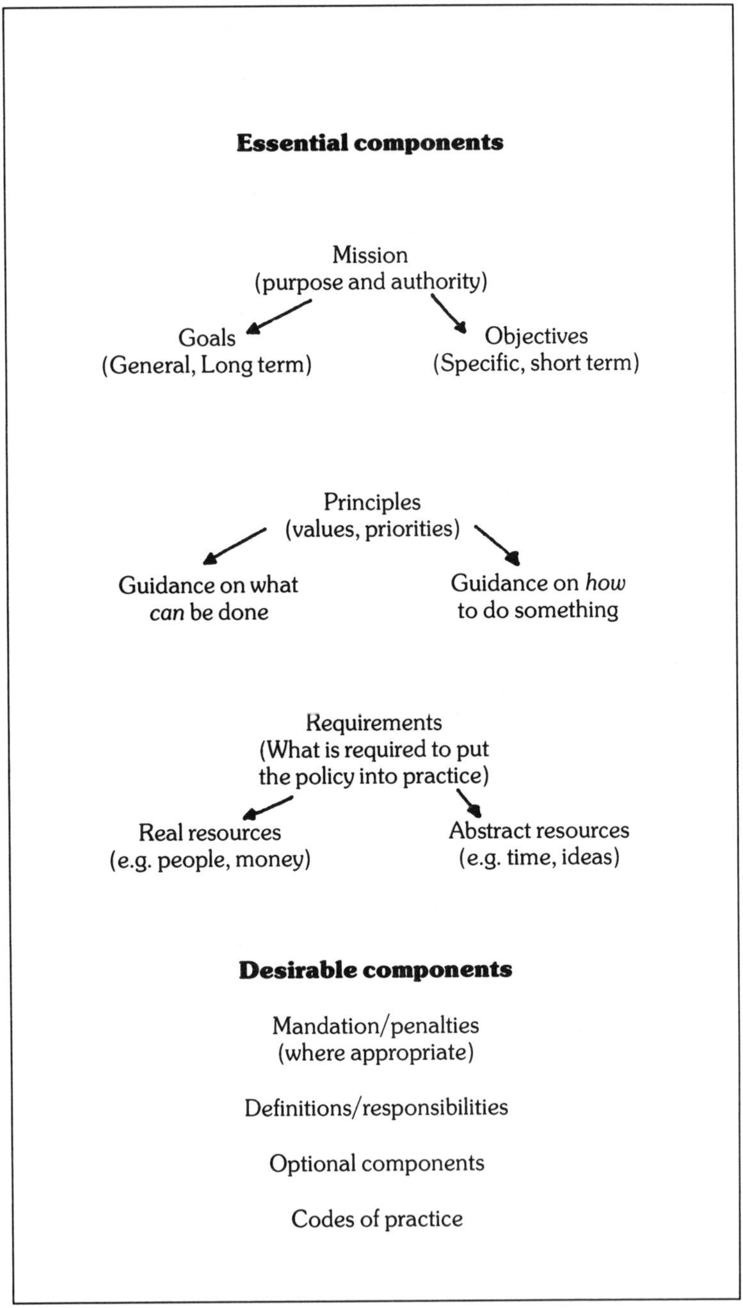

Figure 4.2 Components of policy

Given by argument above, this analysis appears to confuse policy with planning. In my view, policy certainly includes item (4) and might also include (1). Items (2), (3) and (5) fall into what I have defined as planning. It is sometimes the case that a different set of people make decisions about how and when a set of actions is to be put into effect, from those who decide why those actions are defined and what their purpose is. I would therefore suggest that one component that is essential to policy is a statement of purpose or intent. Most writers agree that statements of goals are a characteristic element of policy. The following components of policy are summarised in **Figure 4.2**

Goals

Policy attempts to lay the foundations of a system: it should therefore set out very clearly the goals – aims and objectives – from which operations should flow. Policies in law enforcement and criminal justice should state the purposes of those systems, for example, that policing or prosecution should reduce crime or that the courts should try defendants fairly and with due regard for the law. Most criminal justice agencies now have stated goals: reference has already been made to the statement of national objectives for the probation service, and the Crown Prosecution Service has a set of strategic goals that are published in its annual reports. These are, however, broad purposes of public policy. For local organisations, more specific goals and objectives can be set. Goal setting is an important part of the policy process. Policies that portray a clear sense of purpose are more likely to be effective than those that impart a vague or confused sense of what they are trying to achieve.

Aims and objectives are two varieties of goals. Aims are broad expressions, general statements of what policy is to achieve. Objectives flow from aims and are detailed and specific. Aims will usually break down into clusters of objectives. Aims may be achieved in the long term; objectives should be capable of being achieved in the short to medium term. Aims and objectives should not be confused with methods: aims and objectives are the 'ends' to which methods are the 'means'. Objectives might also take the form of targets; these are time-limited and specific and should be measurable (see **Figure 4.3**).

Principles

A principle is a guideline or set of guidelines that can provide a reference for decision making or action. We can refer to, for example, the principle of proportionality or the principle of minimal intervention. Principles can be located in expressive policy as well as in permissive or operational policy. Such principles express values but

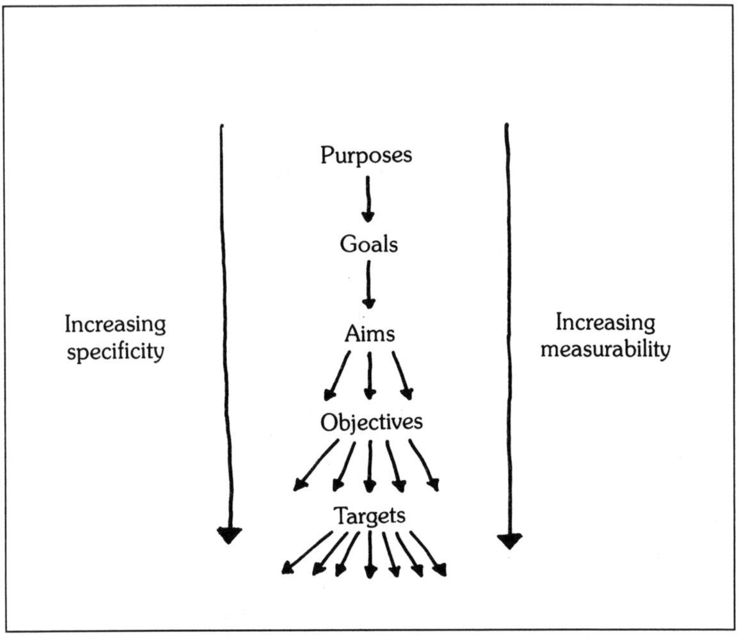

Figure 4.3 Aims and objectives

Figure 4.3

also provide an operational reference for decision making by practitioners. The importance of principles is that they provide an alternative to a set of rules; in this sense they are permissive rather than prescriptive. If we take sentencing as an example, we can see that decisions made by judges or magistrates must relate to a wide range of circumstances presented in criminal cases. It is extremely difficult to set down a comprehensive body of rules that would prescribe what sentences should be made in such a wide range of possible circumstances. A set of principles provides guidance that allow judgements to be made according to a system of values and conditions.

Principles therefore address values and assumptions in policy and act as settlements (for the time being) of conflicts or confusions. They can also represent consensus about values and modes of conduct. Some principles also bear similarities to *standards*, references that seek to impart a consistent way of doing things, maximum or minimum levels, conventions of procedure and so on. Principles are therefore able to convey what things (actions or decisions) ought to result from defined conditions. Principles are, I would argue, of considerable importance in crime and justice policies. There is, in public debates about crime and justice, considerable moral posturing about offending and how offenders should be dealt with. Because certain crimes engender moral outrage, it is sometimes suggested that any response, however punitive, is legitimate. Fears about the prevalence of crime and its affects on victims sometimes lead to overreactions and extravagant claims as what should be done. Such hot responses easily lead to violations of rights and liberties which are as detrimental to society as the crimes those responses are aimed at. Unprincipled and unethical practices cannot be justified by the need to respond to crime. Two wrongs do not make a right – just two wrongs. Policy provides a way of ensuring that means are justified by ends and that the practices of crime control and justice are determined, not by the values and prejudices of individuals, but by public or organisational decisions.

Requirements

Operational and programmatic policies (those that allow something to be *done* as opposed to those that *say* something) usually involve *requirements*: what is *needed* to do the job. Some operational policies are concerned with procedures (*how* something is to be done) and this might not require any change in resources. Operational policies requiring work to be carried out, however, require (a) people to do the work, (b) finance to pay the people and (c) buildings or equipment for the people to use in doing the work. Finally, work requires time and this is also a resource (albeit a fixed one). Other kinds of resources include knowledge, skills, running costs and information. These we can call the operational *requirements* of a policy.

Policies need not necessarily prescribe exactly what requirements are needed in order to achieve their goals or targets. These are details that are often left to planners. But what *good* policy must do is to ensure that sufficient resources can be made available to those that must pursue or implement the policy, to allow policy goals to be achieved to an acceptable standard. It is not good policy to set goals and then not provide sufficient resources for those goals to be achieved.

Mandates and sanctions

Any management policy system should be based on authority and should make clear the basis of its authority. Those to whom it applies need to be aware of its status and to be able to recognise the degree to which it is enforceable. Policy statements can be purely advisory or they can be mandatory. If a policy is mandatory then it should clearly set out any sanctions that will apply to noncompliance and the conditions under which infraction will occur.

If a policy statement lies somewhere between being advisory and being mandatory, then there could be uncertainty or confusion about whether the policy can be ignored or must be applied. The choice of words is important: 'may', 'must', 'can', 'could', 'should', etc. have explicit meanings and implications. Policy statements must state what sanctions will apply if policy is not followed. Of course, policy makers would prefer it if their policy is followed voluntarily – they wish for commitment rather than compulsion. We can see that there can be degrees of mandation: highly mandatory policies will impose severe penalties for nonconformity. Such penalties will be explicitly stated in the policy. However, in cases where there is a low degree of compulsion in the policy, sanctions are less formally organised. Policy makers have to decide whether or not a specific policy or piece of policy will be sanctionable, what sanction may be applied and the degree to which penalties can be imposed. Sanctions can also be applied to discretionary policies where there are codes of conduct or guidelines that set boundaries around discretion. These factors are depicted in **Figure 4.4**. When we considered what policy does we saw that policy can be used to resolve conflicts. Policy that imposes mandates should also provide for arbitration, appeals against the imposition of sanctions and for settlement of disputes between managers and practitioners.

Mandation	Application	Sanction	Example
High	Specific	Explicit	Criminal law
|	|	|	|
Low	General	Absent/informal	Professional codes

Fig 4.4 Levels of mandation in policy

Levels of policy

Policy relating to responses to crime can be seen to cover both national and local levels. National and public policy is laid down by institutions of government and by national organisations and groups. In specific localities, three levels of policy can be identified: local public policy, corporate policy and agency policy.

Public policy

Criminal justice policy begins, as indeed it should, in the public arena, in that criminal legislation is laid down by Parliament and policy circulars are issued nationally by government departments. Also, the political parties have policies about law and order, justice and crime control and these are part of public policy. Criminal justice issues and problems are matters of public concern and debate and are extensively discussed in the media and in many other forums.

Public policy has been defined as the 'implicit or explicit intentions of government and the expression of those intentions entailing specific patterns of activity or inaction by governmental agencies' [Barrett and Fudge, 1981]. Intentions are, for the most part, explicit if they are communicated either in verbal or written statements. But policy can be said to be implicit in decisions or actions that are taken; in other words 'actions speak louder than words'. The extent to which agencies that produce or influence public opinion are governmental is arguable, since many of the interest groups that contribute to the process of public policy making stand in opposition to the government. Government policies reflect what government wishes to do as much as what it is prevented from doing. There is a difference between public policy and public opinion. Policy is, I would argue, essentially written and documentary whereas public opinion is the sum total of what people think. Policy is the product of organisations whereas opinion is the product of individuals.

Public opinion is difficult to measure; even so, policy makers need to make judgements about what public and political opinion will bear in many areas, not least that of crime and justice. Some policy makers prefer to deal only with party political opinion since the wider public have no organised way of impacting on what an organisation does or what its policy is, other than through the political process.

Falkin regards public policy as being the main input to criminal justice policy [Falkin, 1979]; it provides guidance in the form of priorities for the allocation of resources and sets constraints on policy makers. He argues that policy scientists can improve the formulation of public policy by offering analyses of the outcomes of policy proposals. Falkin defines public policy as: 'an authoritative ranking of objectives combined with an official set of rules to guide decision makers and resourcers to enable them to achieve the objectives' [op cit, p 13]. At local level, elected representatives make decisions about budgets, resource allocation, and planning and thereby will influence

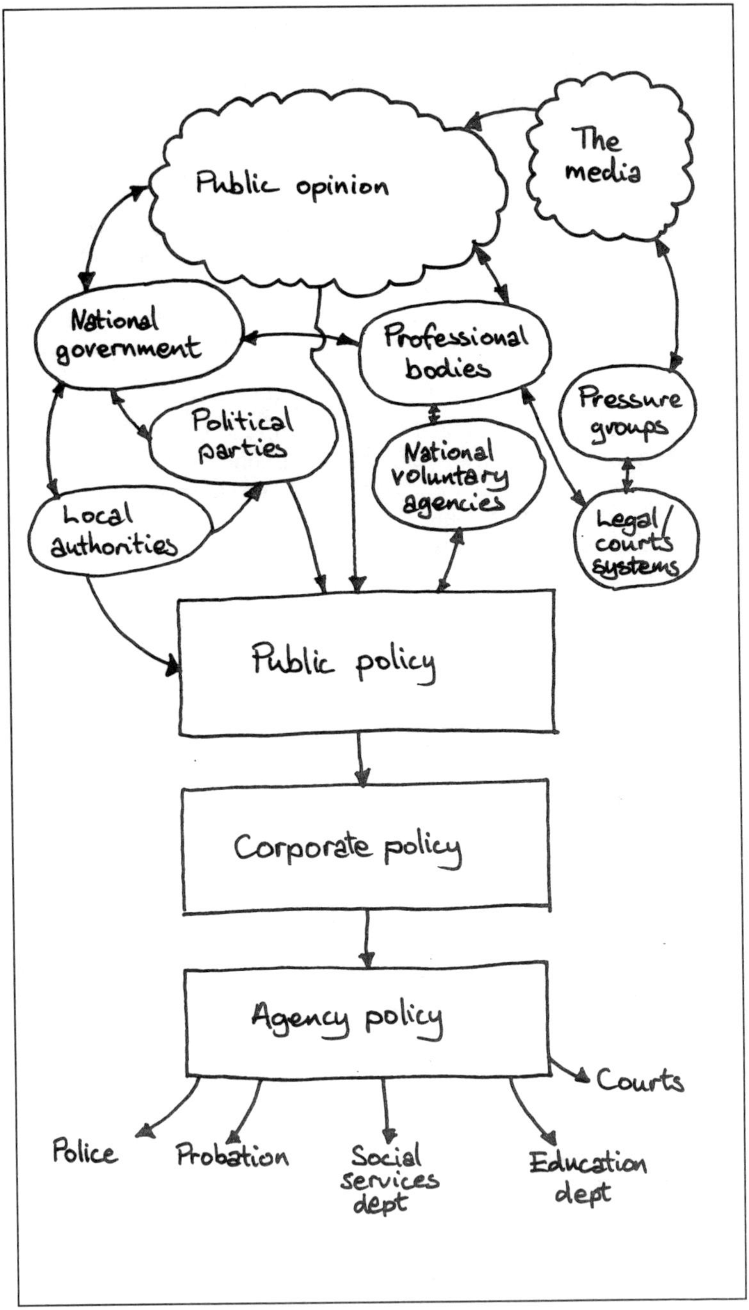

Figure 4.5 Influences on policy

the operation of the local justice system, police force and organisations dealing with offenders.

Local public policy might take the form of statements issued by the full council or by its subcommittees, particularly those that have a service delivery brief. Local political parties, pressure groups, trade unions, community groups and voluntary bodies are also potential participants in the formulation of public policy. The media shape and influence public opinion. A sketch of the influences on public crime and criminal justice policies is offered in **Figure 4.5**.

Where public policy has been stated, it provides a baseline on which to formulate organisational or interorganisational policies. It is not unknown for organisations to formulate progressive justice policies that are in advance of public thinking and this can run them into problems. Public opinion is likely to change less rapidly than organisations in a local area. The contribution of the analyst of public policy is to identify gaps in current policy and to bring these to the attention of politicians. But analysts might also find contradictions in existing policy. A policy formulated by the education committee, for example, might have unintended consequences for work with juveniles in the social services department. Policies tend to be formulated by departmentally-based committees and it is often difficult or impossible to formulate policy on a subject basis. The role of officers in public policy formulation is to assist politicians in the creation of a clear, coherent and comprehensive statement of policy.

It is often the case that policy makers and the specialists advising them have a more developed technical knowledge of the problems they are dealing with than do the general public. Crime is a major problem and prominent in public interest, but few members of the general public know the facts about crime.

Policy and politics

Policy formulation is a political process. Policy formulation by professionals takes place in a political context. It is sometimes thought that politicians make policy and professionals simply carry it out. This is an oversimplification and many studies stress that professionals (for example, civil servants and local government officers) often influence policy formulation to a large extent. When there is competition for resources, conflicts over alternative options and debate about which option is the right one to adopt, or the promotion of one set of values against another, then we have politics. Both policy and politics involve the application of values, and setting of gaols and priorities and the making of value judgements. To some authors, politics and policy formulation are interchangeable terms [Carley, 1980]; for others, politics is one of a number of processes involved in policy formulation. Yet, the process of policy formulation is in essence an attempt to resolve these conflicts. Policy authorisation brings debate to a conclusion – if only for the time being. There is a complex relationship between politicians and professionals; sometimes it includes conflict and this often occurs where their roles are confused. It has been suggested that the political/professional dichotomy might be losing its value and too the distinction between policy making and management [Clarke, 1987]. Both chief officers and politicians engage in policy making functions, sometimes in different arenas and for different purposes,and the process of policy formulation might engage both sets of actors in a collaborative exercise. This might involve politicians, as political managers, going beyond generalised attempts to establish the style and culture of the authority to setting clear objectives for senior officials [op cit, p 24]. A new professionalism is seen to be emerging in local government, and in central government also, management practices and the relationships between civil servants and political leaders have been undergoing considerable change during the 1980s. In this context, the concept of *policy management* has developed to integrate policy and executive functions [Metcalfe and Richards, 1987]. This demands the closer integration of policy analysis into the management process and the greater use of performance measurement to improve policy evaluation [op cit, p 192].

Corporate policy

Public policy lays the foundations for corporate policy. Several organisations are involved in crime management and criminal justice: the courts, the police, social services, probation services, voluntary organisations, and so on. It is now increasingly acknowledged that a collective strategy is required in order to address the problems inherent in fragmentation and in order to increase the effectiveness of individual organisations within the field. A collective strategy requires that representatives of each of these interest groups work together to formulate a corporate policy that will provide a framework on which individual organisations can hang their own policies. Such corporate policies can define the roles and responsibilities of constituent organisations, provide a basis for overall resource allocation, facilitate medium and long term planning and lay the ground for shared and joint information systems.

Agency policy

Each organisation operating within a local justice system - probation services, police, social services, etc. - should document their policies. Such policies should set guidance on internal operations and services and also relate to that organisation's relationships with other bodies within the system. But it is also important for all the key organisations to set a common policy that they will share and it is from this that the policies of individual organisations should flow.

However, the first problem in the formulation of such policies is that of scope. A policy can be oriented to crime, to justice or to the offender. The police might require a crime related policy whereas the social service department might be more concerned with services to offenders. The policy might have implications for the youth service, for education, for unemployment services and these implications might be quite different from those that relate directly to the management of crime and the processing of offenders through the justice system. The aim of policy formulation should be to address the key factors that cut across organisations.

One function of policy formulation might be to clearly define an organisation's boundaries and responsibilities. Each organisation derives its responsibilities (its 'mandate') from legislation and from council policies. Sometimes the exact demarcation of an organisation's responsibilities is unclear and it can require a policy statement to make this clear.

Policy formulation

So far we have looked at what policy is, what functions it performs and what it should contain. Our next task is to consider how it is made. The making of policy is usually referred to as policy formulation. Most policy is not new but is continually reformulated. It has been argued that 'most policy making is actually policy succession: the replacement of an existing policy, programme or organisation by another' [Hogwood and Gunn, 1984]. Policy comes into being in three stages:

(1) *initiation* - someone suggests that a policy should be devised or an existing policy should be revised; or it is suggested that an existing policy should be abolished.

(2) *Formulation* - ideas are worked with, drafts are written, options are evaluated, consultations take place, alternatives are short listed or eliminated and priorities are set. At this stage the task is to prepare a final draft statement ready for the next stage, which is

(3) *Authorisation* - the final draft is authorised or adopted. Policy can only be made by bodies that have the power or authority to make it.

In order to produce good policy it is essential that the process of policy formulation is well designed, thorough and systematic. Policy formulation and creation are continuous processes since everything is subject to change, review and re-evaluation. Because most policies are not freshly coined, it is more likely that reformulation will be engaged in than formulation.

The process of policy formulation

Some writers have defined policy as being the product of government [Burch and Wood, 1983] or as being the product of a process [Pollitt et al, 1979]; others choose to distinguish between policies and effects and goals [Smith, 1976]. This seems to confuse policy and planning; for most practical purposes policies are where goals and effects are defined. In arguing that policies involve a 'deliberate choice of actions designed to reach those objectives' Smith is in danger of fudging the important distinction between policy and planning, that is that policy defines the ends and planning the means.

Policy statements are the tangible products of an intangible process of debate and decision making. When a policy statement is issued (assuming that it is, since not all policy making processes commit themselves to paper) then the process of formulation is finalised, at least for the time being. A statement is thus the product of a policy process. This should not be confused with the out-turn of a policy which is what comes about once the policy is put into effect.

One of the starting points of policy formulation is to make a statement of the goals involved. Any organisation or interorganisational group, intending to formulate a policy, should identify those public policies that are relevant to this exercise. We must begin with a clear understanding of the current situation before moving on to the creation of new policies or to the reformulation of existing policies. We should consider the context of the policy, that is, those influences, factors, considerations or other aspects that are outside the terms of reference of the policy but which nevertheless might have a bearing on its content or mode of formulation.

A social services department could be one example of an organisation which, although having a managerial hierarchy, also permits participation in the policy process at all levels. A police force, however, could be an example of an organisation in which policy is made at the top and handed down through a chain of command for implementation. In most organisations we can see reactions to policy processes, ranging from enthusiastic acceptance to resistance and conflict. Policies that are oriented to change are most likely to incite resistance, and the more changes upset the balance of power or cut across vested interests, the more likely it will be that people will resist them.

Policy makers desire adherence to their policies and the degree of adherence depends to a large extent on the ownership of the policy. Democratic or participatory policy processes tend to spread the ownership of a policy thereby generating adherence to it. Ownership of a policy is therefore a condition of motivating people to implement it. Policy processes in organisations are frequently viewed as being hierarchical and made at the top and handed down for others to implement. This view has been questioned [Barrett and Fudge, 1981] in that policy making could be a reaction to what is already happening within the organisation or, indeed, to pressure and changes in its external environment. Some policies create change; others follow on from change and simply authorise it. Policy change could also be a process of expressing or authorising innovations and changes that have been caused by processes, other than those generated by policy. In terms of public policy, and indeed where interorganisational relationships are concerned, some policies are expressive, requiring other organisations to implement them.

Policy formulation requires ownership and commitment, particularly on the part of those who are to implement the resulting policy. Policies that are formulated by those at 'the top' without consultation with those who are to implement them, and handed down, stand the risk of being ineffective. Where commitment of practitioners is required, it is wise to involve them in the formulation of the policy. This is not just to allow for 'democracy' nor is it just as a mark of a participatory style of management. Good policies often rely on experience and insight and, in this respect, practitioners have as much to contribute as managers.

Boundaries and limits

An early task in the process of formulating policy is that of setting the boundaries and limits of a policy. We must be able to decide what the policy is about, what it relates to, what should and should not be in it. We must be able to define the boundaries of the system. If we are to formulate a sound policy on, for example, juvenile justice, we must be sure to set appropriate boundaries between this policy and any neighbouring policies, such as child care, education, the youth service, welfare, the family or unemployment; such overlaps are of course very important. But we do not wish the objectives of one policy to be thwarted or nullified by other policies. We would not wish separate policy systems to work against each other. Boundaries are important, even where we wish to create an integrated set of policies.

The context of a policy was referred to earlier. Part of that context consists of other policies that are relevant. This can become a complex picture, particularly where crime prevention is concerned. Crime preventive strategies involve a network of local authority policies. The possible scope of policies relating to crime prevention is very wide. Setting out a crime prevention policy for any organisation is likely to involve looking at quite a wide range of policies in other departments or organisations. The degree to which this can be done depends on the time and patience available to those formulating the policy. Clearly, it is wise to start with the most immediately neighbouring policies and deal with those first. So, for example, a crime prevention policy for a housing department would need to look at any relevant policy in the education department (including the youth service), the policy, recreation and leisure departments, chief executive's department and any key voluntary organisations in the area.

Policy formulation and decision making

One of the functions of policy is to provide guidance to decision makers. This poses a dilemma: those making decisions about individuals in the justice system must base those decisions on the particular circumstances of the case. However, the sum of all these decisions adds up to the performance of the system as a whole. As noted earlier, a decision not to do something can be as significant as a decision to do something. In the systems view of policy and planning decisions can have far reaching consequences. Floyd argues that, in defining change within a system, 'the actions of one individual, or an organisation' can have effects on the 'system as a whole or on other parts of the system' [Floyd, 1984 p 2]. Knowing how far and where these effects will be felt is clearly important to managing the performance of the system. It is often a seemingly impossible task to coordinate the objectives of a policy system as a whole with decisions made about any one individual. This dilemma is resolved when we understand the role of policy in individual discretion. Policy sets the boundaries around discretion and provides principles of practice on which good decision making in individual cases can rest.

Many of those who write about policy regard decision making as being one of its main characteristics [for example, Etzioni, 1968]. We have already noted that policies are permissive, allowing the exercise of discretion within a framework of goals and principles and some are restrictive, seeking to limit what is permissible. Policies can be categorised by their degree of openness or closedness [Floyd, 1984]. An open policy sets guidelines but allows for a free range of professional judgements to be made; a closed policy is prescriptive and rule-oriented and prefers not to allow much discretion to be exercised. Regulatory policies are often primarily concerned with decision making, seeking to control what decisions can or cannot be made, by whom and under what conditions. Programmatic policies set out to implement a system of actions or schedule of work and require or allow planning decisions to be made according to the purposes that have been stated by the policy.

What such policy sets out to do is to create consistent decision making, to reduce uncertainty, curtail arbitrary decision making and provide a means of coordinating those decisions that need to be related to each other. Decisions often need to be made on the basis of information. Decision making requires collection and analysis of information. It also may require options to be set out and tested for their feasibility, consequences, cost-benefit, etc. Good and thorough information analysis might widen the choice of options; it could equally well narrow them by showing that some of these options are in fact untenable. Policy, planning and information are thereby interlinked but policy sets the overall framework for the system.

Evaluating policy

Evaluation is essential to effective policy processes. If policy is, as has been argued previously, a continual process of modification, then evaluation should also be a function that is performed regularly. There are two stages at which policies can be evaluated: prior to and after their implementation. The first of these is part of policy analysis, where policy options are evaluated as part of the process of policy formulation. The latter is concerned with considering the extent to which a policy has been successful. In formulating policy, choices have to be made between alternative options. One purpose of evaluating is to see if the best decisions have been made about options. Those who have formulated policy should ideally have looked at all the alternative options and have made choices between these. The thoroughness of such an analysis will of course depend on the availability of information, on political contingencies, amount of time available and so on. Evaluating the options that have been made involves looking at the constraints under which policy makers have operated.

Policy evaluation should take into account the political feasibility of the policy and the administrative feasibility of its implementation. Policy evaluation requires consideration of the degree of commitment likely to be secured to the policy, the extent to which intended goals are likely to be achieved, and in respect of possible unintended consequences [Nagel, 1980].

Evaluation of policies in process of formulation can be achieved through policy analysis; post hoc evaluation requires monitoring of implementation. The results of such evaluation provide a basis for further policy formulation. One study found that evaluation research concentrated on firstly, the assessment of benefit or cost to the client, consumer or community and secondly, improving the design and internal operations of programmes and organisations [Wilner, 1974].

There are several methods of evaluating policy; one of them is to compare its intended aims and objectives (its outcomes) with what was actually achieved (its out-turns). This assumes that a policy statement has presented a clear set of aims and objectives that can be evaluated. Not all policy statements do this. This might involve a before and after assessment, showing what change has occurred as a result of the policy being implemented. There is very often, however, a problem of determining whether observed changes occurred as a direct consequence of the policy or as a result of other influences. Resolving this problem might require us to look carefully at the means by which the policy was implemented. We might select indicators or measures that demonstrate the impact of the policy.

If evaluation is to be built into a policy and planning process, monitoring and recording should be designed into the process so that evidence can be collected from the outset. If a policy seems to have been a failure, even though its aims and objectives were satisfactory, the evaluation might look at the resources that were made available to implement that policy. If there were insufficient resources, relative to the requirements of the policy, then its failure might have been due to this. Well formulated policies present details of their resource requirements; if resources are limited, then policy objectives might need to be restricted to fit with them. Similarly, the policy may have been well formulated but those responsible for implementing it could have performed inadequately. Evaluating policy therefore requires that we separate policy, planning and practice and that we be clear which of these is being evaluated.

But were the aims and objectives right in the first place? To explore this question we can look at the original options that were considered to be available and compare them with the options that were actually chosen; this would indicate whether the original options that were chosen were in fact valid. By this process it is possible to see whether the policy as formulated has addressed the options and has shown why choices have been made.

We may consider the extent to which policies have been implemented, since a policy that has not been fully implemented cannot be said to have taken effect. Neither can we say that a policy is ineffective if it has not been fully implemented. A policy might not have been implemented for long enough to achieve its intended outcomes. A policy that has been fully implemented and has not achieved its goals may be evaluated as being ineffective, though other factors might have to be accounted for. Impact evaluation will be concerned not only with intended consequences but also with any unintended consequences, whether these are positive or negative. Most evaluative research is costly both in time and effort. If it is to be of value, it must produce useful and directly relevant feedback into organisational processes, particularly to the policy formulation process.

A main theme in policy evaluation has been cost-benefit or cost-effectiveness assessment of programme objectives. This approach concentrates on assessing the efficiency or the effectiveness of the policy when implemented [Carley, 1980]. Such approaches can be valid but assume that the policy outcomes can be quantified and measured in cost terms. Some analysts prefer to assess the social benefits of policies in terms of their social values. Costs need not be confined to finance; time, effort, and resources are expended in the implementation process as well as money.

Policy analysis

Policy analysis aims to identify and evaluate the options that are available, to set out alternative ways of achieving goals or the options that are relevant to putting policies into operation. Dunn defines policy analysis as:

> 'an applied social science discipline which uses multiple methods of inquiry and argument to produce and transform policy-revelant information that may be utilised in political settings to resolve policy problems' [Dunn, 1981].

It has also been defined as the systematic study of rules in order to explain how alternative configurations effect differences in human welfare [Gregg, 1976]. Policy analysis should enable policy makers to clarify their aims and objectives and how these will be translated into principles of practice. It is concerned with the nature, causes and effects of decisions or policies designed to cope with specific social problems. Such analyses could focus on (a) determining the causes of social problems; (b) determining the relationship between social forces and social problems; (c) determining the effects of policies and (d) determining how policies will maximise goal achievement [Nagel, 1980]. Such analysis should also provide policy makers with the information that will enable them to make sound choices. It should examine costs and benefits of alternatives, and evaluate the best alternative from a set, given values and criteria.

Methods of policy analysis can be grouped into those which are quantitative and those which are qualitative. The latter can include descriptive or journalistic accounts, philosophical analyses of normative values or ultimate social causes, historical descriptions of attempts to deal with problems, how policy problems are handled in diverse cultures and legal and judicial interpretations. Quantitative analysis involves either inductive statistical analysis or deductive reasoning based on causal models [Nagel, 1980].

Policy analysis reveals the effects of policies, both those effects which are intended and those which could be unintended. It should predict the effects of introducing a policy or change of policy. Policy analysis requires a framework, such as that offered by Falkin [1979]: (1) identify the key variables and model them: to enable this, variables should be quantifiable. The model should be compatible with the generalised statement of goals and targets, methods of operation and structures. (2) Rank order objectives and priorities: sets of objectives can be compatible, complementary or competing and the analysis should reveal the relationships between objectives. (3) Show how the policy can be implemented: instrumental variables are those that policy makers can manipulate. Costs are key instruments. Alternative programmes should be subjected to cost-benefit analysis. (4) Show how the policy relates to the organisational structure: look at the interrelationships between policy makers, particularly in closely related agencies. The analysis should reveal the internal and external constraints and should seek optimal results and outcomes. Policy analysis should also bring out and discuss the political and social issues involved in the proposed policy.

Policy analysis, according to Dunn [1981], is much more than the production of information. He argues that analysts seek, not only to produce different kinds of information, but also to transform this information as part of reasoned arguments about public policy. According to Dunn, policy argument has six elements: (1) policy-relevant information: information about policy problems, alternatives, actions, outcomes, and performance. (2) Policy claim: the conclusion of a policy argument. (3) Warrant: an assumption which permits the analyst to move from information to claim by providing a reason for the claim. (4) Backing: the backing for a warrant consists of additional assumptions or arguments that may be used to support warrants which are not accepted at face value. The backing for warrants allows the analyst to go one step further backward and state underlying assumptions. (5) Rebuttal: a second conclusion, assumption or argument that states conditions under which an original claim is unacceptable. This helps the analyst to anticipate objections. (6) Qualifier: expresses the degree to which the analyst is certain about a policy claim [Dunn, 1981]. These elements are represented in **Figure 4.6**.

Given that policy is written and that words and language are fundamental tools of policy analysis, policy statements can be subjected to textual, terminological and literary studies. Policy analysis requires the use of language as a tool for thinking through policy problems [Ostrom, 1976]. A fundamental function of such analysis is understanding how certain key terms are used, both in policy statements and in the discussions and verbal communications which take place in policy debate and formulation. This is not so much an exercise in semantics as one in which social and political processes are examined. If words and terms are tools, then it is important to understand exactly how they are used.

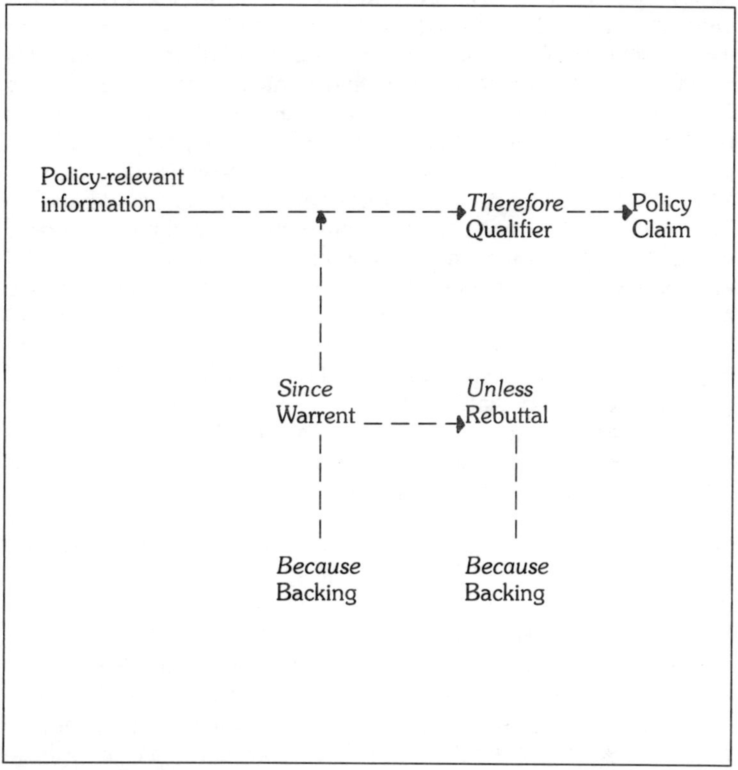

Source: From Dunn, 1981, page 43

Figure 4.6 Policy argument

Policy statements

It is surprising but nevertheless true, that very few studies of policy consider the way in which written policy is documented. Examples of familiar policy documents include: party manifestos, acts of parliament, departmental circulars, or pamphlets issued by organisations that state what their policy is on a particular issue. Whilst there have been studies of the content of policy documents (as a method of policy analysis), little regard has been paid to the format, structure and styles of writing policy statements. In organisations, policy statements are the instruments through which policy is expressed and implemented. A policy statement is a management tool; it provides a basis for planning and practice. The structural features of policy statements are important if the policy is to be used effectively by a large number of people working in an organisation. If a policy statement is to be clearly understood then the style in which it is written will either help or hamper its useability.

A policy statement is a document that sets out an organisation's policy on one or more subjects. Within a statement there are a variety of sections, paragraphs and sentences. In analysis of such documents it is sometimes difficult to decide what writing is the policy and what is background material, or argument around policy issues. Acts of Parliament are very tightly constructed and accurately worded policy statements. We do not find Acts containing large chunks of policy debate or justifications: these are confined to the pages of Hansard. I am not suggesting that policy statements issued by a probation service or a local authority department should be written like an Act of Parliament (heaven preserve us from that) but much could be done to improve the approach that is taken to the preparation of organisational policy statements.

A policy statement is a product of policy formulation and represents a snapshot of policy at the time it was produced, since the policy process is likely to be continuous. A policy statement therefore represents a resolution of the formulation process for the time being. This being so, provision needs to be made for issuing new and updated versions of policy statements. The way in which policy is documented should make it easy for users to incorporate revisions into their policy files.

What should we expect to find in a policy statement? There are a number of components which are essential to any statement of policy and a variety of other components that are desirable but not always necessary (see **Figure 4.2**). These components are similar to those we discussed when we looked earlier at the components of policy. Documents that set out policy – statements – should be structured and presented bearing in mind how they are to be used. The aim of a policy statement should be to inform users and to allow them to implement it effectively. A good deal of time spent thinking through the layout and presentation will be a wise investment. The structure of such documents must allow them to be digested and understood and permit ease of reference. A good policy statement will make clear what the policy is; too often, however, statements fail to distinguish between supportive argument and the actual writing of the policy itself. Statements intended to set out operational policy too often appear to be like essays, recounting arguments, cataloguing facts and statistics and leaving the exact policy to be implied from the discussion.

Statements of operational policy need to be well structured, precisely formulated and carefully worded, if they are to be used effectively in practice. The paragraphs that are the actual statements of policy should be easy to identify; where explanatory notes are essential these should be separated to avoid confusion. Explanations, interpretative notes and other material could be placed in the margin or included in a footnote. It is helpful to provide a contents list at the front and a detailed subject index at the back, with related topics being cross-referenced in the text. Supporting evidence or descriptive explanations which are not part of the policy should be confined to appendices. The style of writing should be clear and precise and technical terms should be avoided, unless they are widely known by the users of the policy or fully defined in a glossary.

Good policy writing should avoid being descriptive, except where this is vital to making things clear and understandable. A policy statement is a technical document and like all technical documents it must avoid confusion, confer certainty and be clear in what it says and easy to use. Sometimes organisations produce general statements of policy on a broad issue and supplement these by more detailed documents that specify what is to be done and how it is to be done. These are often referred to as *codes of practice*. Codes of practice are concerned with the details and rules of practice and explain what procedures must be followed. Codes of practice are very similar, if not identical to, procedure manuals. These are used, for example, in some social services departments to communicate regulations governing specific practices and often pose considerable problems in keeping them up to date and ensuring they are properly used. Rule books and standing orders will also be familiar to police officers. For lawyers, books of rules are bread and butter. Those who are responsible for revising procedure manuals face a daunting task and the products of such tasks often reflect the cynicism and despondency with which they are approached [Scott and Miller, 1987].

There are a variety of types of policy, as described above. Most policy clauses will be prescriptive. The most common statement of intention is expressed by the words 'shall' (obligatory), 'should' (conditional) or 'could' (discretionary). If the policy states that something 'should' or 'could' be done, then the conditions under which it is permissible need to be made clear. This might require the statement of a set of principles or guidelines which can be used by those exercising discretion.

Some policies however relate to outside bodies over which the originators have no power; thus, some expressive statements might say 'we urge the government to ...', or we 'recommend that the local authority ...'. Policy statements often require a certain amount of sifting through in order to find the sentences that actually express the policy amongst those that are part of the policy argument. Certain key phrases indicate policy expressions, such as 'we agree ...', 'in our view ... ', 'we welcome ... ', 'we affirm ...', 'it is important that ... ' and so on. If those who write policy appreciate the language and style of policy writing then, I contend, it is more likely that well written policy will emerge and, if a policy is well written, it is more likely that it will be understood and put into practice.

The objective of the manager is to enable practitioners to achieve the best standards of practice and this also is what practitioners themselves wish to achieve. Policy is therefore something that equally concerns both those who manage and those who are managed. Policy provides an appropriate framework for standards for all parts of the organisation.

Policy and organisations

Mention has been made above of the close association between policy and organisations. Policy was described as both producing organisation and as being a product of organisation. On the one hand policy lays down the fundamentals of an organisation's structures and purposes and on the other hand policy is produced as the organisation changes and, in so doing, modifies its existing policies. An organisation that implements policy can be understood both by policy analysis and by organisational analysis. Meltsner and Bellavita [1983] link policy and organisation together through a study of how public policy is implemented and formulated by governmental agencies. They look at how managers and officials work with policy and how they relate to policy makers. They describe the 'organisational control of policy' by looking at the processes of communication and organisational behaviour.

Since policy is closely connected with organisations it is necessary to analyse them in order to appreciate how they affect the policy process and how they influence policy implementation. Policy is put into effect within organisations and, in this process, managers play a crucial role. Communications theory provides a tool to investigate how policy-related meanings are negotiated, transmitted and received. Meltsner and Bellavita offer eight categories that describe the functioning of an organisation:

(1) Goals
(2) Members
(3) Environment
(4) Structure
(5) Resources
(6) Tasks
(7) Decision making
(8) Communication

Policy is relevant to each of these. The categories provide headings under which policy processes within an organisation can be analysed. Policy is formulated and communicated within organisations and three views of policy communication are offered:

(1) the *issue view* - the communications surrounding the policy issue,

how people are persuaded to accept the policy and how ideas get into policy.

(2) The *policy network view* - looks at components of the policy arena, how patterns of communication are established and how information is processed.

(3) The *management view* - synthesises the first two views and shows how managers play a part in the policy network, how policies continually evolve and how preferences are linked to organisational resources.

Thus, connections are made between an organisation's structure, its internal processes and its patterns of communications. Policy is therefore a function of the organisation and of its management [Meltsner and Bellavita, 1983].

Since policy is found in organisations, some have preferred to see this as an association with bureaucracy or with administration. Much attention has been given to the role of professionals and to the impact of professionalism on policy formulation. Professionals have been characterised as acting as gatekeepers in the task of allocating power or resources and this has had profound impacts on the implementation of many policies. But has policy acted as a mechanism for the distribution of power or has this power distribution simply created policies that have reinforced it? If we are to engage in policy practice then we might wish to define what is good practice.

Putting policy into practice

Policy is a tool of management. It is also a tool of practice. Policy can be used to define good practice and to provide the resources required by practitioners. There are three levels of policy in criminal justice systems:

1. for the system as a whole;
2. for individual agencies within the system;
3. for individuals within agencies.

The problem of policy formulation is working out how these three levels interrelate, how they reinforce each other and what consequences a policy at one level will have for policies at other levels. We should analyse how our policies will affect discretion, that is, the freedom of judgement that practitioners have within the rules that have been set for practice. The extent to which individuals know the policy, understand it and are committed to adhering to it will affect the impact of the policy. Policy answers questions about what to practice, how to practice it, when to practice it and above all why the practice is to be done.

Policy may well show strong and weak influences and these may vary according to the level of the system. Strong influences are the law, agency rules and procedures. Discretion operates within boundaries and these dictate what is possible and what is not. Weak influences refer to matters of judgement where multiple choices are involved and particularly where there is no necessarily right answer or absolutely correct way of doing things. Practice is often a matter of judgement but judgement by individuals reflects their values, idiosyncrasies and personal preferences. How do we reconcile these individual judgements with the policy requirements of the system or organisation as a whole? Strong and weak influences vary according to the level of system, that is, whether we are considering the justice system as a whole or individual practitioners operating within it. We might use for analysis the kind of grid illustrated in **Figure 4.7**. This could be used in analysing the potential impact of a policy option and how it might affect practice.

We have already considered the issue of mandation. We might wish to consider whether policy should be mandatory (a strong influence) or advisory (in which it might be a weak influence). *Interagency* policies are unlikely to be mandatory. *Intragency* policies are more likely to be mandatory and some components may be sanctionable. If a policy is to result in a system of operation then, at an early stage in the process of its formulation, a specification for that system should be written. For example, if a department is formulating policy for a juvenile justice scheme, then a specification for that scheme should be written. The specification would set out the operational objectives, purpose of services to be delivered, define the target groups, and set the financial and other resource parameters of the scheme. Principles of practice should be laid down.

The implementation of policy requires planning and this will involve education and training. Training in specific aspects of practice is required but training in the use of policy is also a requirement but one that is often omitted. It is one thing to understand what a policy statement is saying but another to know *how* to use it is in practice. We might, for example, understand the principle of minimal intervention but how do we use it in the writing of court reports? How do we use it in the administration of cautioning or in the design of day centre programmes? There are also questions about the extent to which practitioners will agree with the policy, since controversial policies often result in attempts to block or undermine them. Policies imposed by senior management without the commitment of practitioners are unlikely to work unless managers are able to secure that commitment from those who are to receive and implement those policies. The same is probably true of bottom-up policies where practitioners have formulated a policy and have sought to put it into effect without the active involvement of management. One of the components of policy that we identified earlier was mission. Effective policies require

	on individuals	on organisations	on systems
Type of influence			
Strong impact			
Weak impact			

Figure 4.7 Analysing influences on policy

authority as well as commitment. Effective policy implementation requires commitment across the board.

Planning is the key concept in policy implementation. Many good policies have withered before their fruition because their authors have failed to realise that planning is essential to implementation. Planning the implementation of policy requires time, careful attention to detail, monitoring, training and evaluation. In most cases this will be a continuous process, since policy is usually established and what we are considering are not new policies but continual reformulation of policy problems and issues. The policy, planning and practice cycle should have built into it procedures that allow experience to be fed in and used. Too often the experience of practitioners is lost because managers fail to capture and use it and feed it into the policy revision process.

Policy in criminal justice systems

The administration of justice is not an exact science. Policing has its scientific aspects but often involves art and creative flair. Most of the decision making found in the field of crime and justice relies on judgement rather than on calculation. Most of those who work in the justice system, are allowed a considerable degree of discretion. Laws exist to provide a framework for sentencing; but within this framework magistrates and judges base their decisions on personal judgement and the law allows them considerable discretion in doing this.

One of the reasons for having policy is that it sets boundaries around such discretion and provides guidance for those who are to make judgements within those boundaries. For example, if magistrates were to change their sentencing policy, whether by design or by default, then the consequences of such a change should be predicted. Such a prediction will only be accurate and reliable if the model of sentencing is itself accurate and reliable. If the assumptions about the relationship between the sentence and its impact are misjudged, then the sentencing policy change will be unlikely to result in any intended outcome.

If, for example, magistrates were to impose heavier penalties for a certain type of offence, hoping that this would deter others from committing such offences, then they must be sure that there is a reliably predictable relationship between sentencing and the incidence of that offence. Those who believe in the deterrent effect of sentencing, hold particular beliefs about the relationship between criminal behaviour and punishment. Monitoring and research can reveal if such a model is valid. It should be possible to predict the outcomes of a change in sentencing policy and such a prediction should be or will be confirmed by the results of monitoring.

The length to which a chain of possible outcomes can be pursued is a matter of judgement. Policy changes could result in ripple effects through other parts of the justice system. A change in sentencing lengths, intended to deter offenders, would result in changes in the prison population, in prison regime, and in the costs of custody, in the family problems of prisoners and so on. The outcome of such a policy change might be to increase rather than to decrease the level of offending – an example of an unintended consequence. Policy analysts have to decide how far they can go in predicting the effects a policy change will have on other parts of the justice system. This kind of exercise can be of great importance, since the cons of some policy changes can outweigh the pros.

Conclusions

My reading of policy theory, policy analysis and the relationship between policy and planning has revealed the existence of a vast and diverse literature. Discussions of policy can be found in politics, sociology, social administration, town planning and management science. How useful is this wealth of literature to those concerned with criminal justice and the organisation of responses to crime? The answer to this question must depend on the degree to which those who organise crime response agencies wish to improve their performance, increase their effectiveness and achieve their goals. Policy studies have contributed to a very wide range of social problems including justice and crime. Much of the literature on policy is theoretical and far removed from the immediate concerns of social workers, policemen or magistrates. Those who work on a day to day basis in the justice system do not share a common set of theories about policy. Policy issues are frequently debated but policy theory is not so often considered. Policy theory can be used by those who engage in policy formulation and implementation to improve the quality and impact of policy and planning processes. If a criminal justice policy has been a failure, then part of the reason for this might lie with the absence or deficiency of policy theory in those who made it. Policy making and implementation is a practice and like all practice can be improved by the use of theory.

In much of the public debate about crime and justice, various myths and prejudices are encountered which, in terms of rational policy analysis, are invalid and counter productive. If policy makers are sincerely concerned to address problems of crime and its reduction, then they might wish to equip themselves with such knowledge and skills as are required to engage in good policy practice and this will increase the effectiveness of the policies they produce. Increases in the effectiveness of policy formulation, analysis and implementation will contribute to better responses to the problems of crime. Such increases will be achieved, in part, by drawing on the considerable wealth of theory and research on policy and planning across a range of disciplines. If policy is to be effectively implemented then considerable attention must be paid to the process of planning. Reliance on conventional wisdom or common sense does not provide a reliable basis for the improvement of policy processes in criminal justice organisation and management.

It has been suggested that policy makers and planners face a paradox: the more that people become aware of new possibilities offered by policy and are thus more able to predict its consequences, the greater is the range of action available to them. The greater the range of available action, the more difficult it is for planners and policy analysts to predict the outcomes of their plans or policies [Bish, 1976]. The better planners can predict, the more possibilities there are, and the more difficult their task is. If policy is a way of managing choice and discretion, then we must be able to predict the decision making behaviour of people in the system. Such predictive analysis becomes increasingly complex and as a result policy makers will become either increasingly abstract or increasingly specialised. In certain parts of the justice system we have witnessed the emergence of 'systems management' and the growth of the control of decision making processes, such as those involving social inquiry reports, gatekeeping or tariff related activities.

In conclusion I offer my own definition of policy: policy is the organised communication of intentions (goals, aims, objectives, purposes), of principles guiding action in pursuit of those intentions and of the authorisation of means (resources, methods and systems) through which intentions should or could be realised.

Suggested reading

There is a vast literature on policy, particularly in government and on social policy issues. Choosing from this wide range of material is difficult. A general introduction to policy, along the lines of this chapter, is offered by William Dunn in *Public policy analysis: an introduction*, 1981, Prentice Hall. This is a very thorough study and offers a good grounding in the theory of policy. A contrasting work and one that will suit the more practically inclined reader is *Policy analysis for the real world* by Brian Hogwood and Lewis Gunn, 1984, Oxford University Press. I like the scope of this book and its approach; it will probably suit those interested in applying policy in management. Similarly, *The policy organisation* by Arnold Meltsner and C Bellavita, 1983, Sage, although not widely known, offers some very interesting insights into the role of policy in organisational processes and will appeal to managers working with policy in large organisations. Lastly, the literature on criminal justice policy is also very considerable and nearly all of it deals with issues rather than policy theory. I find it difficult to recommend anything here other than Gregory Falkin's book, in which so many of the ideas I have used have originated.

5 Planning for justice

Introduction

The aim of this chapter is to introduce some fairly basic ideas about planning theory and techniques, illustrating the methodology of planning responses to crime. Apart from looking at the conceptual foundations of planning, some examples are given of practical techniques that can be used. The majority of this chapter is oriented to planning at the interagency level, although the approach is equally relevant to planning within individual organisations.

What is planning?

Planning is the process of translating policy (purposes, ends) into practice (operations, means). By definition, planning is oriented to the future; it is about what will happen or what we want to happen. The future is tomorrow, next week, next year, or five years hence. What happens today is the result of past planning. The implementation of policy requires planning. That is not to say that policy and planning can be easily separated; in some respects the distinction is theoretical but if that distinction enables us to analyse what is happening in practice, then it will be of some value. In many respects, policy is about organising change. Keeping something going *as it is* involves management or administration rather than planning. Policy provides the purposes, principles and priorities for an organisation or a system. If the policy is clear then the practice is more likely to achieve the intended results. If purposes are confused or ill-defined and principles are not offered, then practice will reflect those characteristics. Planning, therefore, sets out to make those changes that are intended by policy. As has already been noted, policy and planning are two of the main elements of strategy.

Why is planning important?

Being able to make things happen requires organisation and planning. These functions depend on each other: we cannot plan in a totally disorganised situation. Planning is a function that is inherent in all levels of organisation – from the overall architecture down to the 'bricks' and 'bolts'. Planning is embedded in the task of maintaining and developing organisation. Planning produces organisation through the exercise of control and the creation of ordered activities. Planning is only as effective as the degree of control that can be exercised. If the planning function is weak, then the consequence will be increasing disorganisation, failure and drifting.

Ability to organise is the key to achieving purpose, to being effective. In socially based systems, the exercise of control poses many problems. Behaviour is often unpredictable; even if we give a body of people very clear goals and very precise instructions, we cannot be sure that every one of them will do exactly what is expected of them all of the time. We cannot program a body of people as we can a computer. Control is necessarily about probabilities. Planning in organisations is about trying to increase the certainty that people will behave in a certain way. One of the most important aspects of organised behaviour is decision making. What planning tries to achieve is ordered and consistent decision making. Where planning is weak, decision making will tend to be arbitrary and unlikely to achieve the purposes set by policy makers. In such circumstances, decisions tend to be made idiosyncratically, with different decisions being made using different criteria.

Why planning is important in criminal justice systems

If planning is about the achievement of purpose, then what is the purpose of the criminal justice system? And how does it plan to achieve that purpose? The same questions can be asked for each criminal justice organisation; for example, what is the purpose of the probation service and how does it plan to achieve its purpose? The criminal justice system is an organised body of people and all of them make decisions on a day to day basis. To what extent are those decisions related to the purpose of the organisation? Or are those decisions made idiosyncratically, using personal rather than organisational values? If an organisation has a policy, then does that policy provide an adequate framework for decision making? Is there a process of planning that is capable of ensuring that decision making is consistent with policy?

Planning takes place within all criminal justice organisations - at the level of the system, through the activities of central government down to the level of the beat police officer or probation officer. Those who plan the system and who plan organisations within the system are not specialist planners (these are generally a rare species); planning is undertaken by policy makers, managers and practitioners as part of their everyday work. Planning is part of everyday life. The significance of this is that, although we can theorise about planning (in isolation from everyday reality) we cannot practice it in isolation. In order to improve our understanding of planning we need to extract it from the other functions to which it is closely related – such as policy. We also need to look at how it relates to those other functions and how improvements in planning feed back to improvements in policy making, management, performance and so on.

The other thing that we should note about decision making in the criminal justice system is that decisions are not solely determined or influenced by purely criminal justice values or criteria. We need to look at the environment of the system in order to understand the decision making process. For example, resources for criminal justice organisations are allocated by politicians. The mission of the system as a whole or of any of its organisations is derived from parliament, from ministries, local authorities and so on. These provide the external inputs to the system. Even at the level of the individual decision maker, these external influences are at work. The judge, in sentencing an offender, can be influenced by public opinion about certain types of crime, by the media or by broad political pressures.

The Home Office, for example, allocates public revenues to the police services and its policy has been to try to equate resources with effectiveness: 'if the police service is to deal with this situation and retain public confidence it is essential that it should make the most effective use possible of the substantial resources now available to it' [Home Office, 1983b]. As a result of their planning, police forces submit proposals for increases to their establishments to the Home Office. In its circular of 1983, the Home Office stated, in regard to requests for manpower increases, that it 'has to form a judgement about which should be given approval and with what priority' [op cit]. Police forces plan in an environment that includes political policy and planning decisions.

The environment in which the criminal justice system operates is constantly changing (as we recognised in the chapter on strategy). Crime is constantly changing. These changes require that the system respond with its own changes, through policy reformulation and through planning. Even if the policy framework remains constant, planning must respond to external events and processes. Planning must also be a response to changes that take place within the system but which are external to intended policy and plans. Trade unions, professional associations and pressure groups can create or demand changes. People change in their expertise, attitudes or personal motivations. The population working in an organisation changes as employees enter and leave it, grow older and so on.

So what does planning achieve?

The purpose of planning is to increase the effectiveness of a system or organisation. We can think in terms of a system's or organisation's performance: what it does, how it does it. Effectiveness is a way of looking at that performance, of evaluating it. The task of planning is to improve performance, to increase the effectiveness of organisations in achieving their purposes. If we assume that the purpose of the criminal justice system is to control and reduce crime (not everyone would agree with that but let us assume this for the sake of this discussion) then the purpose of planning is to increase the success of response systems in achieving reductions in crime. To be successful, performance must be effective. Planning sets out to organise the system so that it is more able to control crime, to identify what needs to be done to reduce crime and to control the activities of criminal justice organisations so that they can perform effectively. Coordination is therefore a key component of planning. The criminal justice system as a whole is very complex; each organisation within it is complex. Many processes and functions are involved. Organisations have complex structures and employ thousands of people and resources are always at a premium. Planning therefore seeks to identify the strategic aspects of complex problems: those aspects that are most important to effective performance. These aspects need to be coordinated with each other if they are to work together rather than against each other.

In chapter two we discussed the importance of coordination and how the fragmentary nature of the criminal justice system makes it extremely difficult to achieve the level of coordination that is required for effective action. Performance is also related to the allocation of resources: what level of resources are available and how they are distributed (by resources, I mean finance, personnel and equipment). Lastly, performance is also related to decision making; the better the decision making the higher the quality of performance will be.

Planning will be engaged in if specific benefits can be foreseen and these can be summarised as follows: (a) improved coordination of the various agencies responsible for responding to crime; (b) achievement of goals and priorities set for the system and its organisations; (c) effective allocation of resources based on needs, targets and agreed priorities and (d) increased impact of service delivery agencies based on evaluated performance.

Resistance to planning

If planning is such a good thing, then why do some people seem to resist it? Managers often encounter resistance to their plans; colleagues might hold different views about the right way of doing things or feel that their interests are being compromised. Sometimes there is a feeling that planning is a waste of time. What creates resistance to planning is often frustration caused by failure. If people plan to do something and the plan goes wrong or fails to happen as expected, then people tend to blame planning in general. Such problems often result not from planning but from bad planning. Good planning techniques require operational problems to be predicted in advance so that solutions to those problems can be formulated before they happen, thus avoiding crises or 'knee jerk' reactions. The solution is not to reject planning but to improve it. Just as problems will be encountered when we attempt to implement plans, planning might often be a reaction to problems. Not all planning however is problem driven. A reliable model of the system will allow us to test its behaviour in simulation, to see how the system will perform under various stresses and to identify pressure points and possible weaknesses. Clearly, in the real world, the most difficult problems to handle are those which modelling cannot predict.

In Chapter three, I considered the loss of faith in strategic planning during the 1970s and how this has recently been regained now that a different approach has been developed. Some of this decline in strategic planning and in planning in general has been generated by uncertainty; this has been particularly true in local government which has been and still is subject to considerable uncertainty. Planning becomes a seemingly hopeless endeavour in an environment of constant change and upheaval. But it is change and uncertainty that planning attempts to respond to and control. Far from being the basis of resistance to planning, uncertainty should be a rationale for it. This problem will also be encountered elsewhere in this chapter. If, as I have suggested, planning is about change, then resistance to planning is one and the same with the resistance that can be anticipated when people are confronted with any kind of change. The resistance is to the change rather than to the planning.

Resistance to planning can also be seen to be inherent in organisations. The organisation can be viewed as a social territory dominated by a variety of power groups. The dynamics of such groups are often inconsistent with rational and systematic planning processes. Planning creates change and, in this view, the organisation reacts to the imbalances that are caused. The task of planning within an organisation might therefore be to manage the internal dynamics of change. This might involve securing commitment to the process of planning. This would seem to require an analysis of why resistance to planning is being experienced, using an analysis of the organisation. Organisations have also been viewed as learning systems that can respond positively to change, provided that the right kind of culture is cultivated.

The case against planning

Resistance to planning can be generated by those who are suspicious of planners. Sometimes such suspicion is justified, particularly where there has been bad planning practice in the past. There are several arguments in the case against planning; one of them is that centralised planning can lead to a consolidated bureaucracy in which innovation and experiment are stifled. Planning would lead ultimately to totalitarianism and the concentration of power in the hands of a very few people. Centralised planning can, for instance, redistribute power away from local people into the hands of experts, professionals and officials. Planners can de-skill those who previously took planning decisions. Worst of all planning could lead to planning for planning's sake. Such extreme instances emphasise how planning can be used for ill as well as for good and point to distinctions between the effects of planning which is based on good practice and that which is based on bad.

It has been suggested that there is a problem in reconciling corporate planning with democratic accountability. There is, according to Saunders [1981], a tension between economic planning and democratic accountability. This idea was put forward in a discussion about the conflict between corporate business interests and the competitive sector of small firms. But, it suggests a broader tension between the policies and plans developed by a corporate state and the policies put forward in the manifestos of political parties. This is not a criticism of planning as such, but of the need to make planners democratically accountable. The case against planning appears to be a case against bad planning and the abuse of planning. Saying that planning is a bad thing is like saying that management is a bad thing because there have been bad managers.

To sum up the argument thus far, planning is undertaken to put policy into practice, to increase the degree to which an activity or system is organised and to ensure that future activities or outcomes can be predicted with greater certainty. There is a theoretical basis to planning in so far as we can think about what planning involves in a general sense and can apply this thinking to any kind of organised activity or system. Our next task is to consider what theories of planning exist that can be applied to responses to crime.

Can responses to crime be planned?

In posing this question I am not suggesting crime responses are at present totally unplanned. Rather, my suggestion is that they are ineffectively planned. Planning does take place within criminal justice organisations (such as police forces, probation services, the Prison Service, etc.). There is, I suggest, a lack of strategic planning in the system of responses to crime as a whole.

It has been argued that criminal justice is a non-system or a network. I have already described it as a fragmented system of autonomous yet operationally interdependent subsystems. It would therefore seem to follow that such a non-system is unplannable, there being no coherent organisational structure or central management through which planning of criminal justice and responses to crime as a whole can be pursued. At local level at least there is no central authority responsible for planning and administration of the criminal justice system.

To tackle the complex problem of managing responses to crime, each organisation needs to operate collaboratively in order to maximise its effectiveness, both for itself and for the system as a whole. We have already seen that collaboration amongst agencies does happen at present but it tends to be confined to a narrow set of operational issues. The need for corporate, authority-wide planning in local government generally was acknowledged in the early 1970s:

> 'we have heard from a number of sources that, in the past, local authorities have given too much attention to operating the services for which they are responsible and too little to planning them. It is of the essence of the corporate approach to management which we are advocating that there should be a realistic attempt to plan ahead on an authority-wide basis, to formulate objective, evaluative alternative methods of achieving those objectives and measure the effectiveness of ultimate performance against those objectives' [HMSO, 1972].

For the criminal justice system to be plannable, it must be controllable, or at least capable of being managed. It is impossible to plan a system over which there is no opportunity for control. Since there is no structure for the corporate management of the system at local level, there is little chance for comprehensive strategies to be developed. Another problem with planning in criminal justice agencies was pointed to by one author when he wrote:

> 'planning can help criminal justice agencies to respond to crime more effectively. It has however been argued that planning, as it is currently practised, tends to be too short term. Long term planning is needed to counteract those forces which favour short-term methods of crime control' [Tormedd, 1987].

The Home Office has suggested to Chief Police Officers that they might '... find it help it helpful to develop their manpower planning over a longer period and the Home Secretary will so far as is possible take long term plans into account ...' [Home Office, 1983b].

Blumstein has commented that most planning efforts have been notoriously weak and ineffectual. He argues that a major reason for this failure is the inadequacy of the knowledge base on which to develop rational planning and of the tools available to planners [Falkin, 1979]. This argument assumes that planning is necessarily rational, objective and scientific and that if only the tools of the job can be improved then the job will be done more effectively. There is perhaps a tendency for planning to reflect the irrationality and turmoil of the real world; indeed as Friend and Hickling have pointed out

> '...the view of planning as strategic choice is found to offer more of a challenge to such idealised principles of rationality than it does to the idealised judgements and compromises that seem characteristic of planning practice' [Friend and Hickling, 1987 p 1].

Rationality in policy and planning is a much studied issue [see for example Dunn, 1981, p 225 who offers five categories of rationality and Dror, 1973 who puts forward six]. We must be able to differentiate between rational planning and the idea of planning as an inherently rational activity; as Friend and Hickling argue, it is not always bound to be so [Friend and Hickling, 1987].

It might be argued however that what often makes planning ineffective is that it fails to take account of the real world. In the real world there are always forces or conditions which will work against planning. No matter how rational the planner may be (an intellectual descendent of Immanuel Kant or a clone of Dr. Spock) planning must be undertaken in a seemingly irrational world and one in which social and political currents and forces run deep. Given that crime and justice evokes fundamental emotions and the politics of law and order often pander to fears and myths, it might well seem to be the case that the justice system is unplannable. The real world of criminal justice and responses to crime is governed largely by political forces, by personalities in small local systems and by the dynamics of agencies operating in a fragmentary environment. To what extent is it feasible for even the most cunning of planners to develop effective criminal justice strategies?

To answer this question we need to look at the conditions under which planning would be feasible. Firstly, responsibility for planning will need to be located with an identified group of people. The current lack of system wide planning is due to there being no clearly located responsibility for this function in local systems of response to crime. The creation of interagency planning groups, as suggested in the final chapter, will enable responsibility for planning to be clearly located. Secondly, the effectiveness of planning will depend on the degree to which it is approached comprehensively. Partial planning will be unlikely to achieve the best results. The system wide approach requires that responses to crime be treated comprehensively if the problems inherent in fragmentation are to be overcome. This suggests the need to develop a corporate strategy and a set of plans within individual agencies that can be consolidated by and through that strategy. Thirdly, the effectiveness of planning requires an improvement in planning techniques and skills on the part of those setting out to undertake planning. This is true for all kinds of planning in all fields. It is particularly true for those planning in criminal justice systems largely because their professional backgrounds offer little in the way of planning or management theory either in pre-service or in-service training.

Planning responses to crime is likely to be no less complex than responding to any other form of social problem. Access to the best available knowledge about planning methods and to training in appropriate skills will enhance the performance of those planning criminal justice systems as much as in business or other branches of public administration. But both the knowledge base and the portfolio of practice skills available to planners ought to address the political environment in which planning must take place. The problem of how planning relates to politics will be addressed again later in this chapter.

At what level should planning be undertaken?

In the previous chapter we looked at three levels at which policy needs to be developed: the national, the local and interagency level and that of the individual agency. This three-tier approach follows through into planning. If policy is created at these levels, then the planning of policy implementation needs to be carried out at these levels. In the following discussion we also consider the smaller unit of local planning, the neighbourhood.

Three levels of planning are suggested: the macro-level (national), local (local authority and individual agency) and the micro-level (community or neighbourhood). These divisions represent different levels of complexity and planning problems. Each level has a different environment, involves different organisational settings and requires differences of approach. Macro planning is the responsibility of national government and that responsibility is divided amongst a number of national organisations. Such planning involves developing national policy, legislation and issuing guidelines to local organisations. Promotional and advocacy elements can form part of this task. National planning requires that a foundation is provided to enable and facilitate planning at lower levels. National government therefore needs to understand and to be informed of local planning initiatives. This is currently achieved by Departments issuing circulars and by local agencies making reports.

Local planning takes place, in most areas, at the level of the local authority, though the boundaries for planning in criminal justice vary between Police Force or Commission of the Peace areas. National policy provides an initial input to local planning. Micro-planning can take place at the level of the neighbourhood, estate or other small socio-geographic area and the choice of boundary will depend on local circumstances.

Macro-planning

The Home Office policy paper on criminal justice [Home Office, 1986] indicated that the concept of a strategic approach did exist in Home Office thinking but the paper reflected the reluctance of its author(s) to address the issues of fragmentation, autonomy and interdependence. The paper did have a section called *Working Together* in which was acknowledged the 'need for a coherent and systematic approach to the problems of crime and to the administration of justice' and concluded that the independence of criminal justice organisations is well established and sensible. The paper did not include any substantive treatment of how planning can assist in enhancing the effectiveness of responses to crime. In the more recent strategy statement [Home Office, 1989c] it is clear that thinking about how to organise criminal justice services has moved on but there is still little indication that a strategic planning methodology has emerged in the Home Office, at least in relation to the business of response planning. There is no evidence of national government taking any initiative to set in place systematic local planning structures. The main orientation of criminal justice planning is with national rather than local levels. Trends towards greater interagency coordination are however beginning to show up and the strategy statement refers to some of these (some were referred to in chapter one). As we saw in chapter two, various governmental agencies have, however, urged cooperation between local organisations, most notably in juvenile justice and crime prevention but this does not of itself constitute a strategic approach to responses to crime.

More and more elements of planning are beginning to appear at national level in the criminal justice agencies. The Crown Prosecution Service, for example, has a set of strategic goals and objectives and its annual report addresses the extent to which these have been achieved. There is also a set of 'future plans' and a set of performance indicators [Crown Prosecution Service, 1989]. It has an annual planning cycle that involves a 'strategic planing and resources review' of their strategy statement, command planning surveys and a director's review [Crown Prosecution Service, 1988]. This suggests that strategic planning is applied in this particular agency. The next stage of development in criminal justice planning will, I hope, be that of applying it to the interagency level rather than just within individual organisations as part of management.

The area of the criminal justice system in which planning is inadequately addressed is that of the courts. Recent work on the management of magistrates' courts [as reported in Justice of the Peace over 1989, the report of the Home Office scrutiny team being published by the Home Office in July 1989. See also Raine, 1986] has been concerned almost exclusively with their administrative arrangements in term of the 'three Es'. Planning in the magistrates' courts service is difficult because of the fragmentary nature of its management structure. As the scrutiny team pointed out the questions 'who manages?' and 'to whom are they answerable?' seem not to have been addressed when the present legislative framework was put into place in 1949 [Home Office, 1989a, para 4.1]. The team's solution to this problem was to propose the creation of a national agency with a Director General and a management board accountable to the Home Secretary. The national framework agreement would then constitute in effect a strategic plan for the service. This might address the management of the service but will not be able to address the planning of the judicial functions of the courts. This side of the equation is considered by the proposals for a national sentencing, as yet not accepted by the Government although accepted by the opposition and a variety of non-governmental national bodies.

As we saw in chapter three, the Home Office does have a strategic plan for dealing with crime. However, judged by the standards of strategic planning practice currently seen in commercial organisations and indeed in the Crown Prosecution Service and other governmental agencies, the Home Office's approach to strategic planning appears to suffer limitations. There is clearly a lot of policy, a lot of planning of sorts in the various departments but as far as can be seen, none of the advanced applications of planning have yet been developed in this particular branch of government in relation to the overall response to crime. Strategic planning on this scale is, of course, a highly challenging and complex task. But this is, I would argue, the very reason why it is needed. It is the sheer scale and complexity of the task that demands the use of the best available planning techniques.

National strategic planning of responses to crime could be achieved if: (a) the public policy framework is more clearly shaped and articulated; (b) effective structures are created to enable national agencies responsible for responding to crime to engage in planning and (c) there are mechanisms in place that will allow plans to be implemented, particularly at local level but with coordination between national and local planning. Unless the fragmentation problem is addressed then the last of these conditions will not be met.

Local planning

Local planning may be developed if: (a) the organisations involved agree to cooperate in a corporate approach; (b) a central coordinating structure is created; (c) individual organisations see the merits of coordinating their internal planning with that which has been agreed corporately among the participating bodies and (d) there is an understanding of the benefits to be gained from comprehensive planning of responses to crime.

If there is to be planning at the local level, then how will that relate to planning at the national level? As mentioned above, national government currently has only tenuous and indirect control over many localised planning initiatives. The task of central government is to formulate and implement public policies concerning crime; because its powers over local areas are limited, it must seek the commitment of local organisations to its policies if it is to see them put into effect. Central government has chosen to rely mainly on advocacy and encouragement, rather than on direct management, to secure the implementation of its criminal justice policies at local level.

This degree of voluntarism is necessitated by the fragmentation and autonomy of local agencies and by the delicate balance of political forces that characterise the various agencies of criminal justice. The development of a sound basis for local planning requires the backing of central government and legislation. However, a local planning process could be established voluntarily, that is, without legislative mandate. But a voluntary approach would be constrained by the lack of a complementary national planning approach and the implementation of any corporate planning at local level would be constrained by existing powers and public policy (i.e. political) parameters. In this scenario, planning would focus on coordination, information exchange and the setting of interagency targets and objectives. Even without a complementary national level planning approach, much could be achieved through this kind of voluntary corporatism.

It is at the local level that we can most usefully think in terms of corporate planning processes and structures. One possibility is that local crime response and justice commissions could be established to promote and develop a corporate response to crime and this is discussed in the final chapter.

Micro-planning

Planned responses to crime at neighbourhood level are already evident in crime prevention and community policing. In planning local responses, the police play a central role but magistrates, probation officers, social workers and others who are either directly or indirectly concerned with crime or offenders also have an important part to play. Magistrates play a key role in crossing agency boundaries: some of them sit on police authorities, some on probation committees, some are active in local schemes and projects, some (as private citizens) penetrate a wide range of community organisations and networks at a variety of levels. In many localities, there are networks of officials and professionals who meet each other on a regular basis. But few areas engage in comprehensively coordinated planning of their crime responses. What we tend to find is activity that is limited to crime prevention, juvenile justice, probation or policing. There is no local ownership of the response as a whole.

It has been suggested [NACRO, 1987a] that local authority chief executives could play a central coordinating role in consolidating the work of local statutory and voluntary organisations and the various departments of local government in the prevention of juvenile crime. NACRO has gone some way towards the development of a comprehensive planning structure in setting up Juvenile Crime Consultative Groups in ten areas of the country [NACRO, 1985a].

The need for local approaches to the planning of crime prevention measures has been emphasised by a number of groups and studies; for example, in its report on the play and recreational needs of young people on housing estates, a NACRO working party recommended that

> 'at a local level, we would like to see every local authority create a body for planning, co-ordinating and reviewing approaches to juvenile crime' [NACRO, 1988c p 8].

The same report went on to make a series of recommendations about the improvement of the management of local authority housing estates, many of which stressed the planning aspects of this kind of work. Planning in this context can relate to monitoring, agency coordination and to the design of facilities for children and young people and to environmental planning.

Local planning can be seen to have an economic dimension. Crime costs money; it has social costs but it also has economic costs and these are quantifiable. Crime has direct costs in terms of the value of property stolen, damage done, income lost, increased insurance premiums, repairs and replacements, etc. Injuries caused through personal violence and traumatisation of victims also involve costs and losses. These costs should be monitored and evaluated at all levels as part of the planning system. Responding to crime through policing, justice, prisons and probation involves considerable costs. Priorities for the distribution of resources need to be decided on and this is a key function of policy and planning.

What is the right level?

We can plan at a number of geographical levels but which one is the right level? This must depend on the kind of problem that is being tackled. Primary responses are delivered through organisations that are structured and have systems of control and management. These are therefore relatively easy to organise. Secondary levels of response, such as communities, families and parents do not have a line management structure and a different approach is therefore required. Primary responses have relatively immediate effects on offenders. Secondary levels might have immediate effects but if we wish to enhance and promote these, that might require a much longer-term effort. Crime prevention, delivered through organisations of one kind or another, exhibits effects over all terms. Some methods of crime prevention, such as increasing security or even the organisation of neighbourhood watch schemes can, under certain conditions, have fairly immediate effects on opportunities for crime. For example, mounting a surveillance scheme in a car park could fairly quickly reduce a high incidence of car theft. This is likely to happen more quickly than, for example, deciding to launch a response to car thieves through the justice system.

Another factor in the selection of appropriate planning levels is that of consistency. For example, there is a high level of variation in sentencing around the country. From a justice point of view, it might be suggested that national government should plan to even out these variations (see for example Ashworth's proposals for a sentencing council [NACRO, 1989e and elsewhere]). Local planning could equally result in more consistent sentencing practice. The issue is whether national or local strategies would achieve better results. Setting the number of police officers that should be employed in a local area, as a matter of national dictate, might solve one set of problems but it might equally create others. Consistency, imposed nationally, might be good in one case and bad in another. Some planning processes are only available to national bodies such as Parliament (for example, the making of criminal law). Some systems might need to be split between national and local levels: the prison system could have national prisons for high security inmates and local goals tied into local courts. Most policing must necessarily be provided and planned at local level but some have suggested that there is a case for a national police force to deal with terrorism and organised crime. These debates suggest that the level at which responses are organised and planned needs to be related to the geographical level of the crime problem. It is easy to understand the problems of responding to nationally organised crime through 43 local police forces. But is there a valid case for saying that there is an optimum size for police forces? Arguments have been put forward for consolidating the 43 forces in a much smaller number of large forces; an opposing analysis sees some forces as being too large and too weakly linked into local government structures, thus reducing public accountability and increasing the problems of cooperation with other more locally organised bodies.

What would local planning look like?

If those working in the local system of responses to crime are to be convinced that they should engage in interagency planning, then we must be able to suggest why responses should be planned, what such planning would involve and how it would be carried out. Some of this has already been touched on. The following offers a very brief sketch of what a local planning initiative might look like.

If a group of local people want to improve planning in their area, then they need to be clear what it is that they want planning to achieve. Representatives of criminal justice agencies, the community, the local authority and voluntary groups might meet to discuss the rationales for planning, how such planning could be developed and what contribution each agency can make to a planning initiative.

Local planning would entail a range of functions such as coordination of 'front line' agencies (e.g. police, courts, probation) to ensure that key components of the local response to crime are effectively targeted. A comprehensive system of information about crime and response performance would enable policy and planning to be evaluated. The planning initiative might also involve coordination of other relevant policies and services (e.g. schools, youth service, housing, employment, drugs and alcohol projects) in support of 'front line' work. This would link into prevention, diversion and offender programmes. Local authority policies and plans could be reviewed to see what contribution they make to crime reduction. This would result in a better and a shared understanding of local crime patterns and of the linkages between prevention, diversion, policing, sentencing and probation. Policy analysis could contribute to the development of corporate goals and priorities and ensure that the policies of each organisation reinforce each other. Impact and cost benefit studies could be undertaken. The costs of local crime and justice services should be known, analysed and evaluated. This might require research to be commissioned into the costs of crime in a local area. Routine monitoring can provide one level of information but longer term, more complex problems often require research programmes to provide results before action can be taken. Research should be planned and coordinated and the results shared between those agencies that can apply them.

This assumes that there is modelling of the local problem of crime, monitoring of the current response systems, evaluation of existing operational tactics, interdependence studies (e.g. cautioning and sentencing) and studies of the pattern of interagency collaboration (as suggested in chapter two). These functions require, on the one hand, considerable technical expertise, operational and servicing resources and, on the other, interpretation, management of response and commitment to implementation by those within organisations who have responsibility and accountability.

In conclusion, it is possible to plan responses to crime given that a range of conditions can be met: the benefits of planning need to be identified, there needs to be a determination to confront the problem of fragmentation, a valid understanding of what planning entails and of how planning can be implemented in practice. Improvements to the effectiveness of responses to crime are not dependent on planning alone but this is one of the fundamental elements of development that should be addressed.

The rest of this chapter looks at what theories and techniques are available to planners that can be drawn on in order to improve the practice of planning.

Theories *of* planning. Theories *for* planning

To what extent is theory for planning available to those concerned with planning the justice system and with crime control? Of what value is planning theory to practices, methods and techniques in justice administration? Theories *for* planning are many: general systems theory, organisation theory, decision theory, management theories and so on. There is probably nothing which is unique to the business of planning justice systems or crime control. Planning, like administration, engages similar skills, encounters similar problems and requires similar approaches in almost any branch of human activity. What we are unlikely to encounter are theories of planning which are indigenous to crime and justice; if we are to transport theory into the field of responses to crime, we need to plunder a wide variety of disciplines.

It is possible that a theory *of* planning in crime or justice could be constructed but it is doubtful that it would involve conceptual material which is radically different from any other planning theory. Those in the fields of crime and justice are more likely to be searching for theories *for* planning. Planners who do not utilise theory are unlikely to maximise the potential of their planning practice. Theory alone, however, is not enough because planners also require specific skills and these need to be utilised and developed within a framework of theory. There are dangers in assuming that all that planners need is common sense. What is missing from the current approach to planning responses to crime is a coherent framework of theory on which practice can be based. The remainder of this chapter attempts to identify, discuss and analyse the requirements of practical criminal justice planning.

A general approach to planning

The following brief description of a model of planning in criminal justice is based on that offered by Robert Cushman [1980]. He offers an overview of the planning process (see **Figure 5.1**) in which three stages of planning are outlined and, for each, a set of questions that orientate us to the nature of the exercise. This kind of process can be applied to what ever level of work we are engaged in - whether public, corporate or interagency planning. Policy provides purpose, principles and priorities. Planning examines alternative methods and options for putting these into practice. Policy answers questions about 'what should we do and why?' Planning responds to the answers provided by asking 'what can we do and how?' And 'what will we do and when?' As Cushman points out, the process is concerned with assessing the feasibility of alternative courses of action, developing operational systems and developing guidelines for action. Planning addresses the allocation of resources, the utilisation of methods and 'tools' and the design of day to day operations.

This process is considered in more detail in **Figure 5.2**. Here there are three key elements to the process: what should be done, what can be done and what will be done. The process involves elements which are standard to policy analysis, particularly that of considering and evaluating alternative options and possibilities. The weight given to each stage of the process is of some importance, for, as Cushman points out:

> 'Today, some sort of planning process is regularly applied by many local governments and criminal justice agencies. Unfortunately, most spend a disproportionate amount of time and effort in operational planning, at the expense of policy program planning. The need to respond to short term workload crises, immediate political events, and a one year budget cycle tends to encourage a focus on operational planning and the allocation of resources' [Cushman, 1980, p 23].

If these three essential elements are to work effectively, then emphasis must be placed by senior managers on the policy and operational levels of planning, if practice is to be firmly grounded. Short-term operational planning alone is not enough to maximise effectiveness. Practical planning takes place under pressure and

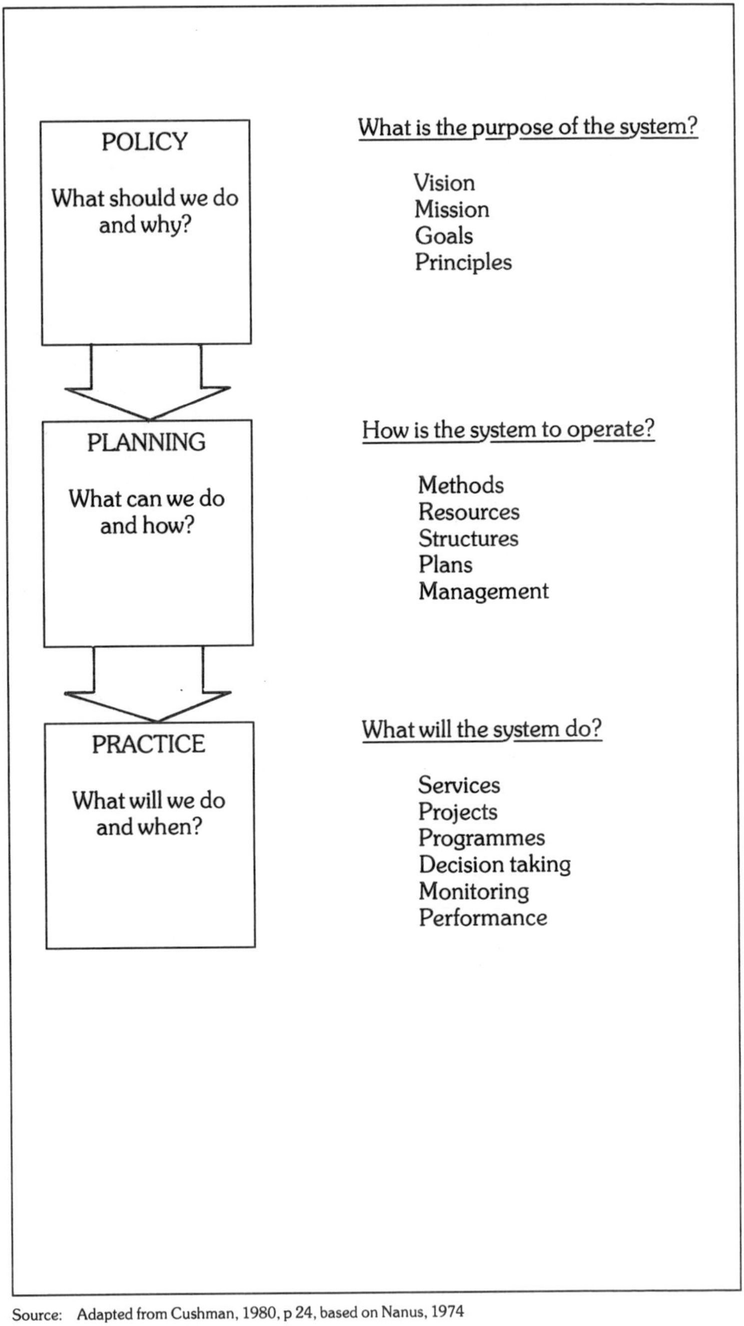

Source: Adapted from Cushman, 1980, p 24, based on Nanus, 1974

Fig 5.1 A general model of the planning process

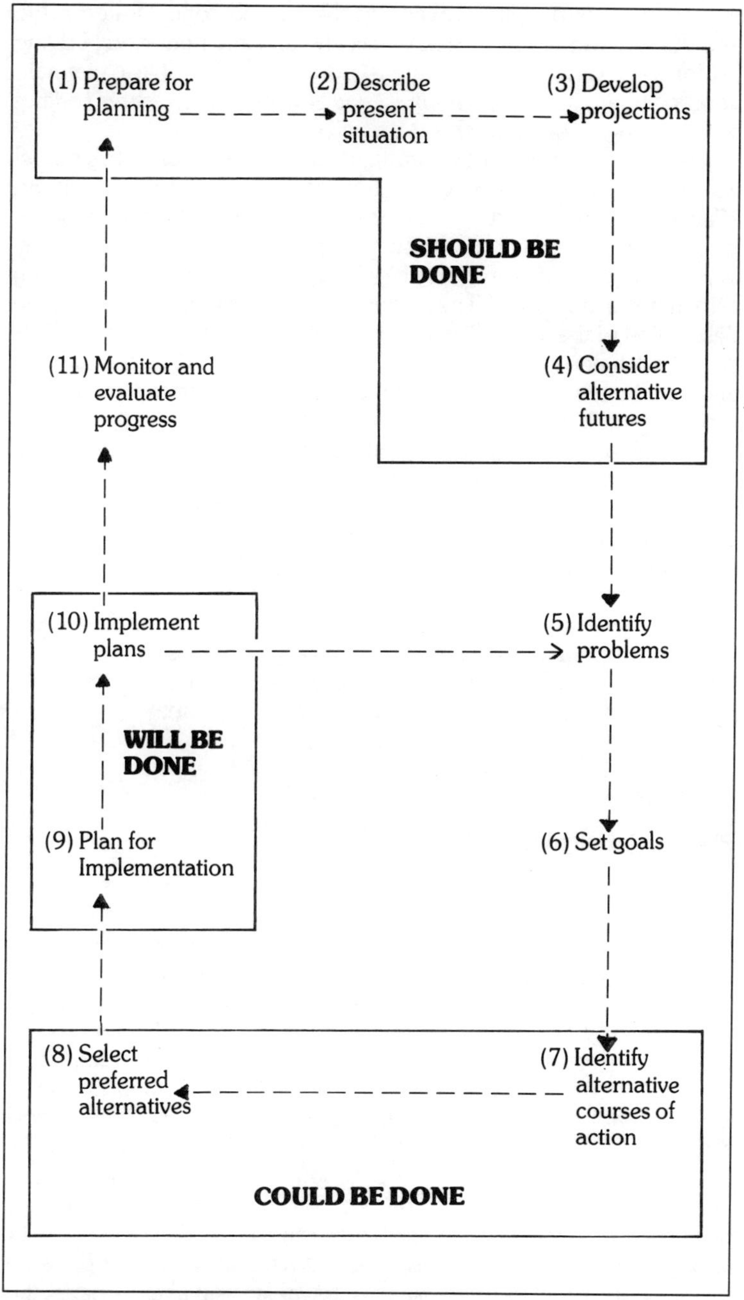

Source: Based on Cushman, 1980, figure 2.2 p26.

Fig 5.2 A general model of planning

this often leads people to abandon theory and concentrate on the immediate compulsion of their practical situation. Friend and Hickling recognise this and have developed ways of helping people to maintain good planning practices when faced with everyday pressures [Friend and Hickling, 1987].

The central importance of monitoring and evaluation in this model will be apparent from its role in the illustration. Without a full and effective method of finding out what is happening in the system, there is little chance that we will know if our plans are being successfully implemented or of identifying blockages and problems and dealing with them as they occur. The starting point of a planning process is the description of the initial situation or problem. The use of area profiles, described below, is one method that can be used at the start of planning local responses to crime to describe the current situation or problem and how it is being responded to.

I would also highlight one other point that Cushman makes: that criminal justice planning should be comprehensive. At several points I have suggested that what happens in one part of the system will have consequences, intended or otherwise, in other parts. Real impacts on crime and offending cannot be made by policing, sentencing or prevention measures alone but only by a strategic combination of all the elements that are available to manage the problem. A systems view of the operations of criminal justice is by no means a new idea nor is it the only way of analysing criminal justice; but it does offer certain useful analytical techniques that can be used in planning.

Planning as a process

Planning is primarily an activity that people do by and large in groups, thus emphasising the essentially social nature of planning. Planning is political and social, intellectual and active and begins with values, attitudes, beliefs and personal goals. Good planning commences with working out the process by which the planning task will be undertaken. Davidoff and Reiner [1982] defined planning as: 'a process for determining appropriate future action through a sequence of choices'. They view planning as a 'set of procedures' involving three levels of choice: (1) selection of ends and criteria; (2) identification with a set of alternatives consistent with these general prescriptives and (3) guidance of action towards determined ends. They regard planning behaviour and its decision making process as rational, purposeful and capable of objective scrutiny. But, 'man operates with imperfect knowledge'; the options and alternatives facing decision makers might be too complex to be able to make a 'perfectly' reasoned choice. Information might be lacking about all the possible consequences of any option. The manager might often take the best available option on the basis of best available knowledge. Planners might not themselves be decision takers; they might service the needs of those who are, by providing information about alternative options and their consequences. They might be trying to formulate an *optimum* plan, where conflicting goals or means are resolved.

Designing a planning process

The design of a process for planning is nine tenths of the task. Design involves making decisions about why planning is being conducted, who will do it and how it will be done. Decisions are also required about what techniques to use, the appropriate time scale for the plans, their scope, what evaluation methods to employ, what kind of information and monitoring systems will be required and so on. The purpose of designing a framework for the planning process is to ensure that it will be as effective as possible.

Planning is a continual process. It can be conducted explicitly or implicity. An explicit process is one that begins with working out what methods will be used. This puts the planner in control of the planning process. In implicit processes, planning depends on intuition and habits and the planner remains largely unaware of the process being worked through. The process controls the planner. As we learn about the operation of the system and become aware of its limitations, we are more able to decide how it can be changed.

An early stage in the planning process is identifying and prioritising options. Given a set of objectives and targets, there can be several ways forward. Once feasible options have been identified, they can be evaluated according to a set of criteria. Options can be assessed for their *suitability*, *feasibility* and *acceptability* [Johnson and Scholes, 1988 p 170]. Some options might be seen to have more *strategic* significance than others. Option selection also requires some degree of forecasting of the out-turns to be expected from the adoption of that option.

For example, in planning a programme of work with offenders who have alcohol-related problems, we might identify that there are two options: either to solve the alcohol problem first and see if the offending problems are also likely to be solved or to curtail the offending behaviour so that the offender remains in the community long enough for the alcohol problem to be treated. Similarly, planning the distribution of resources in a probation service might require decisions to be made about which services or projects need to be increased and which can be decreased in order to allow for transfers of resources. Should day centre programmes be increased at the expense of casework? Should work with persistent offenders be prioritised over that undertaken with people who have committed serious crimes but are unlikely to offend again? Should work with juvenile offenders be closed off in order to provide more resources for work with young adults?

The planning process requires operational decision making to be based on thorough processes of this kind. It also involves integration of direct services with the management of systems. Systems management has become established in juvenile justice and is becoming increasingly widely practised in the adult justice system. Offender management involves both direct work with individuals and work with the system of decision making, program planning and processing of cases. Which of these aspects of practice will most effectively realise the objectives that planners are trying to achieve? This is not an either/or question but one that requires the relative merits of each approach to be assessed.

To give another example, if a limited budget is available to establish a new probation project, which group of clients should be selected to benefit from it? Should it be available on demand for all offenders or should it be targeted at those most at risk of a custodial sentence? What criteria are to be used to decide who should benefit from a limited resource? Once criteria have been agreed, what is the best way of ensuring that those criteria are applied effectively and in a way that will secure commitment from managers and practitioners alike?

All of this is the day to day stuff of operational planning. Planning requires us to have a set of budgets, or a budgetary framework within which to operate. Evaluation can include some kind of cost-benefit assessment and much emphasis is currently being placed on value-for-money. Planners need to know if there are sets of rules which must be followed and the likelihood that those rules will be followed. Where these rules involve expenditure or costs (including time), then how will they affect the financial or budgetary plans of the organisation?

Planning is often related to the budgetary cycle. Planning generally works in cycles and such cycles often commence with setting targets and objectives and working out the resources needed to achieve them. Often these need to be prioritised. Operational systems need to be designed that relate goals and resources together, and services delivered that will reach the targets that have been set, within the constraints of cost and efficiency. The operation must then be evaluated and the results fed back to a new planning cycle.

Planners need to be able to predict the problems that will arise when plans are implemented. Some of these problems arise from the overspending of budgets, failure to achieve a desired level of funding, failure to meet targets and so on. The more we can learn about how a system operates and how it performs, the more able we will be to control it. Dealing with problems such as these has led to the development of scenario planning in which sets of possible performances are constructed to show the best possible, optimum or worst possible out-turns.

Structures for planning

How do we design structures through which planning can be developed? Let us begin with the assumption that the system does not already contain such structures and that they therefore need to be created. Large scale planning is best undertaken by a small group of people (because of the complexity of the task and the need for intellectual grasp of the total situation). It is also best done intensively, otherwise it tends to become bureaucratised and stale. Good planning requires vision and imagination and an environment in which people can work creatively. Whilst I would tend to emphasise the importance of the planning *process*, the need for appropriate structures (such as planning committees or units) should not be forgotten, particularly where planning involves a number of organisations. Within a single organisation, planning can reside within the existing organisational structure. But planning systems that are delivered by a range of agencies require the creation of some infrastructure in order to allow planning processes to be properly established. I will be returning to this issue in the last chapter, where I will make some suggestions as to what kind of planning structures would be required in a developed strategic planning approach.

Cooperation among agencies

The key to solving many of the problems inherent in interagency planning is the development of collaboration. I am not arguing that there should be, at local level, one overall administration responsible for the strategic planning of the police, probation, courts and so on as *individual* agencies. What there should be is willingness and commitment on the part of those agencies to engage in a process from which strategic planning will emerge.

Collaboration was viewed, in chapter two, as a continuum. As the level of integration increases more and more functions are shared, resources are developed collectively and there is a corporate or mutual approach to policy formulation. These levels are theoretical constructs designed to help us understand the various patterns of integration that we find in local areas. Moves towards collaborative planning might require development of collaborative processes and structures.

The cooperative infrastructure

Planning in a multiagency environment requires extensive collaboration at all levels; the function of this is to integrate the strategies of each of the organisations involved. The task of integrating strategies seeks to maximise the impact both of individual agencies and of the response system as a whole. This is the kind of result that system-wide planning would try to achieve and would be consistent with the goal of maximising the impact and performance of the system as a whole. Clearly, system-wide planning requires the development of collaborative infrastructures through which people in a range of agencies pursue a corporate approach.

The corporate crime response plan represents the policy and planning environment in which the various agencies that respond to crime operate. There will still be some areas of operation within individual agencies that lie outside the scope of the corporate strategy. As integration increases, each agency surrenders some of its independence but it never forgoes complete self-determination. In any federation, commonwealth or consortium there is a balance between the requirements of the system as a whole and the requirements of the individual parts.

The practice of planning

Planning, as an activity, requires knowledge, skills and techniques. Planners (those whose functions include planning) can perform better in the practice of planning if they understand something of the 'theory' of planning (that is to say, if they have a set of conceptual tools that will enable them to think about what planning is, why it is done and how it is done). All practice (activity, performance) requires skills and we can point to those that are characteristic of planning. Specialised skills are not necessarily the backbone of planning, as they are in many aspects of organisation and management. Planning largely draws on general skills of communication, analysis, using information and being able to think clearly about how events or processes relate to each other. Often effective planning is more a matter of attitude or approach than of specific skills: being able to attend to details, being objective, being patient – these are perhaps some of the personal qualities that characterise good planning practice.

Planning does however have at its disposal certain techniques that represent specialised tools for the planner to use. The assumption has been made in this discussion that planning in the criminal justice system is not nor needs to be a specialised practice. There is however a case for saying that planning (as a specialism) could be improved in many parts of the system and in the management of the system as a whole. This would be achieved by increasing the performance of those who plan criminal justice agencies as part of their general management task. In the arena of interagency work there is a particular need to increase the effectiveness of planning. Is there also a case for developing planning specialists in criminal justice organisations? Such specialists could support the work of those for whom planning is only one aspect of their overall task. Specialised aspects of planning, such as information processing, training or evaluation, could be seen to be supportive skills that could be used by policy makers and managers. Some large businesses employ strategic planners and a few are beginning to appear in some local authority departments and voluntary organisations. Planning *units* or *departments* are already fairly familiar. Planning can be specialised within an organisational structure; but, as a function of management and operational practice, it is a task for everyone. There is a growing tendency for criminal justice agencies to hire management consultants and other external specialists to advise on the more technical aspects of operational development and planning. I would argue however that more needs to be done to equip justice agency managers and practitioners with advanced skills in planning. Outside consultants can contribute to this if their brief includes the development and training of those in the agency who need to be able to master planning or technical aspects of the job.

Operational planning

The location of the responsibility for interagency planning in criminal justice systems presents major difficulties. If there is to be planning of crime responses, at interagency level, then who or which body should be responsible for doing it or seeing that it is done? Or indeed, for coordinating it? For example, most of the work with young offenders (aged 12 – 16) is carried out by social service departments. In some areas, work is also undertaken by the probation services. Where juvenile work is well developed, planning, monitoring and coordination is often led and developed by social services. To approach their work effectively, social workers need to involve the police, the courts and a range of other organisations. In many local authorities, interagency steering groups have been formed for this purpose. The role and remit of such groups varies considerably around the country. In some cases, their members are relatively senior; in others, they are drawn from middle managers. Because they are *interagency* groups they have little or no authority; their role is to enable the exchange of ideas and experience, to provide opportunities for liaison and to provide a forum for the discussion of policy issues. Planning, on a day to day basis, is often the responsibility of intermediate treatment or juvenile justice coordinators or of

Principal Assistants responsible for child care services (in the social service department). Where young adult offenders (aged 17–21) are concerned, work is primarily located with the probation services but this age group has not so far been so highly targeted as have juveniles.

Where crime prevention is concerned, the police play a leading role but a wide variety of interest groups, particularly those in the community and neighbourhoods, are also often involved. In many areas crime prevention panels have been established and the work that they do contributes to planning and coordination. Many of the duties and services of local authorities can and do contribute to crime prevention. Businesses, private and public housing estates, sports grounds and many other locations can be targets for preventive measures. Whilst the police often take a lead in promoting and coordinating preventive strategies, there is no single agency in the criminal justice system that can represent the planning interests of all these disparate groups and organisations. The wide spread of preventive measures necessarily requires a multiagency strategy but finding a suitable location for responsibility for this poses problems, particularly at the level of the local authority area.

Operational planning is a function of individual agencies, such as police forces or probation services, but the interdependence of the criminal justice system requires planning to operate across agency boundaries. The problem is therefore how the delivery of a wide variety of services that impact on crime and offenders can be coordinated and evaluated. Response management will not happen corporately unless some means is created through which it can be pursued.

Operational planning also requires financial and budgetary management. Once a plan has begun to operate, it must be monitored. Data must be collected to determine the operating costs of the system and this requires the selection of a range of performance indicators. This data can be used in reviewing progress and to evaluate the extent to which objectives are being achieved. Financial management requires information to be supplied from a strategic information system. Review, assessment and evaluation form part of the process of policy formulation and reformulation and these elements also draw on the system's information processes. Financial management is an integral function of overall strategic planning.

All this is a growing feature of the management of particular criminal justice agencies but it has not yet begun to happen extensively or comprehensively in the multiagency arena. Most criminal justice organisations now have performance indicators: but there are no instances (as far as I know) of local systems having developed *corporate* interagency performance indicators. Corporate performance indicators are being used within organisations and are developing within local authorities where there is a commitment to interdepartmental strategy. Corporate responses are often required to tackle problems that cut across a variety of departments. For example, a local authority strategy to tackle poverty has been devised and this requires *inter-corporate* approaches, since a variety of departments and organisations must be involved in such a task [McGill, 1988]. Increasing the effectiveness of crime responses in a local area requires a corporate approach to planning; one aspect of this would be the development of a strategic information system and we will be looking at this in the next chapter. That is perhaps the next phase of criminal justice management to be developed over the next ten years.

Techniques in planning

For many managers, planning is more of an art than a science. As with policy formulation, in planning there are few general techniques that exist independently of the fields in which they have been developed. Planning is necessarily a complex process and therefore requires use of techniques that will permit planners to cope with that complexity. Some planning techniques can, however, be relocated from their original fields and brought into use in criminal justice planning. The following sections provide only examples of the many practical techniques that can be used in planning.

Maps, charts and diagrams

Planning requires a great deal of information to be accumulated and analysed. The task of planning a system often involves being able to accurately visualise that system and the way that it operates. A range of methods are available to assist in this task such as flow diagrams, maps and charts. Flowcharts are fairly common in criminal justice and will be familiar, for example, to juvenile justice specialists and probation officers in analysing or representing the processes through which offenders go, between arrest and final sentence. Similarly, we could draw a chart of an organisation's structure or of the resources that it has at its disposal. Current responses to crime in an area can be charted in terms of the organisations involved or the economic dimensions of those responses. Flow charts are often drawn to make clear the routes by which offenders enter the criminal justice system. Many of these flowcharts are, however, poorly drawn. The development of more precise flowcharting would increase the usefulness of this technique as an aid to planning and analysis. A system of symbols could be used to depict certain types of events within the chart and some attempt has been made to standardise these generally. Certain principles can be used in increasing the accuracy of flowcharting. For example, in drawing a flowchart, it is important not to mix or confuse different aspects or functions of the system. If the flowchart represents decision making, then only decision making events should be included. Other events in the process, if they need to be included, should be drawn in a different colour or picked out and distinguished from the substantive design.

Reference is made later to simulation and modelling and a map is a kind of model. At its simplest level, *mapping* is a pen and paper exercise. As the map becomes more detailed, more sophisticated techniques can be used. By mapping the local response system (either as a system or in its spatial dimensions), planners can visualise how the system is structured and how it operates. This is helpful in analysing and setting operational boundaries, monitoring flows through the system and locating key decision gates. The relationships and dynamics of the system can be worked out. There are various kinds of maps; the most usual is simply a pictorial representation of a geographical area against which a variety of characteristics can be plotted, such as population density or distribution of crimes. *Mental* maps depict people's attitudes or beliefs about an area and these can be quite useful in planning crime prevention or policing operations. A wide range of graphical techniques are available that enable complex and abstract patterns, processes and events to be clearly understood. Where very complex mapping or charting exercises are required, computers can be used and a wide range of computer-aided design and graphics software is now available. Constructing information based maps manually is a time consuming business. Software packages are now available that can print maps and use databases to show the distribution of various factors across selected spatial grids. These enhance the usefulness of mapping techniques and take a lot of the drudgery out of the process. Crime mapping aids operational planning, particularly resource distribution. It is used extensively by the police both in policing operations and in crime prevention. Mapping techniques can help to target areas where there are high rates of particular crimes and be used as diagnostic devices in assessing the impact of programmes and initiatives.

Critical path analysis

Strategic planning is necessarily a complex activity; it therefore requires the use of techniques that can assist us to cope with that complexity. Critical path analysis (CPA) is a technique that could be used by criminal justice planners. Sometimes this is referred to as *network analysis*. Lockyer [1969] explains that CPA proceeds in three distinct phases: planning, analysing and scheduling/controlling. CPA emerged from the development of operational research in the 1950s, particularly from the need to plan the development of large-scale engineering projects. These projects involved complex networks of decision making, resource marshalling and production scheduling.

Methods were required to manage and control these very large and complex systems. As CPA developed, it began to be used in diverse fields, such as town planning, marketing, office administration, consultancy assignments and computers. CPA offers a 'technique for planning projects by breaking them down into their component activities and showing these activities and their interrelationships in the form of a network' [Johnson and Scholes, 1988 p 251]. In a complex project certain events cannot take place until preceding events have occurred. Resources have to be brought into place in a certain order and at specific times. The construction of a building provides an example of a project that requires a wide range of tasks to be performed according to a specified schedule. CPA provides a technique for calculating the total amount of time required to complete the whole project.

If the time taken by each event can be estimated, then CPA offers a means for estimating the total duration of the whole project. The shortest possible duration for the whole sequence can then be calculated. Some sequences could increase, at the same time that others could decrease, without affecting the overall time taken to complete the project. Lockyer explains that 'this determining sequence is critical to the performance of the project and is hence drawn as the critical path'. CPA thus enables effort to be concentrated in the most useful way. CPA is usually applied to time limited projects but it could be applied to continuing organisational processes if the whole process can be broken down into a series of time-limited events.

Part of the CPA technique involves describing a network or system in terms of activities, events and the interactions between these. There are conventions in drawing up these descriptions. The critical path is isolated as the network is analysed. Lockyer explains that this exercise 'imposed a discipline on planners, forcing consideration of WHAT has to be done, WHEN, by WHOM and in what TIME'. Lang [1977] described CPA as the

> 'organised application of systematic reasoning to planning, scheduling and controlling practical situations, where many separate jobs, which make up the whole task, can happen simultaneously, almost simultaneously or in sequences, such that it is difficult intuitively to establish the relationship between the separate jobs'.

In complex plans or systems, one small activity could have a disproportionately large affect on overall performance. CPA offers a diagnostic tool for locating bottlenecks and blockages in a system. Our ability to draw a map or plan of a system, accurately and in good technical detail, can determine the depth of our understanding of how that system works. The use of conventions in drawing graphical representations of systems and processes permits a greater accuracy than where an indisciplined approach is used. Johnson and Scholes point out that there are a number of developments of network analysis, such as 'programme evaluation review technique' (PERT). This allows uncertainty about the times of each activity to be taken into account [Johnson and Scholes, 1988, p 253].

CPA might, for example, be used to reduce delays in processing cases through the prosecution or courts services. The design of complex research projects that need to be completed quickly might also use CPA techniques. It could be used where an agency is building and equipping a new centre or setting up a new scheme of service delivery. It might also be applied to the organisation of the planning process itself. CPA is a long established and widely applied technique. It requires quite some time to learn but has much potential for practical application.

Planning and training

In planning the implementation of a strategy, emphasis should be laid on staff training and professional development. Planning is an activity that requires knowledge, skills and specialised techniques. But not all those working in the criminal justice system need these in equal proportions. Some criminal justice organisations may need to employ people who can undertake some of the more complex and skilful aspects of planning. But personnel at all levels can and should participate in planning. Training is of central importance to planning, especially with respect to systems that rely heavily on skills and expertise and on a large number of practitioners making day to day decisions. People are the most vital resource in a criminal justice system and one of the many factors that influence their performance is their capacity to respond to change. In order to respond to change appropriately, flexibly and effectively, those working in the field of crime responses must have and be able to exercise a wide range of skills. Those responsible for planning need to ensure that these skills are developed and this requires training to be built into planning at all levels.

Planners themselves need skills, both in terms of managing and developing crime response initiatives and in the art of planning itself. Much more could be achieved if training courses in planning were to be made available to the police, probation officers, prosecutors and others who have responsibility for the development and implementation of crime response policies and programmes. The implementation of plans often requires retraining of personnel, training in new techniques or practices, in the use of new equipment or technology and in working out the implications of changes to legislation. Training is therefore an aspect of planning that should be placed high up on any list of priorities.

A groupwork approach to planning

Most planning is carried out in groups. Large-scale organisational planning involves a wide variety of people and a complex consultative process. In the strategic planning of responses to crime, a variety of agencies are required to collaborate and that requires groups of people from various organisations meeting together to make planning decisions. For the process of planning to work effectively, planners need to function well in and as a group. Some planning must be done in formal committees; but these are not necessarily the most productive forums for creative planning. Small informal groups can work more flexibly and creatively with complex planning tasks. In this way the groundwork can be done for the more formalised process of committee decision taking.

Much planning is routine and requires patience rather than creativity. But there are always times when a premium must be placed on creative and imaginative planning. *Synectics* is a technique for enabling creative working to take place. It has been described as a 'joining together of different and apparently irrelevant elements' and was devised in 1944 by Gordon, who had made an intensive study of individual and group processes [Stein, 1975]. The technique is based on improving people's comprehension of a problem through analogy and metaphor, allowing access to more creative solutions than are possible through conventional analytical methods. Problems can be restated in alternative ways and this can provide new insights and innovative conceptions of how problems can be solved.

Problems in planning

Problem solving often requires creative thinking; planning is often viewed as a process for solving problems. Planners will often be faced with difficult problems in trying to implement policies or when organising the development of a new service. Certain problems are of strategic importance in achieving effective planning, particularly the problem of dealing with uncertainty.

Planning and uncertainty

Planning is a process of reducing uncertainty. Most organisations operate in environments that contain uncertainties that are beyond control; planners must respond to these uncertainties as much as to those that are within their control. In one study of creative strategic planning, it was suggested that

> 'during the next decade, public and private organisations will experience increasing environmental uncertainty and turbulence as modern Western society continues transition from the post-industrial world to the information/service orientation of the future. Managers and strategic planners will face even more complicated future planning and forecasting tasks as these changes evolve' [Maddox, Anthony and Wheatly, 1987, p 118].

The effectiveness of planning relies on identifying these uncertainties and working around them. Friend and Hickling define three types of uncertainty:

> Uncertainties about the working environment,
> uncertainties about guiding values and
> uncertainties about related decisions.
> [Friend and Hickling, 1987, p11]

Policy development, at one level, attempts to reduce these uncertainties by providing definitions and principles. At another level, planning seeks further reductions in uncertainty through its function of coordination, scheduling, preparation and feedback. At another level, information seeks to reduce uncertainty by increasing knowledge. Planning is about reducing uncertainty; if it cannot be reduced then it must be accommodated. How a problem is seen, conceived or imaged is part of the process of devising a solution to it. Uncertainty often lies at the heart of a problem: uncertainty about what the problem really is as well as how it can be solved. Crime is very much a problem shot through with uncertainty. Our knowledge of the influences on crime rates is somewhat uncertain and this is often because the information we have about crime is uncertain. Forecasting crime rates is very difficult, partly because of the inadequacies of the knowledge base and partly because of the deficiencies of criminal statistics. Forecasting changes in the environments of criminal justice systems poses many uncertainties. Clearly, these need to be addressed and worked with if planning is to be successful.

Dealing with uncertainty and engaging in prediction requires both rational and intuitive capabilities. Planners should be able to use 'individual and collective imagery to identify future scenarios that will impact on the strategic plan and develop strategies that address these future scenarios' [Maddox, Anthony and Wheatly, 1987, p 119]. Forward thinking and predicting the future cannot be based exclusively on rational, mathematical or deductive modelling. Techniques of the kind suggested by *synectics* (as mentioned above) can also be used. Creative thinking allows the future to be seen or imagined as acceptable, desirable or ideal. This provides an evaluation of what we think will be probable or possible. Formulating strategic *vision* can require creative thinking and looking at things in a new way.

It is through organisation that many of the problems caused by uncertainty can be addressed. Policy, planning and information are organisational processes that anticipate what will or might happen, analyse the implications of events or conditions, increase understanding about what is happening or what will happen, and which devise predictive scenarios. The underlying process is that of decision making, particularly the making of decisions about which options are likely to achieve intended outcomes. Some uncertainties are due to randomness in the system; they can only be predicted through techniques involving probability. Planners need to know which components of their plans they are reasonably certain about and which they are less certain about. This requires skills in forecasting.

Predicting out-turns

The ability to predict out-turns is essential to good policy formulation and to policy analysis. It is perhaps important to distinguish between outcomes (what is intended to happen) and out-turns (what actually happens). Criminal justice policies have sometimes been ineffective or counterproductive because those who formulated them had not correctly predicted the out-turns of those policies. Alternatively, the out-turns were not those which had been intended. Often, it is the unintended consequences of a policy that are the most significant. Policy analysis includes predicting all possible out-turns for sets of conditions, variables or pressures which will produce one out-turn rather than another. Such prediction requires us to have a model; moreover, it requires an accurate and reliable model before our prediction can be both accurate and reliable. The art of good model building requires correct selection of component parts and correct determination of the relationships among them and how these contribute to the dynamics of the system. The same is true of planning; being able to successfully implement plans requires accurate prediction of their consequences. We must, however, use the term 'prediction' cautiously; some would prefer the term 'forecast'. A meteorologist can forecast what weather patterns might occur; but not predict what they will be. Those who engage in prediction often need to calculate the probability that an event will occur, given a certain set of conditions. Hogwood and Gunn [1984] have commented that

> 'given the differences between prediction in science and forecasting for public policy-making, we would argue that forecasting in policy analysis

should always indicate the sensitivity of forecasts to assumptions, and in particular should always indicate the extent to which the outcome of forecasts is capable of policy manipulation'.

The models that we use in predicting the results of a policy rest on the assumptions that we employ; if the assumptions are wrong, we are unlikely to achieve the desired out-turns of our policies.

Some uncertainties are due to failures to predict. Unintended consequences result from inadequate information, faulty modelling or insufficient planning. Other uncertainties are simply due to inability to interpret available information. Some uncertainties derive from external influences over which planning can have no control. Planning is about making strategic choices and this is surrounded with influences and pressures (see **Figure 5.3**). To be successful, a coherent analysis of opportunities and constraints is required in order to be able to accurately forecast the consequences that will follow when our plans are implemented.

One increasingly common technique in forecasting is the use of *scenarios*. There are a variety of styles and techniques of scenario planning – the Delphi technique, intuitive logics, trend-impact analysis, cross-impact analysis and so on. These have been reviewed [Huss and Honton, 1987] and now appear in many of the major textbooks on management and strategic planning [for example, Johnson and Scholes, 1988]. Scenarios assist in strategic thinking, particularly in terms of an organisation's future development, although the same technique could be used for crime response planning. Many scenarios focus on what might happen to current trends over the future and alternative pictures of the future can emerge from this. No analytical tool will provide all the right answers:

'Scenarios are best suited for long-range time spans (5-20 years), highly complex situations of many factors of which some are unquantifiable, highly uncertain situations where virtually every factor is a variable and none is constant, and where there are few or no reliable data available for quantitative models' [Millett, 1988 p 61].

Clearly, scenarios would seem to fit well with the task of planning responses to crime. Scenarios can be used in forecasting changes in the environment of criminal justice systems and in the evaluation of strategic choices. Crime reduction strategies can be based on restraint, deterrence, reformation and prevention [Falkin, 1979]. By varying the blends of each of these in potential strategic recipes, we can devise scenarios against which strategic choices about budgets and resource distributions can be assessed. At the level of the system, crime response planning requires that we test a number of recipes to see what impacts each would have on crime rates. This allows us to formulate a strategy that would make the most effective use of resources.

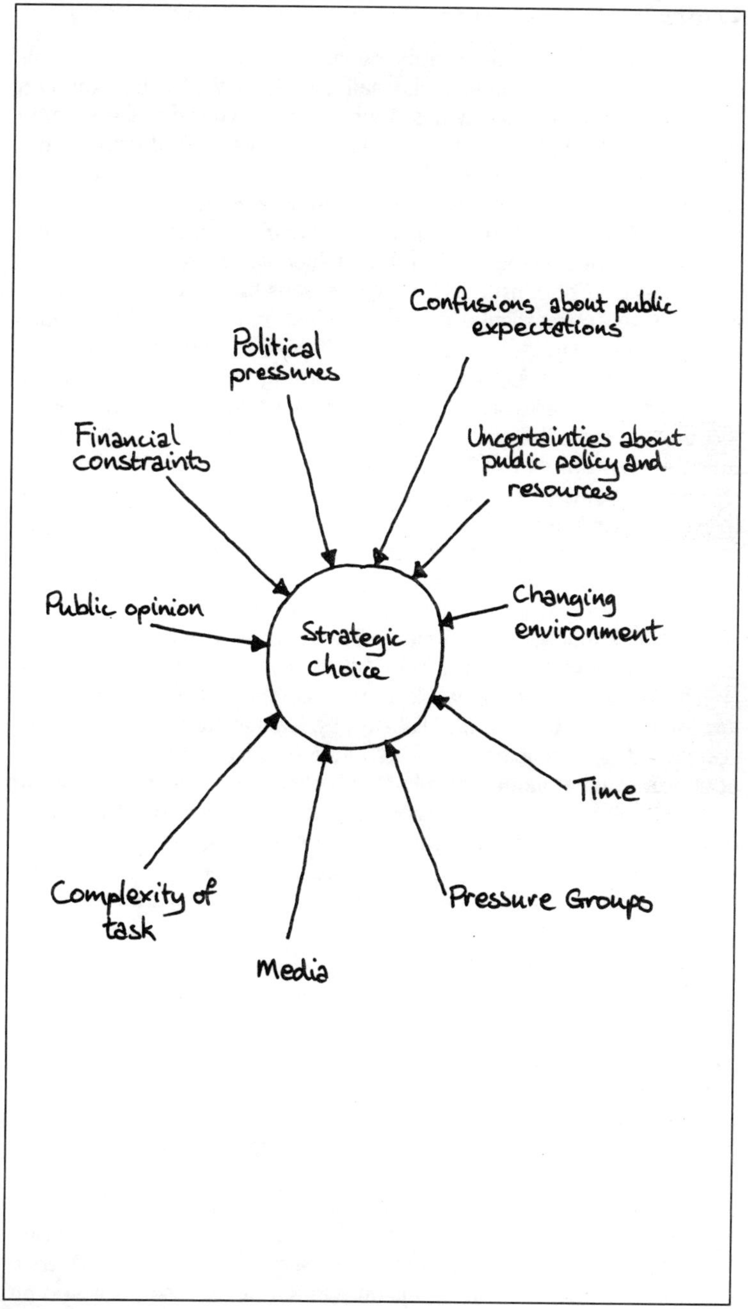

Figure 5.3 Pressures on strategic choice

Values in planning

The planning process necessarily involves decision making; often this is a case of choosing between alternative options. Whilst decisions can be informed they almost always involve values. A good process would be one in which the values involved are clearly understood, not implicit, covert or displaced. Good decision making requires coherent choice, based on values which have been opened out. Whose values? How widely are values held? How intensively is a value held? Can the system of values be mapped to show which values flow from others? Can values be prioritised? There will always be a number of means available to any particular end. The selection of the desired means must be related to values or criteria. Alternatives must be evaluated. Means might also be evaluated according to the probability of achievement. These processes take account of two sets of values: those held within the organisation and those impacting on it from the outside environment. Current values need to be identified but changes in values are equally important. We have already seen that resistance to change can be generated by the culture of an organisation; values can therefore represent barriers to, for example, plans to increase effective performance. We discussed above the problems facing the probation service in adjusting to a role more oriented to criminal justice. Values play a central part in the issues and process currently going on within the service.

There is a complex network of values in the justice system. These are the subject of jurisprudential studies. Values are studied by those concerned with policing practices. Finding value for money requires attention to what value actually is and how it is defined. Criteria are used in evaluation and in decision making and these too are subject to values. The selection of values often involves political rather than strictly managerial choices. The development of a strategic planning approach to crime involves ethical dilemmas; our discussion has pointed only to a few of these.

Politics and planning

There is an important relationship between information and politics. This is particularly true in the field of responses to crime and something that crime and justice planners are likely to encounter. Information is brought to the planning process in a variety of forms: statistics, generalised information and research. It is used in setting and evaluating performance indicators and other systems of monitoring. Since crime is an emotive subject, at least in public debates, and one that is sometimes the subject of party political controversy, information and research results are vulnerable to being hijacked by politicians. Criminal justice policy is notorious for ignoring the conclusions of research and debate is too often ill-informed. In political debates about crime 'facts', as many like to call their beliefs, are used as ammunition in the battle of conflicting views. Politicians seem to have become very fond of firing off salvos of 'facts' at each other in the hope that in this way they will shoot down the other side's arguments. Very often politicians assume that the 'facts' speak for themselves. Making assumptions about the significance of 'facts' is very dangerous; interpretation of research findings and sets of data is a difficult business. But without this careful and reflective approach, investments in expensive research projects can be squandered.

Planning should not become an alternative to politics; nor should politics seek to replace planning. These two processes are interdependent but fulfil different functions. The role of the planner in public organisations, I would argue, is to provide information to those who make public policy but also to assist policy makers to accept that there is much we do not know about crime. Public perceptions of crime often vary greatly from reality. Public policy makers however have less excuses than the ordinary person for not being adequately informed. Simply providing information will not necessarily change a point of view but it might change the strength of that view or its legitimacy.

We have set out to distinguish between policy and planning in various ways, whilst recognising that, in practice, they are closely linked. Both require considerable decision making. There are often problems in deciding which decisions are appropriate to policy and which are legitimate in planning. The idea presented in this discussion is that where policy has been accurately and thoroughly formulated, there is less need for planners to make policy decisions. A clear and well formulated public crime and justice policy (at both national and local corporate levels) sets a firm context for the planning task and locates accountability in the public policy arena rather than in operational bodies.

Boundaries and logistics

In deciding how best to plan criminal justice and crime prevention, geographical considerations are of prime importance. One of the foremost problems in planning criminal justice is that of noncoterminous boundaries. Many police force areas conform to local authority boundaries, as do most probation services. Commission of the Peace areas also fall largely within local authority areas. But in certain areas of the country, most notably London and what used to be the metropolitan counties, things are not so neat. At the local level, within local authorities, boundaries tend to be noncoterminous. Social service departments, the police, the probation service and the courts all have different boundaries and these do not always match up with wards or other local government districts. Such areas might not be related to identifiable communities or neighbourhoods. The formation of interagency groups for the coordination of juvenile justice or crime prevention, face considerable boundary problems.

Whilst a strategy might be devised for the local authority area, operational planning might need to be focused on smaller areas, particularly in the large counties and dense urban areas. It has long been recognised that crime prevention needs to be organised at a fairly local level, within neighbourhoods, on estates or even in certain streets or groups of streets. The task of central planning, at the authority-wide level, is to set the strategic goals, policy guidelines and resource parameters for the system as a whole. Local planning is more concerned with day to day, relatively short-term operational activities and with responding to the immediate needs and problems of people in a small area. The problem of noncoterminous boundaries presents considerable logistical problems to the task of delivering interagency responses.

In criminal justice, an important feature of the planning task is to reach agreement on which agencies are to contribute what services or activities, at local level. Planning attempts to clarify the allocation of specific responsibilities among the various agencies concerned with offenders. Often more than one agency is involved in working with offenders and this is particularly true where juvenile and prevention schemes are concerned. Since there is often a degree of overlapping involvement in a particular area, agencies might find themselves cooperating with others outside their areas in matters concerning those resident in their particular catchment. Lack of clear definition of boundaries can lead to unnecessary conflicts and confusions. In the long term, some of these problems can be resolved by agencies agreeing on area and subdivisional boundaries which are coterminous. Where boundaries cannot be reset, either in the short term or in the future, agreements should be reached about operational responsibilities where there are boundary overlaps and hence confusions.

Suggested reading

There are no books written about criminal justice planning in the English context as far as I know. My main source has been therefore a monograph by Robert Cushman *Criminal justice planning for local governments*, produced in 1980 for the United States Department of Justice. I mention this but realise that it will be difficult to obtain, although the National Youth Bureau, 17 – 23 Albion Street, Leicester LE1 6GD does have a copy which they might be able to lend. A book that I suggested in chapter three and which deserves to be recommended here is *Planning under pressure* by John Friend and Allen Hickling, published in 1987 by Pergamon. This provides a good deal of very practical material which is well organised and full of ideas. The book by Johnson and Scholes, 1988, has been mentioned before and this will provide excellent material to those focusing on planning theory and practice. Faludi's *A reader in planning theory,*1973, is perhaps a bit outdated now but still provides a useful introduction to a range of planning issues and problems.

6 Information for planning

Policy, planning and information

In previous chapters, strategies were viewed as being based on three essential and interdependent components: policy, planning and information. Information is used in policy formulation and in planning; it is used in processes of organisation, management, research and evaluation and is therefore one of the most universal tools in organisations and systems. Information is continually changing and is always on the move. It becomes active when it is communicated. Therefore, information, communications and systems theories, cybernetics and operations research have all been used in exploring the role played by information in organisations. These theories will not be discussed here; instead we will concentrate on some of the principal techniques that characterise information systems planning in criminal justice now, and on the trends that might shape the development of these systems over, say, the next decade. This chapter focuses on information in local systems of criminal justice; the same concepts can, of course, be applied to information systems at the national level.

Information is the catalyst that makes policy and planning work. Policy, planning and information can be studied by linking them together in models. Strategic planning in criminal justice systems, as elsewhere, requires an organised system of information flow to inform decision makers and planners. The organisation of information collection and use requires modelling to be used in the processes of design and system implementation.

Policy formulation and planning depend on being able to model the system. Very often, however, models are implicit and this is probably because managers do not have or give themselves the time to articulate the models they use or because the purpose of accurate and reliable modelling has not yet been established. One of our first tasks is to identify the variables which affect the system, as for example the rate of offending; if this can be achieved, we can then investigate the degree to which these variables can be controlled. Some may not be controllable (and hence, we can call them constants or independent variables). Others may be controlled to varying degrees (in which case, we can call them dependent variables).

The degree to which we can exercise control over a system of variables will depend on the resources available, and the effectiveness of our management of those resources. The effectiveness of our policy and planning will depend on having correctly identified the key control variables. The model will test that we have identified the relevant variables or that we have correctly determined the relationship between variables. The model is a method for translating our assumptions into data and back again.

In justice management, policy models represent the aims, objectives, methods and procedures of the system and set out the application of practice principles expressed in the policy. This model should enable policy makers and planners to understand and to predict how the system will operate. Modelling the system as it is, assists in the formulation of the policies that will enable changes to be made. This model aids policy analysis by allowing us to identify policy options and to begin to predict how these options would affect the system if put into operation.

The role of policy and information in the management of juvenile justice systems has been discussed by the present author and colleagues [Britton et al, 1988]. In this publication it was suggested that dynamic modelling techniques could be applied to the management and planning of juvenile justice systems as a whole. In particular, simulation techniques could be used to predict the impact of changes applied to or taking place within the system [op cit, p 15].

Policy modelling provides a basis for simulation modelling which can be used in planning and management. Simulation models allow the out-turns of changes to be predicted, reveal how the system will perform dynamically and show how far various subsystems will interact with each other as a result of these changes. However, we must appreciate that justice is not a wholly determinate system. Because it is largely a human, decision making system, its operations are highly probabilistic. The model must be able to predict the chances that given out-turns will occur to the extent that the governing conditions are known and controllable.

Models are an aid to human beings. For data to be of value, it must be interpreted and this is something that cannot be replaced, even by the latest generation of artificial intelligence software. Interpretation requires judgement. Policy modelling allows us to increase our ability to interpret the data gained from simulation models and to do so in an organised way. Simulation models should be designed on the back of policy models, since it is the policy model which provides us with a foundation and a framework for interpreting the results obtained from simulation models. This assumes, of course, that the two models are compatible. Computerised models *support* human thinking:

> 'In addition to solving complex computational problems, computers also are used to aid human intelligence by providing a tool for handling and manipulating information. This will probably continue to be the most important use of computers in the future' [Tsichritzis and Lochovsky, 1982 p ix].

We can rest assured that computers will not replace human intelligence.

Information and knowledge

I referred earlier to the comment made by Blumstein about the inadequacy of the knowledge base for criminal justice planning. It is significant that he did not refer to a lack of information. This is something that the criminal justice system is swimming in. What is needed more than information is knowledge. For information to become knowledge it must be analysed, interpreted and evaluated. Planning consumes large quantities of information; this can only be put to effective use where there is a reliable body of knowledge. A collaborative approach to planning requires a collective knowledge base, the development of which involves identifying gaps in what is known and how and which gaps should be filled. These gaps can sometimes only be filled by undertaking research and by synthesising the results of research. Collective knowledge is important; as knowledge increases, so individuals become increasingly ignorant.

Accurate and reliable information is a prerequisite at all stages of strategic planning. In order to obtain reliable information, we must design good monitoring systems and we can only do this if we have well constructed and reliable models. Without a full and effective method of finding out what is happening in the system, there is little chance of knowing whether plans are being successfully implemented or of identifying blockages and problems and dealing with them as they occur. But information alone is not enough: in order to decide what information we need, how to collect it and how to use it, we need to devise and utilise models.

What are models?

Models are commonly used in research and these very often are sophisticated devices constructed according to established rules. A model is a representation designed to describe, explain, control or predict, as realistically as possible, the essential aspects of a problem, device, object, process, system or phenomenon. The model is structured around specified assumptions and is governed by accepted rules of inference. Thus, a model of this kind is not a reconstruction of something in the real world but a simplification of it that can be comprehended more readily than the complex reality to which it relates.

A model is a means of interpreting and understanding a thing or system. We cannot see, touch, hold or manipulate a justice system: it is a set of abstract ideas. Any representation of an abstract system is a model of that system. The model is characterised by what we choose to include in it or to exclude from it. In constructing a model of a system, our primary concern is to achieve a reliable match between the real system and our abstract, conceptual representation of it.

Models are built from components and these are related together to form a structure. As one component changes, moves or operates, the other components are affected, changed, moved or operated on; this representation of interactive changes is often referred to as *dynamics* and a model that represents change as a *dynamic model.* A model can be constructed through either analysis or synthesis of information about the original system. The success of either process depends on being able to identify the most important components (or variables) involved and how these interrelate. The degree to which a model allows us to study a system depends on the degree to which it accurately and reliably represents that system. In other words, it depends on the degree to which there is a concordance between the properties of the model and the properties of the system it models. Models allow such properties to be investigated independently of the reality or source from which they are derived.

How can models be used in criminal justice planning?

The purpose of a model in planning is to test assumptions, predict effects and to search for unintended consequences. The model should allow us to answer questions, such as: 'to what extent will a prevention policy be effective?' Or 'to what extent will a particular policy affect the rate of offending in an area?' For example, if our aim is to make an impact on the rate and patterns of offending through applying a particular policing policy, then we must have a reliable model of offending, in order to decide what the likely consequences will be of introducing that policy.

We construct models for a variety of purposes: to represent or describe, to simulate, to explain, predict, experiment or to test hypotheses and so on. In the context of our present discussion, modelling is seen as being a method which supports planning and decision making. Models provide diagnostic and experimental facilities and in this respect are tools that can be used in a wide variety of management situations.

Some models perform a function of converting information into knowledge; they help us to structure our ideas about complex and abstract systems and problems. They permit the structuring of quantities of data into intelligible analogues. A model can be constructed in natural language or it can be constructed using mathematical formulae and data. The model can be represented graphically using symbols and diagrams. These are all, to some degree, simulations but the highest level of simulation can be achieved only by using a computer.

For the purposes of local strategic planning, two general models are required: a *crime* model and a *response* model. Each of these will consist of a variety of sub-models. These models can be used in policy, planning and management. Complex decisions can, by the use of models, be subdivided into a series of smaller and more manageable parts. Before we go on to examine these, we will consider the general types of model that can be used in criminal justice information planning.

What types of model will be needed?

A comprehensive consideration of modelling theory and types of models need not be presented here since that is available in a number of works [for example Vemuri, 1978]. It might be sufficient to say that some models will be almost entirely mathematical, some will be based very much on statistics and some can be descriptive, employing a variety of information types. Mathematical models of criminal justices processes are not uncommon [see for example, Butler, 1982].

Analogue models are, in effect, analogies of something, representing not the thing itself but its characteristics or effects. Most crime and criminal justice models are of this type. Analogue models merely imitate a system rather than duplicating it and this imitation is 'necessarily restricted to a subset of the structural features, attributes and behavioural traits of the system' [Vemuri, 1978, p 75]. *Heuristic* models are described as a 'means of identifying satisfactory "solutions" in a systematic way' [Johnson and Scholes, 1988 p 220]. The strategic plan is a kind of heuristic model. In developing a strategic plan a range of options are *searched* until one is found that satisfies all or most of the selection criteria. A *heuristic* is a 'rough guide or principle, rule of thumb, hypothesis or approximation' [Vemuri, 1978, p 103] that can be used in planning and decision making procedures, indeed these procedures are themselves heuristic.

Heuristic models provide a means of exploring problem solving techniques that are aimed at improving performance, such as evaluating out-turns and feeding the results back into decision making [House, 1982, p 114]. These models involve learning how to do things in the best or optimum way. Many computer programmes used in management use heuristic modelling (e.g. decision-tree analysers).

Various types of models that are relevant to criminal justice policy making and planning are described by House [1982]; he describes simulation forecasting models and those that attempt to 'specify what should be done or what path ought to be followed to achieve the "best" result, given a specified goal and known resources and constraints' [op cit, p 112]. Since policy and planning processes depend on human behaviour, they will necessarily include a degree of uncertainty. Models in which there is a high degree of randomness, use probability theory in forecasting out-turns. They can be viewed as *stochastic* models in which the characteristics of the modelling system are defined largely in terms of probabilistic variables.

Simulation models have much to offer to both crime and response modelling. Simulation involves the construction of a model that is analogous to and which behaves like the modelled system (the source). For example, the flow of prisoners into and out of the prison system and the effects of these flows on the size and characteristics of the resident population can be modelled mathematically. If these equations and statistics were to be loaded into a suitable computer programme, it would be possible to simulate what has happened to the prison population over a period of time. This would allow forecasts to be made of what would happen to the population if we changed some of the factors involved in the flow. The process of simulation modelling is widely described in the literature, including accounts of how computer simulations can be constructed [see for example, Balmer et al, 1989]. The latest and most advanced techniques in this field seek to integrate expert systems, simulation modelling and decision making [op cit, p 142]. This has led to the emergence of *expert simulations* (an expert system interfaced with a simulation model). Developments of this kind can be used in policing, sentencing, crime rate forecasting and so on to support strategic planning.

Flow models utilise statistics about the number of people entering and leaving the criminal justice system or a part of it. As mentioned above, the flow of prisoners into and out of the prison system can be simulated in a flow model. The flow of offenders through the criminal justice system, from arrest to sentencing, is a commonly used model and these, in their simplest form, are drawn as flowcharts (an illustration of a criminal justice flowchart is given in **Figure 6.1**). Charts of this kind 'provide the capability to extensively examine the criminal justice system, diagnose criminal justice problems and

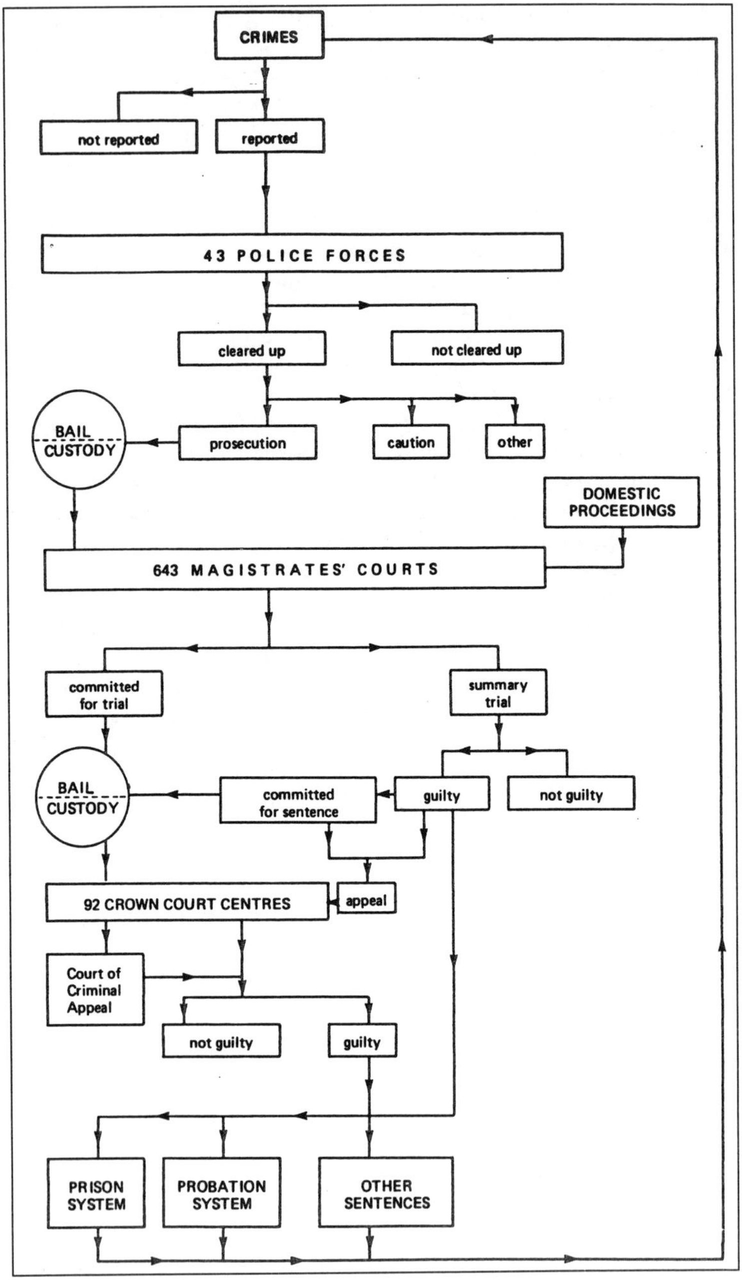

Source: Reproduced from Patricia Morgan *Modelling the Criminal Justice System* Home Office Research and Planning Unit, 1985

Fig 6.1 The criminal justice system

evaluate the effects of changes in programs and policies' [Cushman, 1980, p 34].

In the United States, a model called JUSSIM was developed by Blumstein and Larson [1969] to evaluate changes in the system's resource costs, workforce requirements and criminal population for several types of crime at each stage of the criminal justice process [Falkin, 1979, p 58]. The application of such models has been described [Cohen, 1973] and trial use of JUSSIM II helped to some extent, it is said, in clarifying features of the model developed by the Home Office for England and Wales [Moxon, 1985, p 31]. Work on the development of the Home Office model of the criminal justice system began in 1979 [Barton, 1984].

Flow models are of particular value in investigations of the interdependence of criminal justice processes and will provide a valuable tool in the development of interdependence management techniques. They can be used to forecast changes in the demand for resources by various agencies as a consequence of input variations, such as trends in the detection of crimes or the effects on the system of demographic change (as an example of a flow model, **Figure 6.2** shows part of the model of the criminal justice system developed by the Home Office in 1985).

Two other types of management models have been used in the United States: *workload analysis* models, which enable bottlenecks and imbalances in flows of cases from one agency to another to be identified and corrected, and *system rate analysis* models which relate workload and demand to resource requirements, thus providing diagnostic and policy planning inputs to agency managers and local authorities [Cushman, p 34].

Econometric modelling in criminal justice is discussed by Falkin [1979]; he argues that, although the economic approach to crime offers a very attractive methodology, its shortcomings make it 'impossible to support a criminal justice policy on econometric findings alone' [op cit p 52]. Such models tend to oversimplify complex realities and are 'limited in their capacity to incorporate the necessarily fine detail of program options in complex social systems' [op cit, p 53].

Given this note of caution, it is nevertheless true that economic modelling is of considerable importance in the management of criminal justice systems, particularly since budgets are sometimes the only variables that can be controlled in some policy situations. Here there is scope for using information technology to relate budgetary and financial management with the needs of strategic planning processes.

One study of the economics of criminal justice found that, inter alia, the crime-reducing effects of additional budget allocations for court and prosecution are very high; the crime-reducing effectiveness of an

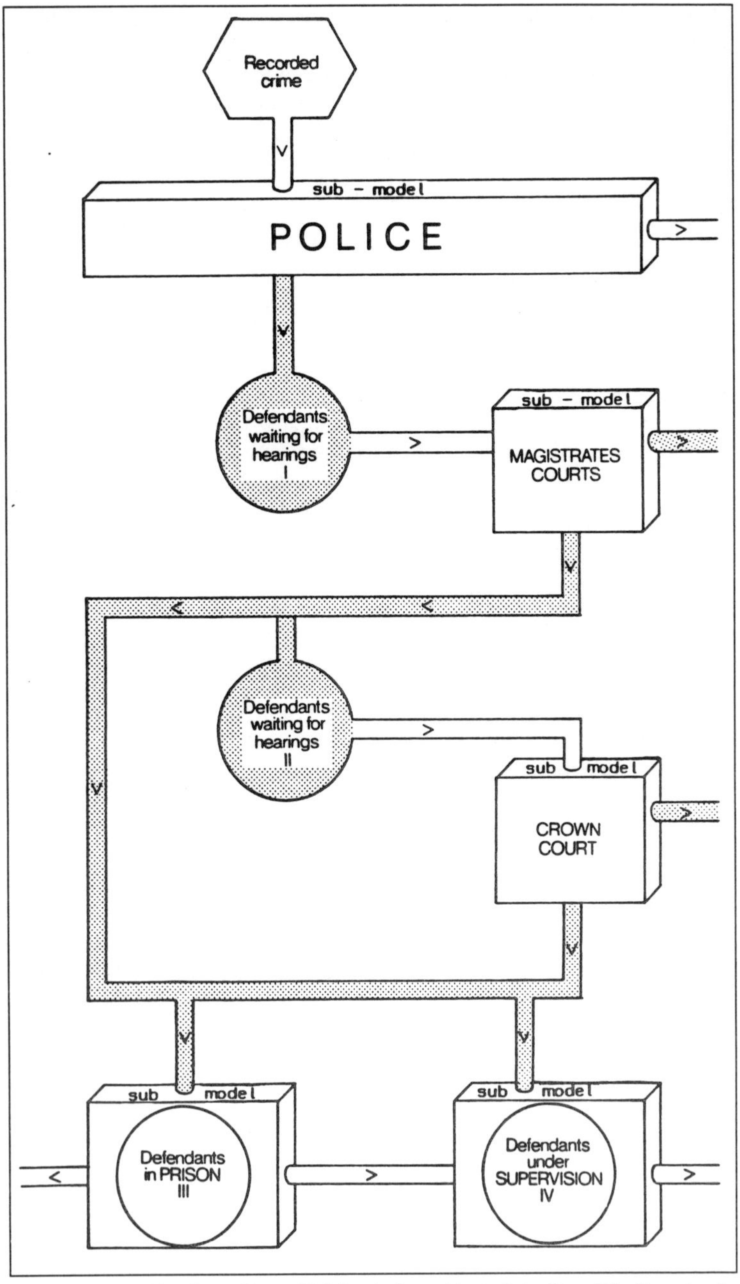

Source: Reproduced from Patricia Morgan *Modelling the Criminal Justice System* Home Office Research and Planning Unit, 1985

Fig 6.2 A criminal justice flow model

additional budget allocation to the prison system is fairly low; a direct relationship exists between increased court congestion and increased sentence reductions; the crime-reducing effectiveness of a trial is higher than that of a guilty plea case; an increase in crime, if unaccompanied by an expansion of the criminal justice system budget, will lead to a further crime increase of 6% of the original increment in the following time period; an expansion in police capacity will be partly offset if other parts of the criminal justice system are not adjusted simultaneously [Noam, 1977, pp 42 – 43].

These findings are stimulating, not necessarily capable of replication in the English system and should not be accepted at face value. But, they illustrate some of the principles of economic modelling. If increased resources in any one part of the system is to be justified, then resource implications for other parts of the system must be analysed. These interrelations can be specified by an interdependence model. The effectiveness factors of budgetary allocations and resource evaluation must be related to a measurable criteria. In the above study, crime reduction effects were the focus and these are arguably good strategic yardsticks although other values also need to be introduced (such as due process, civil liberties, etc.). The author of this study comments that

> 'the interrelated resource requirements of part of the criminal justice system therefore requires integrated planning if reforms in the subsystems are not to be offset by the lack of adjustments in other parts of the criminal justice system' [Noam, 1977 p 43].

Other economic models can be identified beyond those that relate to the operations of the justice system. A model could be devised to quantify the impact of property-related crime on local economies. Some tentative work on this has been done by the present author [Locke, 1989]. This very modest study considers what contribution knowledge of the economics of urban crime can make to prevention strategies in the commercial sector. A pilot survey is described in which data about the costs of crime to businesses could be gathered and evaluated. It suggests that econometric models offer important inputs to the formulation of prevention policies, especially for businesses. The purpose of models of this kind is to provide contextual analyses for policy and planning in crime prevention. This can provide, especially in relation to the prevention of business-related crime, a framework for evaluating the relative cost-benefits of public and private prevention measures.

Expert simulations will also allow for increases in performance in the management of costs and resources. The drive towards effectiveness, efficiency and economy demands that sophisticated costing, budgetary and resource management systems be developed. Existing financial planning and modelling software already exists that can cope with these demands but more needs to be done to develop connections between financial modelling and impact effectiveness as part of the strategic planning process. Economic planning in the context of overall organisation, management and strategic planning is beginning to emerge in criminal justice agencies. As an example of this, the National Audit Office has commented, in a report on the Probation Service that

> 'Increasing demands, finite resources, and the need to harness probation work more closely to central policy objectives mean that the Home Office oversight and monitoring will inevitably assume greater prominence ...'

and it went on to say that

> 'There will consequently be a need at both Home Office and local level for more and better information and analysis about which aspects of the probation service work well and which do not and why; about how resources are being deployed and to what effect; about comparative costs and performance against targets; and above all how far achievements match up to agreed objectives, at both operational and strategic level. At present information on all these matters is incomplete and of variable quality, and this stands in the way of effective management...' [quoted in NACRO News Digest, 1989, p 12].

The probation service has been included in the financial management initiative in common with other public sector bodies and work has been undertaken to develop a Financial Management Information System (FMIS) for the service [Audit Commission, 1989, p 61]. The purpose of this proposed system is to provide information about the efficient, effective and economical use of resources and in one of the reports from the consultants, the absence of integrated information systems was criticised. Apparently, 'thorny problems of integrating cost and statistical information' had not been resolved in stage two of the project [ibid]. To take another example, it is intended to add financial information to police statistical data, to enable H.M. Inspectorate to make judgements about effectiveness and efficiency in the police service [Chancellor of the Exchequer, 1989, p 6].

Modelling crime

We have considered the idea that responses to a problem are dependent on the way in which that problem is defined. If a problem is to be managed, controlled or changed, then it must be defined, analysed and interpreted. The purpose of a crime model is to provide structured information for use in policy analysis, strategy formulation, planning and evaluation. Those wishing to plan responses to crime, need to have a model of crime that can be used as part of the policy and planning process.

Constructing crime models

Crime models should take in what is known or believed about crime and the factors that influence it. A considerable quantity of data about crime is currently collected and provided through the Home Office, in the annual *Criminal Statistics* and in the annual reports of Chief Constables. Data alone does not constitute a model although some of the analytical commentaries provided in these sources suggest that a variety of models are being used in making interpretations of the statistics.

Crime modelling needs to be done locally if the response is organised locally. Some components of crime models will be valid at any level but each locality varies and these variations must be reflected in the model and the data collected. In constructing a model of crime we might begin by asking such questions as 'what affects rates of crime locally?' 'What relationship is there between crime and the demographic characteristics of the area?' 'Are there specific factors that are known to influence levels and patterns of crime locally?' 'How does sentencing in the local courts affect crime?' 'What measures have been shown to have a preventive effect?' Clearly these are very fundamental questions and any answers to them will require a good deal of research and evaluation. It is unlikely that we will either want to or be able to construct one global model to cope with the range of questions that we will want to ask. It is more likely that a series of models will be required to cope with specific aspects of the local response system. A series of small, specific models can be networked together to provide a larger scale of model where appropriate.

Information about crime must be *reliable and accurate.* The procedures used to collect and collate it must be consistent and represent an accurate measure of local crime rates. There are considerable technical difficulties involved in the collection of crime data and these are discussed in a number of studies [For example, Bottomley and Pease, 1986]. Such information must also be *meaningful and relevant* to end users. The choice of which data to collect and how to present it must be dictated by the uses to which it is to be put. There is little point in collecting data that cannot in some way be applied. This suggests that those responsible for the collection of crime data have or need to have a profile of consumer's needs. This poses immense difficulties at national level but the design of information systems at local level can be improved by surveying needs (as discussed below).

The system for collecting and processing data must be efficient and economical, since it is a time-consuming process that consumes considerable resources. The present systems for the collection of crime statistics at local levels result in large amounts of data, some of which is seldom used. There are often, in local areas, problems in gaining access to data that is collected, because police force statistical personnel cannot meet all the demands placed on them. Computing technology should enable freer access to aggregate crime statistics. The present arrangements for the collection of data by and from criminal justice agencies present a number of difficulties, not least that of inconsistencies in definitions and varying data capture techniques. There are also differences between agencies in the way that similar sets of statistics are collected. Some work is in progress, I gather, to sort out these problems in order to provide greater uniformity and standardisation in official statistics of crime and justice.

Analysis of crime data should normally be undertaken by those with the appropriate time and skills to do this to an acceptable standard but research staff time is often at a premium. Computing technology could be used to enable statistical skills to be built into programmes that can be used by planners and managers without having to continually refer to researchers for simple statistical analyses. Statistical software of this kind is becoming increasingly available.

What information should be collected for local crime models?

We will be considering later *how* to answer this question but experience suggests that several factors are likely to be involved. Crime data can have three main bases: firstly, *events*. This looks at what types of crime are committed, where and what targets are involved, when and how frequently and how they are committed. Three types of crime are recorded by the police: reported, detected and apprehended crime; and each of these produces data of different significance (see **Figure 6.3**). Secondly, data about *offenders* looks at who commits offences, their age, sex and race, how many crimes they have committed and of what type. Thirdly, data about the *victims* of crime considers who (or what) the victims are, their age, sex and race. The relationship between the victim and the offender might also be relevant and in some cases the impact of the crime on the offender and his family (we can identify immediate victims and secondary victims who suffer indirectly as a result of the offence). Fourthly, *costs*. What was the value of property stolen, damage done? What were the economic costs of the offence? What was the cost of dealing with the offence to the police or the courts? Some of this information is already collected. Information about costs is generally not routinely available. Information about victims can be obtained but recording practices vary considerably.

These categories raise issues (especially for the police) about the degree of detail that can or should be collected and about the appropriate level of resources (time and money) that should be expended on data capture and collation. Some data needs to be

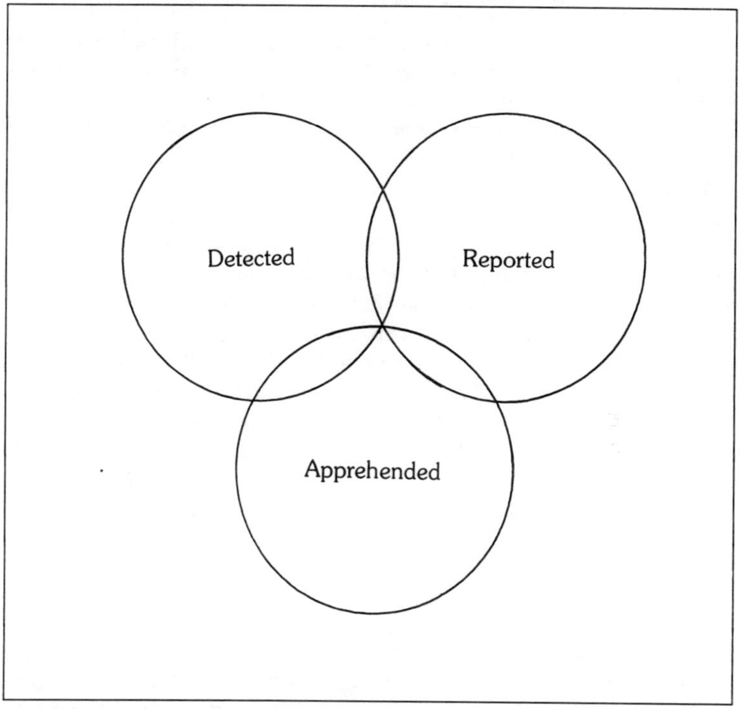

Source: Based on a figure in Bohigian in Nagel, 1977 p23

Figure 6.3 Types of police crime data

collected routinely but some can only be secured through special research projects or surveys. Choosing between these options will depend on the priorities attached to such data. There is also a need to relate data about reported crime to that which is not reported but which can be assessed through special surveys (such as the information made available in the British Crime Surveys that indicates the level of unreported crime). Local surveys of unreported crime have been undertaken in several areas to provide input into prevention planning.

The process of capturing data could be improved by the use of small portable computers. These can be programmed to trap certain kinds of errors at the point of entry, and to interpret a crime event correctly to ensure that data is entered accurately and consistently according to standard criteria. The data collected on these machines could then be fed into larger computers for processing on a force-wide basis. This might allow extra data to be collected as for example details about costs involved in the offence.

Modelling influences on crime

This section assumes that a model is being constructed from scratch - a rather hypothetical situation since most people will already have some kind of model of crime, even though it might not be precisely formulated. How can a model be constructed? A first step could be to bring together a group of local people who work in the law enforcement and criminal justice organisations who, by virtue of their work, know something about local crime. Such a group could include police officers, researchers, magistrates, probation officers and so on. The group could begin its task by sharing understandings about what influences crime locally. This exercise establishes what people currently think about crime. This initial 'brainstorming' should be structured in some way; for example, suggested influences could be grouped under the headings of 'environmental', 'social', 'direct' and 'indirect' influences (see **Figure 6.4**). An alternative method is to use a force field analysis (see **Figure 6.5**). Here, the influences on crime are represented by arrows pointing towards the problem field. The length or size of the arrows is a rough indication of what people feel the strength of that influence to be.

In this initial phase, the process focuses on putting forward beliefs, perceptions, ideas, 'theories', some results from research, practice wisdom, hunches and so on. Some of these ideas might be proved to be invalid by subsequent research and some might simply reflect the collective wisdom or culture of each organisation, but their value lies in identifying the 'models' currently in use in various parts of the crime response system. Some ideas might find a ready consensus in the group; others will generate controversy. This, in itself, is valuable material that can be used in planning, since it will affect the utilisation of any formal model that might be developed later.

How crime models can be used

Crime models can be used in a variety of ways: to reveal patterns of crime to assist in operational response decision making, to test hypotheses about the factors that influence crime rates as part of prevention planning, to relate social and economic trends to crime rates as part of the policy processes in local or national governments, and to predict crime trends so that proposed changes in response systems can be evaluated as part of the management of resources. One method of organising information about crime is described in the section below on 'area profiling' and some of the ideas suggested there about how such profiles can be used are also relevant to employing crime models in general.

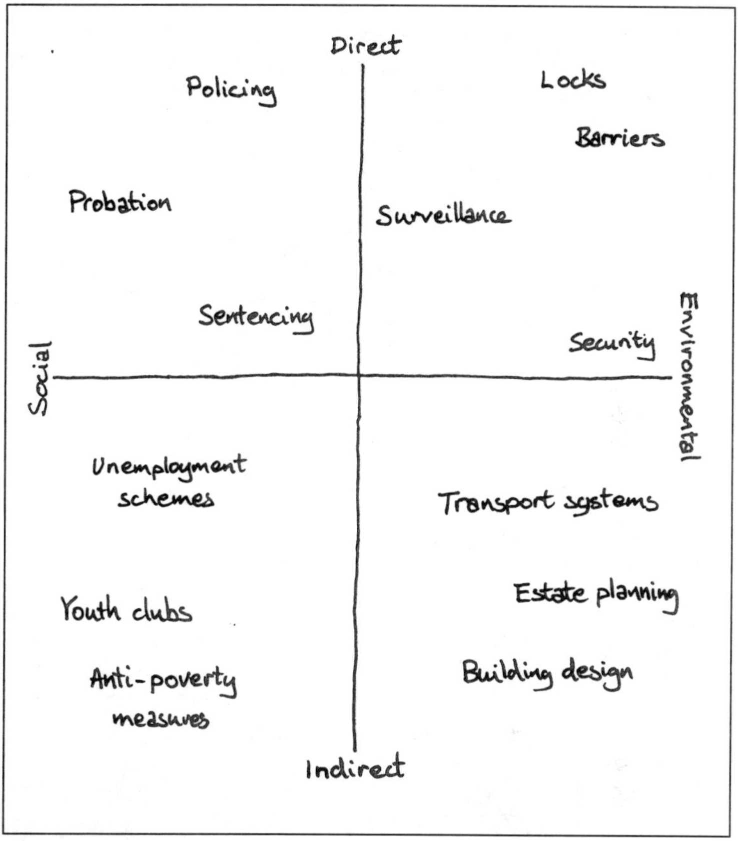

Figure 6.4 Modelling influences on crime. An illustration

Response models

The second type of model that is needed in strategic planning is that which represents the patterns of responses to crime that are made in a local area. Response models should be comprehensive, covering the responses of the key criminal justice agencies, together with those policies and activities of central and local governments, other public agencies, voluntary and community bodies that influence crime and the patterns of response to it. Criminal justice models have been in existence for some time. A summary of selected criminal justice

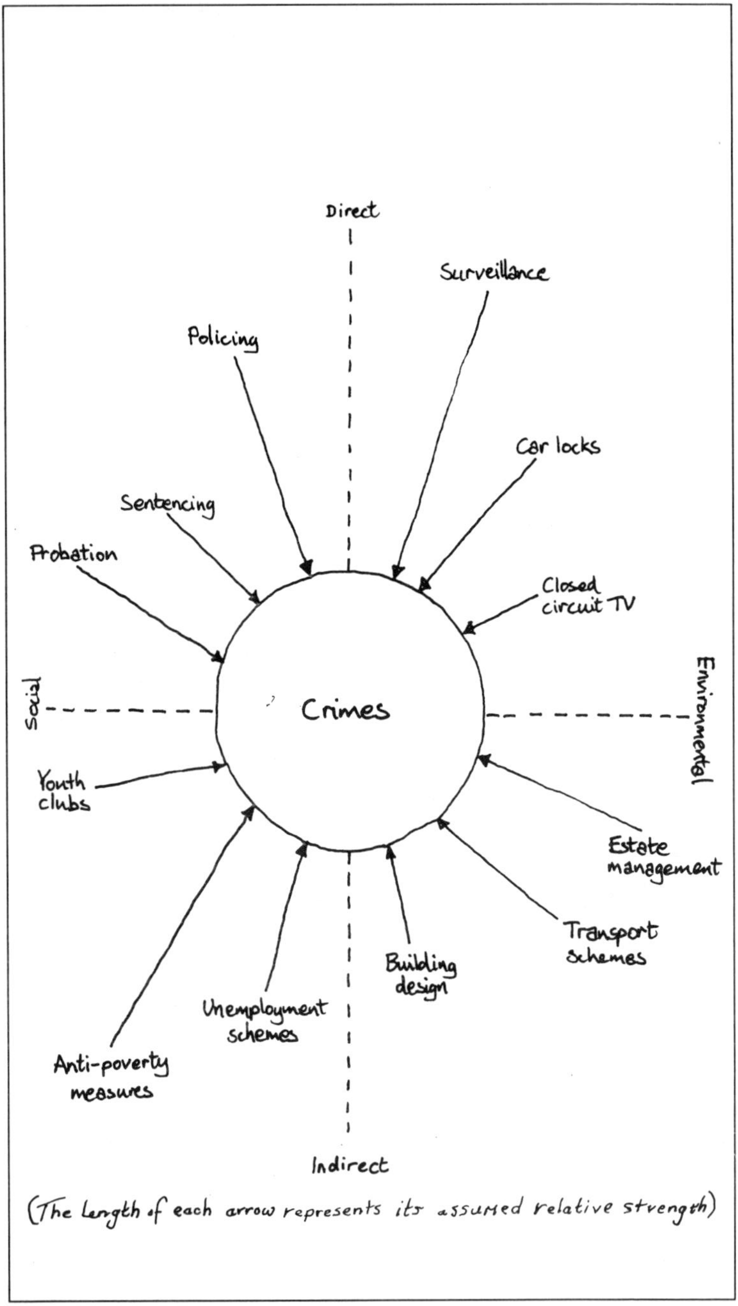

Figure 6.5 Force field analysis of influences on crime

models is included in Nagel's collection of papers on modelling [Nagel, 1977]. This concentrates on models that would help agency policy makers in decision making.

Constructing response models

A fundamental problem in constructing response models is that of determining appropriate *boundaries.* Most local models might satisfactorily be based on police force areas but these do not always coincide with local authority boundaries. Within police force areas, there are, however, considerable problems in finding suitable subdivisions. Operational boundaries of various criminal justice agencies are often noncoterminous and an initial step might be to draw a series of overlay charts to see where the boundary differences occur. This aspect will be returned to below under *Scales, boundaries and maps.*

Another fundamental decision relates to the *scope* of the model. Whilst criminal justice agencies constitute the core of the model, wider environment factors need also to be brought in. Some of these might be national inputs to the system (such as central government funding), some will come from the local authorities (again funding, policy decisions, structure plans and so on) and others will relate to local social and economic parameters (demography, unemployment rates etc.). The task of setting the scope of the model is to achieve a manageable quantity of information without missing out strategically important factors. Given that operations and influences will be interdependent, decisions relating to scope must be made on some knowledge of where networks of interrelatedness fade out.

The third element of fundamental importance is that of being able to use the model to meet its consumer's needs. The construction of such models is not an academic exercise but one of being able to create an information system according to policy and planning needs. A survey could be conducted to find out *which* consumers will require *what* information. This kind of survey can be viewed as an *information audit* the purpose of which is to provide a comprehensive and detailed account of supplies and gaps in current information about responses to crime. Typical consumers might include planners and decision makers in criminal justice agencies, research staff in a variety of organisations both within the system and in local academic bodies. Staff in local authority departments and voluntary agencies might also be included. One important group of consumers is public policy makers – elected members of authorities who contribute to the public policy framework within which the system operates. The survey could be combined with the results of the area profiling techniques discussed below. Once consumer's needs have been audited, the current supply of information can be evaluated and this will begin to reveal the relationship between information supply and demand.

In general, a response model should show, comprehensively, what responses to crime are made, how they are made, which organisations make them and very importantly, why they are made, since this last item links directly into policy. Connections, patterns, interrelationships and significant lack of desirable connections can be drawn into the model (see example in **Figure 6.6**).

Using response models

The purpose of a response model was aptly stated by one of the researchers who developed the national model for England and Wales:

> 'The objective in developing a model of the criminal justice system is to provide an aid for strategic planning over a period of up to ten years' [Barton, 1984, p 16].

Whether his idea of an appropriate planning period is realistic or not is arguable. It has been argued that political timescales are short and politicians need to react to the events of the day or week – 'governments as a whole cannot plan beyond the lifetime of a parliament' [Croft, 1982 p 5]. The principle involved here is clear enough. By modelling the current responses to crime, a baseline is established, against which any future situation can be compared. A forecasting or forward planning model pictures what response patterns should be if crime is to be reduced in the future. The task of planning is to change the current situation and to effect the outcomes set down in policy.

Some models can be descriptive; others can be econometric or generally statistical; some could analyse the resources available to primary responses currently and in the future. This could assist in the task of targeting resources. The exercise could well help to identify the most appropriate targets for response systems. Analysis could suggest which targets would generate what levels of effectiveness or impact and over what term of time. Some models can be predictive: distinguishing between those responses that are certain to be effective from those where effectiveness is less certain.

Criminal justice models as diagnostic devices

Models of the criminal justice system can be used to simulate the performance of various parts of the system. Two broad categories of such uses are described by Falkin: *operation research* models and *system dynamic* models. He identifies four system models: police, court, corrections (i.e. probation, prisons, etc.) and total subsystem

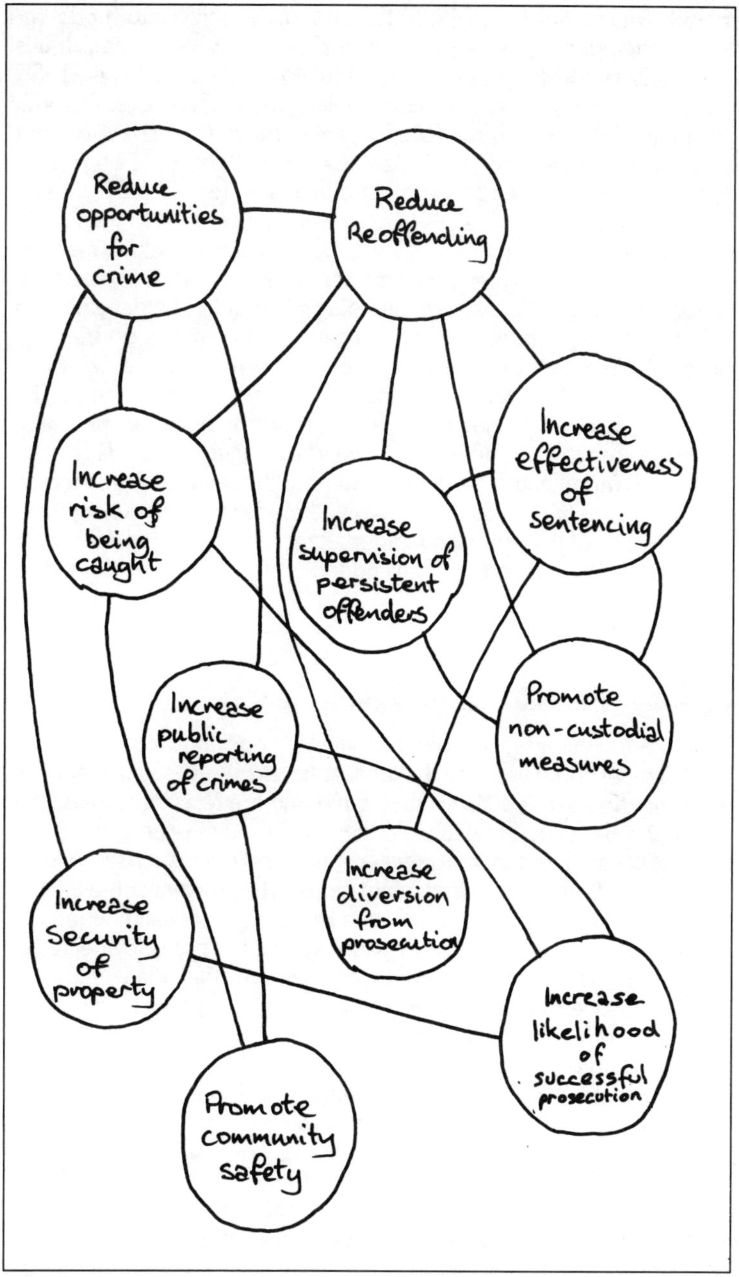

Figure 6.6 Networking of responses to crime. An illustration

models [Falkin, 1979, p 57]. In this country, a police sub-model has been developed by the Home Office [Barton, 1984], a magistrates' courts sub-model [Rice, 1984], a system flow model [Pullinger, 1985] and an overview of the systems modelling project has been provided [Morgan, 1985]. Sub-models for the Crown Court, Prison and Probation Services have also been described [Morgan, 1985 pp 25 – 35]. Both the court models described by Falkin (op cit, p 57] and the Home Office [Rice, 1984] are mainly concerned with the management of case flows, including the reduction of delays, resource allocation and increasing the efficiency of case processing. These are national level models but local planning will require the development of local level system that reflect indigenous circumstances. Planning systems will also require the development of sentencing models or the incorporation of sentencing factors in aspects of systems modelling generally. Less work has been done of the modelling of probation although some of the work on caseload management tends towards the use of modelling. The development of the systems management approach to juvenile justice has involved modelling to some degree or other. Not all of the modelling undertaken so far has relied exclusively on statistical data; some of it has added a broad range of descriptive information.

Relating crime models to response models

Two models have so far been suggested: one that focuses on the modelling of crime and one that concentrates on systems of response. It has been suggested above that crime and the responses made to it are interdependent. How then do these two models relate and how do they reflect the relationship between crime and the responses made to it? An important concept that might be used here is that crime and the responses made to it interact. Crime levels are not solely dependent on the responses of the criminal justice system but they are affected by the way it operates. If we take, for example, that idea that some criminal justice measures exacerbate crime (e.g. prisons) and some diminish reoffending (e.g. certain probation programmes), we can see that the emphasis placed by the system on these factors will act as inputs to a model of crime. In this analysis, the model represents a response system that does not simply react to crime rates but seeks to influence them by making strategic choices about which measures to increase and which to decrease.

A full crime model will reflect what people believe about crime, as well as what is known about crime, influences on crime and forecasts of what might happen to crime rates in the future. The response model likewise reflects current patterns of response (at various levels) and what might happen to those responses in the future. The response model should also reflect the mission of each of the organisations involved in the response system and should map the resources available, economics of the response, some measure of its impacts (as far as these are known) and how policy outcomes compare to practice out-turns.

In the process of constructing these models, agreements and disagreements between policy makers, planners, practitioners and researchers will inevitably occur. These conflicts reflect what is known and what is unknown and the degree of certainty or uncertainty implicit in that knowledge. There should be some degree of fit between the crime and response models, so that modelling of crime can be related to modelling of responses within the development of the area strategy. However, any inconsistencies between the two models should be carefully noted and analysed, particularly those between assumed ideas about how the system operates on crime rates and what the response models tell us about how the system actually responds.

This procedure of modelling, testing and analysis is part of the methodology needed to improve approaches to planning. Also, as a result of the process, we hope to see improved impacts on crime. As with all techniques and methods, they can be applied to varying degrees. Perhaps it would be fairer to say that we should try to find the right level of application for a technique. Crime modelling could well engage a whole research department solely in that task for years. What is more realistic is to get a rough model into working order and then refine it as we use it. There are 'costs' to this type of approach: time, patience, workloads, other things not being done etc. People and organisations will only commit themselves to this approach if they can see the eventual payoffs. These models offer powerful analytical tools for strategic planning and allow policy makers to analyse strategic options on the basis of the best available information.

Using Models

Modelling brings together the elements of a system and challenges us to think through how the system operates. Models are conceptual tools that can be used in policy formulation, in planning and in the design of monitoring and operational systems. Once a model has been established it can then be used in a number of ways. One of these is diagnosis: where a problem is identified and the model used to find a solution to or test the performance of alternative solutions. Models have been used to study the effects of making changes in systems and to evaluate proposed modifications to or new initiatives in policy, planning, provision or procedures [Morgan, 1987]. There is often a basic assumption that the relevant components can be accurately and reliably quantified. Criminal justice modelling often requires qualitative information; many crime prevention surveys, for example, have investigated fear of crime and how local people feel about the problem of crime in their area.

If we have a reliable model, then we should be able to predict the consequences of changes in policing or sentencing. If our model is valid for certain types of offences, it might not be valid for offending as a whole, since offending is a very heterogeneous phenomenon. Again, it must be stressed that prediction needs to be probabilistic. Modelling is a technique of fundamental importance in the development of successful criminal justice and crime reduction strategies.

Using information locally

Information can be used, at local level, to develop policy and planning of responses to crime. The first stage in the general planning process is to describe the current situation. In order to make full use of information in local planning it is necessary to gather it together in a readily accessible form. This can be achieved by the preparation of an *area profile*. A profile presents a snapshot of the current situation; it represents 'where we are now'. The aim of a profile is to provide policy makers and planners with a catalogue of information about the local area (this could be a local authority area or a smaller area within a local authority). The profile can draw on a wide range of information, in order to provide a comprehensive picture of the local area, its crime, social characteristics and facts about what is being done to respond to crime. The profile, therefore, gathers together widely spread information into a readily accessible format. Statistics should, wherever possible, be presented graphically, using such devices as maps, diagrams and charts. Some of the information might be in the form of narrative text, describing the area and the problem of people who live in it.

Profiles can be constructed in a number of ways depending on how they are going to be used. The first step is to draw up a series of headings. Some headings will be concerned with setting out the characteristics of the area, some with patterns of crime, some with the operations of the justice system and some with local organisations and resources. Some of the more common headings that might be used in a profile are shown in the **appendix** to this chapter.

These broad headings can be subdivided depending on the degree of detail required. Where a profile is presenting a range of crime and justice information, it is helpful to put that data into context by providing a number of social and economic indicators. Population is an obvious indicator since demographic changes can have direct bearings on the rate of offending in an area. This blank list of headings, or 'template' can then be used to gather the information that will be required.

Area profiling and modelling

The process of compiling a template clearly requires the use of crime and justice models. We have already discussed the significance of modelling and of underlying assumptions, definitions and values. Embedded within a template profile will be a series of hypotheses about the relationships between various sets of data. Some of these hypotheses will be based on fairly reliable research findings; others will be more tentative, offering information to a speculative process of listing relationships or of exploring possible connections between factors. Crime templates are already being developed to provide a method of analysing offending in small localities [Davidson, 1988].

Our discussion of modelling shows that this is seen to be a centrally important technique in strategic planning. Two main models have been proposed: one that represents crime and one that represents the response to crime. In constructing an area profile it is assumed that a model of each of these has been devised (in some form or other). The profile collects information that is based on the framework of the model. Since the task of collecting a large amount of information is costly (in terms of money and time) it is desirable to collect only information that will be of value to its consumers. If an information audit has been undertaken, then the task of deciding what information to collect will be easier.

Profiles can be drawn up for particular age groups (e.g. for juveniles, young adults or adults). Much of this information will have a geographical dimension but systems and processes, resources and services should also be included.

In comprehensive profiles a very broad range of information is brought together as part of a process of strategic planning of responses to crime in an interagency context. Such macro-profiles are as yet uncommon. The *scope* of a profile is the extent of its coverage, both geographically and in terms of its depth of information. The profiling technique can be used in very broad perspective pictures as well as in more limited and specific work, as for example, planning schemes of supervision for 14 – 16 year olds [NACRO, 1988]. It is also possible to take a non-geographical approach; a systems profile can be constructed to assemble information about the workings of the justice *system* without necessarily considering subareal dimensions.

Profiles can be constructed at various levels. In a *level one* profile, the aim is to collect together, into an easily accessible catalogue, all the currently available information and statistics that could be relevant to policy and planning at local interagency level. This primarily consists of 'off the shelf' material, that is information that already exists and does not require the origination of new data.

A *level two* profile could draw together information that is already available and add analyses based on the original data, such as rankings, statistical operations, calculations of percentages, means, graphical presentations and so on. Local data can also be compared with national or regional trends or with neighbouring areas. At this level, no new information is generated but existing information is gathered and organised into an easily accessible analysis.

A *level three* profile might include the creation of new sets of data drawn from monitoring systems, the results of research projects or recordings that have been kept but not yet analysed. Research projects and surveys could be undertaken to fill important gaps in current information and knowledge. This level of profiling is concerned with filling gaps in existing information or with extending existing data sets. Clearly, a profiling exercise could begin with a *level one* profile and then move on to further levels. A profile differs from a research project in that a profile is a catalogue of information whereas a research project is a means of arriving at specific findings. Profiles, as conceived here, are information (not research) tools for those who are engaged in planning.

The usefulness of a profile is that it collects together a wide range of information that will represent a comprehensive picture of crime and responses being made to it in the local area. To make the information accessible it should be assembled into a manual, organised in an appropriate way and indexed so that when some particular item of information is required it can be located quickly and easily. Also, patterns and trends should be set out so that they can be easily seen. Statistics and other quantitative data should be presented graphically so that proportions and relationships are easily recognised.

Contextual information

Most criminologists would probably agree that crime or justice processes cannot or should not be studied in isolation. Crime and justice are part of broader social patterns and institutions. Facts about crime often have to be related to wider facts; for example, a true crime rate cannot be expressed simply as the number of offenders committing crimes but as a proportion of the overall population in an area (e.g. offenders per 10,000 of population). In order to put information about crime and justice processes into context, profiles might need to include a range of social, demographic, economic and political information. Examples of such social indicators are given in the sample template profile in the **appendix** to this chapter.

The choice of which indicators to select will be determined by understandings or hunches about the influences on the crime rate, on sentencing or on local practice (depending on the subject of the profile). Clearly a very great deal of information *could* be assembled under the heading of *context*; decisions will be required about how much information could be gathered in the time available and about how meaningful that information will be. For example, much information is usually available about employment and unemployment. Research into the relationship between crime and unemployment is plentiful but highly complex and often inconclusive. Before undertaking to gather large amounts of information on employment the question needs to be asked 'what reliable conclusions are needed about employment (or unemployment) as a variable in crime rates?'

Boundaries, scales and maps

We are primarily concerned here with *area* profiles. One of the most difficult problems encountered in such work is that of finding a suitable unit of mapping. In criminal justice work, data is often gathered according to different boundaries. Whilst census data and much local authority data uses wards as a basic unit of areal scaling, police data and very often social services and probation data are not always prepared using these units. The police often use beats as a unit of areal analysis and these do not necessarily conform to ward boundaries. Noncoterminous boundaries present fundamental problems in preparing this kind of data. Similarly, some data might be available for local authorities or districts but is not broken down into smaller areal units. This makes the investigation of small localities very difficult and sometimes impossible.

Depending on the overall scale of the profile, the electoral ward is often the more useful unit of analysis. Another method that has been used is the postcode system. But population distributions might make this impracticable: some wards have high densities, others low densities [NACRO, 1988 and Unell, 1983].

Crime patterns show considerable variations geographically; even at a small locality level, large variations in crime rates can be detected [Davidson, 1988]. Policies and operations of criminal justice agencies also show significant variations within single organisations; the pattern of SIR recommendations, for example, frequently reveals variations within a single probation service because practice varies among probation teams. Area profiles necessarily require a geographical approach to the collection of data. Area crime analysis is a rapidly developing aspect of crime prevention. Area crime analyses have been used in the development of multiagency crime prevention schemes [Heywood and Hall, 1988] and in the planning of police activities [Davidson, 1988].

The Home Office has published a methodological study of area crime analyses in which mapping is given some attention [Ekblom, 1988 pp 27 – 29]. This refers to the 'grain' of area pictures; the larger the picture the lower the resolution of its definition. Postcode or census enumeration districts provide the 'finest-grain picture'. The use of acetate overlays in mapping offers a possible solution to the problem of displaying data sets over noncoterminous boundaries. Ekblom mentions the usefulness of utilising computers to prepare maps [Ekblom, 1988]. Mapping as a geographical technique in crime analysis is amply covered in a number of studies (see for example [Herbert, 1982]).

Profiles and surveys

The link between profiling and survey work has been discussed within the context of intermediate treatment [Unell, 1983]. Unell described the process of building up a series of socioeconomic profiles as part of a large scale survey of local areas. Housing, population, socioeconomic groupings and levels of unemployment were mentioned [op cit, Appendix II]. Unell concluded that 'an area profile will usually be constructed from standard information sources based upon small geographical units such as electoral wards or the catchments of local agencies'. She also discussed the problems of unit boundaries. Her approach included both hard and soft data and she commented that 'the informed impressions of local people about the structure of their area may be important in qualifying statistical data and filling the gaps in statistical knowledge' [op cit, p 11]. This latter point is echoed in the Northumbria work on crime prevention: 'central to the successful emergence of the North Tyneside CPI as a policy body was the development of a comprehensive spatial database incorporating both the police *and local communities'* perceptions on the composition of crime within the locality' (my emphasis) [Heywood and Hall, 1988]. NACRO's crime prevention work has also laid emphasis on the involvement of local people in initiatives and collecting their views about fears of crime in their area (see for example [SOLACE/NACRO, 1986]).

Choice of data

In deciding which data to select for a profile, definitional issues must be considered. For example, police data consists of reported, recorded and detected crimes. The use to which such data is to be put will determine which kind of data is best used. Timescales are also important. The use of the data will determine what period of time the data is required to cover (e.g. one year, five years, ten years, etc.). The last census was carried out in 1981 and much of this will now be unreliable as populations tend to be mobile in small areas. Some local authorities are able to provide current data based on their own monitoring of populations. Decisions will need to be made about whether complete sets of data will be required or whether representative samples will be sufficient.

Making use of area profiles

The use to which an area profile might be put will depend of course on the needs of those in an area whose task is to develop policy or to plan response systems. Generally, area profiles supply information to the process of strategic planning. If the planning task is clear then the task of providing information will also be clear. Since an area profile provides a reference tool for decision makers, it must provide that information in a readily accessible format. But information is relatively inert; to be of use it must first be interpreted. This is where information becomes transformed into knowledge. What does information mean? How are we to make sense of it? Profiles can be used as a basis for interagency work in which information is analysed and its planning implications negotiated. Steering groups can use a profile to assess and evaluate the current pattern of responses to crime in their area. Having a range of information available makes the task of strategic planning easier. Such profiles are of particular value in devising crime prevention schemes. They can also be used in planning a range of schemes for diversion and sentencing services. Work of this kind will often be undertaken by the police in planning their operations. Results can also be used by the courts to evaluate the effectiveness of various sentencing options.

Apart from making information more easily accessible, a profile can be used as an evaluative tool. By searching for existing information, gaps in what is currently available can be identified. In sorting out what is known about a local area, we can also find out what is not known. This might lead to new research projects or the development of monitoring systems.

Once a profile has been created it can then be used in a number of ways. One of these is policy formulation. The importance of information in this process was, I hope, made clear in the chapter on policy. Once policy has been established and its implementation has commenced, it must be continually monitored and evaluated. If we have a set of policies, we need to know what out-turns they are effecting and this can be achieved through collecting and analysing information.

It is the responsibility of planners to implement policies and this requires the operation of a management information system (MIS). A MIS regularly gathers information about the performance of those who are implementing policies, provides feedback about performance indicators and critical success factors. In large scale and complex schemes, such as interagency justice management or crime prevention, several MISs might be in use within a number of agencies (such as the police, CPS, probation, social services and so on). Interagency management groups might therefore need an area profile to collate a wide range of information and this in itself constitutes a kind of MIS.

Secondly, information is equally important in planning. Profiles can help to analyse the required level of resources in an area, where resources are currently distributed, how the resources of various agencies complement or duplicate each other and what new resources might be required in the future given rates of change or trends in the population or in crime patterns. Information is already used within organisations, such as the police or the probation service. Profiling offers a valuable technique, on an area basis, in the servicing of interagency initiatives. The key characteristic of this kind of profile is its comprehensiveness: it should cover a wide range of information, both statistical and descriptive, and should look very thoroughly at crime in the local area, at systems of prevention, diversion, and justice and at the operation of those agencies involved in responding to crime. It is this broad sweep of information that allows a comprehensive strategy to be developed.

Information, monitoring or research?

Three terms are widely used in the field of crime responses: information, monitoring and research. These are three distinct kinds of activity though it is at times difficult to distinguish between them precisely. As a rough guide, I would suggest that information describes facts, data, statistics and descriptions. I would characterise 'research' as being a method of inquiry that is often an investigative procedure conducted through the use of established techniques such as testing hypotheses, deriving findings from experiments and the like and is usually time limited. Monitoring is a function of management: it is the ongoing, routine collection and utilisation of data as a part of control. Monitoring should not be confused with evaluation which is the interpretation of information through the use of values.

Computers, modelling and simulation

Much of the work of modelling the justice system involves manipulating information and statistics. If the information can be held on a computer then there is more chance that the data base can be used interrogatively and this is obviously the most effective way to build up a model. Model building often requires hypothesis testing, extrapolation and 'what if' investigations, and these activities are performed most effectively on a computer. The modelling technique will usually involve some form of quantitative analysis and this will require a detailed and comprehensive data base.

Some programmes allow flow charts to be designed graphically on the screen and printed out. One such programme has been described by Barry Hope [in Britton et al, 1988, pp 19 – 22]. This is a dynamic modelling package which is capable of building stock-flow models graphically. 'Once such a model has been constructed, it can be run in "real time", the results being output in the form of tables and simple graphs' [op cit, p 19]. A prototype model was devised, using this package, to explore possible relationships between cautioning and custody rates. Such products offer advantages over the pen and paper method, especially when a flow model becomes established as a tool for operational management.

Using a computer simulation of the justice system, we can test the effects of policies and plans. Such a simulation offers a tool kit for creating evaluative analyses of the degree to which policy assumptions are valid. It permits us to predict the effects of changes in policy and to evaluate various policy options in order to find an optimum formulation of policy. The value of the simulation depends on the choice of variables and parameters, and on our assumptions about or knowledge of relationships within the system. The simulation must be able to correctly emulate the performance of the system in order for it to be used reliably.

In the initial stages of designing a simulation, one must decide what it is that is to be simulated. The investigator must decide how states of the system and events occurring within the system are to be represented in the computer, given that the computer will be working only with data [Hamilton, 1976]. A sentencing simulation, for example, will represent the decision making of magistrates in terms of case characteristics, availability of sentencing options and a range of hypotheses about what influences their sentencing practice. A court monitoring system would simply churn out data about which sentences were given for which offences but a simulation will go much further in assisting with interpretation of what happens in courts.

Computer simulations are constrained by programming considerations; this is not about how much data a computer can handle but is about the sophistication of the software. Criminal justice simulations that are relevant to policy analysis and systems management need to be interpretive and diagnostic and this requires functions that are more advanced than those available in the traditional data management system. With databases, the simulation remains in the analyst's head; with an advanced simulation, the model is incorporated into the programme, freeing the analyst for more creative activities.

It would be wrong, however, to focus too much on the functions inherent in processing because the value of a computer simulation also depends very much on output – the presentation of the results. It is not an asset to have yards of figures flowing out of a printer; modern software offers more scope than before for colourful, pictorial results, the significance of which is more immediately clear.

The selection, specification and processing of data should be closely related to how the results of the model are intended to be used; that is to say, there should be a close fit between the data and its interpretation. Data should be coded and processed with regard to its interpretive functions. A good modelling technique should be able to enhance the user's ability to interpret the results obtained from the model. It must be born in mind, when designing data models, that the process of interpretation requires us to attach meaning and significance to the results obtained from them. Workload analyses, for example, enable decision makers to identify bottlenecks and imbalances in the flow of cases from one agency to another, to take action to correct any problems identified, and then to monitor and evaluate the results of actions taken [Cushman, 1980].

Trends and developments in criminal justice computing

Computers can assist in both the collection and interpretation of data. The era of data processing has now been superseded by that of knowledge processing. That is not to say that data processing has been made redundant but that developments in computing technology, particularly in the practical application of artificial intelligence to planning and decision making, have brought about fundamental changes to what computers can do in organisation and management. What has come about is the introduction of the *knowledge-based* system and its application to the processes of strategic planning [Mockler and Dologite, 1988].

There are many decision support systems in computing and some of these provide systems of expertise. An *expert system* is an example of an *interpretative* package that can help to make sense of large and complex sets of data or conditions in which there is a complex body of rules that must be applied in the process of diagnosis and interpretation. An expert system for use in the sentencing of offenders has already been devised [Bainbridge, 1988]. This package presents all the rules that apply to the sentencing process in a structured way for the sentencer to use. The sentencer is helped by the system to determine the availability of disposals and to select the disposal that most accurately corresponds to the criteria entered by the sentencer.

Information about law and appeal judgements is also supplied by the system. The system takes the sentencer through the sentencing process in a rational and structured manner. Given the current developments in structured decision making in courts, this is likely to be a useful device. The system also provides a probability function so that information about the case being tried can be entered and 'the relative use of the disposals for similar offenders committing similar offences is calculated in percentage terms' [op cit, p 346]. In summary the system 'gives assistance to the sentencer by applying the rules in an organised fashion and giving the sentencer access to all the relevant materials and guidance concerning those rules and their scope and meaning' [p 346]. The system does not replace the skills and intuition of the sentencer but improves the exercise of discretion without imposing rigid standardisation. Bainbridge has conducted extensive surveys of this system to determine its potential in practice.

Expert systems and knowledge-based software can provide powerful support tools for management decision making and for the diagnosis of complex problems in crime response. Unlike conventional databases, they are based on knowledge rather than information. Such knowledge-bases can be written in English rather than numbers. Probability functions often have to be included since some questions cannot result in an absolutely true or false answer. These packages offer more powerful forecasting facilities than those based on databases, spreadsheets or statistical processing alone. Expert systems can be designed to be interactive so that the solution of problems involves a dialogue between the user and the computer. This is not to say that expert systems can or should replace databases, but that they offer some advantages over the latter or could be used in conjunction with them. Knowledge-based systems have already been developed for use in supporting strategic planning [Mockler and Dologite, 1988] and their introduction into the criminal justice field would be feasible and opportune, once strategic planning becomes firmly established. There is of course always a relationship between the application of a method (like strategic planning) and the means for applying it. The emergence of planning technologies might in fact enhance the take up for strategic planning processes but the role of computers in this depends to some extent on the level of 'computer literacy' amongst those who might use them in this particular field.

Computers are already extensively used in magistrates' courts and this use has recently been evaluated by the Home Office [Maclean 1987a and 1987b]. This evaluation showed that (at the time of writing) the Home Office spent some £3 – £3.5 million a year on the purchase of computers in magistrates' courts and a considerably larger sum on their upkeep and operation. Most of this equipment is used in the administrative duties of the courts, rather than in relation to their judicial functions. The report recommended that the aim of computerisation in the courts might be 'to enable the courts to process cases as rapidly and efficiently as possible with due regard to the quality of justice and to the statutory obligations of courts' and 'to reduce as far as is practical the delays to members of the public, including defendants and specifically those in custody, and to representatives of other agencies...' [op cit, 1987a, recommendation 5].

The report also included as one of a set of aims the promotion of the 'smooth introduction of new functions and procedures resulting from changes in legislation or policy' [ibid]. These objectives suggest that increased resources of this kind in the courts will have impact on parts of the system. Given the ideas presented by Noam [in Nagel 1977 pp 42 – 43] about the interdependent nature of resource changes in the criminal justice system, it would seem desirable that any new technology strategy in the courts service should be analysed for its impacts elsewhere in the system. The same model suggests that changes in the efficiency of court administration will have affects on the judicial functions of the courts. Speeding up the flow of cases through the courts, according to this model, will affect sentencing behaviour.

The report also considered the strategic role played by the magistrates' courts in the criminal justice system [op cit, pp 67 – 70] and acknowledged the interdependency between them and the Crown Courts, Crown Prosecution Service, police and other agencies (e.g. probation service). The flow of information around the system is one aspect of this interdependency. Because of their central position in the system, the courts offer a good target for the centralisation of information. Judging from experience in the United States, the report concludes that the development of integrated information systems based on simple information flows alone have not been very successful [op cit, p 67].

Integration of criminal justice information systems therefore will require a different strategy. But, as the report points out, there is considerable duplication and waste between criminal justice agencies in handling their information. Progress in developing shared information systems has been hampered by the funding of each criminal justice agency being separately controlled [op cit, p 68]. There is a suggestion here that area technology systems could be developed if corporate funding mechanisms were a possibility. The report recommended the establishment of a specialist team to advise and support the courts and the Home Office on matters relating to new technology; one of the services such a team could provide is 'strategic planning to integrate computerisation in the magistrates' courts with the use of computers elsewhere in the criminal justice system' [op cit p 79]. This would seem to be an essential requirement if the full potential of information in the overall strategic planning of crime responses is to be achieved. The companion report [Maclean, 1987b] also recommended that

> 'the setting of computerisation strategy for individual agencies and for the criminal justice system as a whole should not be delegated to information technologists or data processing specialists; it requires the combined and committed involvement of both local and central management of agencies concerned, support as necessary by a range of specialist staff including both computer technology skills and management consultancy or analytical skills' [op cit recommendation 3].

This view is supported by experience in the business field and accords with what is said elsewhere in this chapter, based on that experience, about the role of information technology in policy and planning.

The report goes on to support the view that the provision of statistics to central policy or funding agencies should not be regarded as separate from locally-based or agency-based operational systems. The same statistics that are passed to central government agencies can be used locally as inputs to agency or corporate planning. In addition, the report recommends, that statistical systems should be developed into 'interactive planning systems' with forecasting and testing capabilities of the kind referred to in our section on modelling. The information requirements of criminal justice policy making and planning, as suggested in our current discussion, suggest that an information strategy needs to flow from the overall development of a strategic planning framework (hopefully, of a corporate nature) rather than from the need to collect and process statistics for administrative reasons. The report also recommends that system design standards should be developed for all criminal justice agencies and notes that 'various initiatives along these lines have already been undertaken, but none adequately pulls together the interagency needs' [op cit recommendation 11].

These reports are of considerable value and importance in the development of information strategies for criminal justice systems in this country (despite not being widely available) and underscore the need to set such strategies in the context of the overall development of strategic planning of crime responses.

Current analyses of information technology in criminal justice have however focused overmuch on the mass storage and processing of data, to the exclusion of interpretative and policy/planning requirements. The potential of knowledge-based systems lies in their ability to facilitate and support research and decision making. One of the most widespread problems in the utilisation of information in criminal justice and allied organisations is, in my experience, the inability of end users to interpret and apply information effectively.

These problems can be addressed by training and by the introduction of personalised and knowledge-related computing.

Processes such as modelling, simulation and forecasting have, up to now, been limited to research departments. This means that decision makers have only been able to apply the results of such processes to the extent that researchers have been able to deliver them. Advanced information technology offers applications of these techniques to planners and decision makers *when* they need to use them and without the need for skilled *intermediaries.* This is tantamount to giving every manager a personal research assistant. This trend has already begun; developments in expert systems are now finding their way into decision support systems [Balmer, Goodman and Doukidis, 1989, p 134].

A computer package therefore needs to offer three elements to strategic planners in criminal justice: firstly, a comprehensive data base drawing in information from a variety of sources; secondly, an expert system that can provide a tool kit of diagnostic and analytical facilities and thirdly, a model building facility that will help to structure information and relationships between variables, provide simulation and forecasting procedures and link information to decision making parameters. The engineering of interfaces between these modules might require innovations in system design and architecture (see **Figure 6.7**).

A package of this kind should include high quality graphics facilities so that charting, mapping and symbolic modelling can be carried out on the screen and the results printed out in colour or monochrome. It should be able to interact with the user without the mediation of technicians. The embedding of probabilist functions, for example, means that the system can be used directly by managers without having to resort all the time to researchers. This would then allow scarce research time to be devoted to developmental projects rather than to the routine servicing of management needs.

From databases to information resources

As was pointed out in chapter three, much of the strength of modern strategic planning is derived from recent developments in information technology. This is a rapidly changing field; new techniques and products are constantly appearing. Database management has become the established standard in information technology but it appears that this has now been absorbed into 'or perhaps replaced by, the broader concept of *information resource management*' [Gunton, 1988, p 72]. This requires a coherent and comprehensive approach to information management. Although there was a growth in end-user technology, a new phase in the evolution of computing seems to be taking place, based on the growth in communications technology. The emphasis on end-users appears to be being replaced by an emphasis on communications between networks of end-users [Gibson and

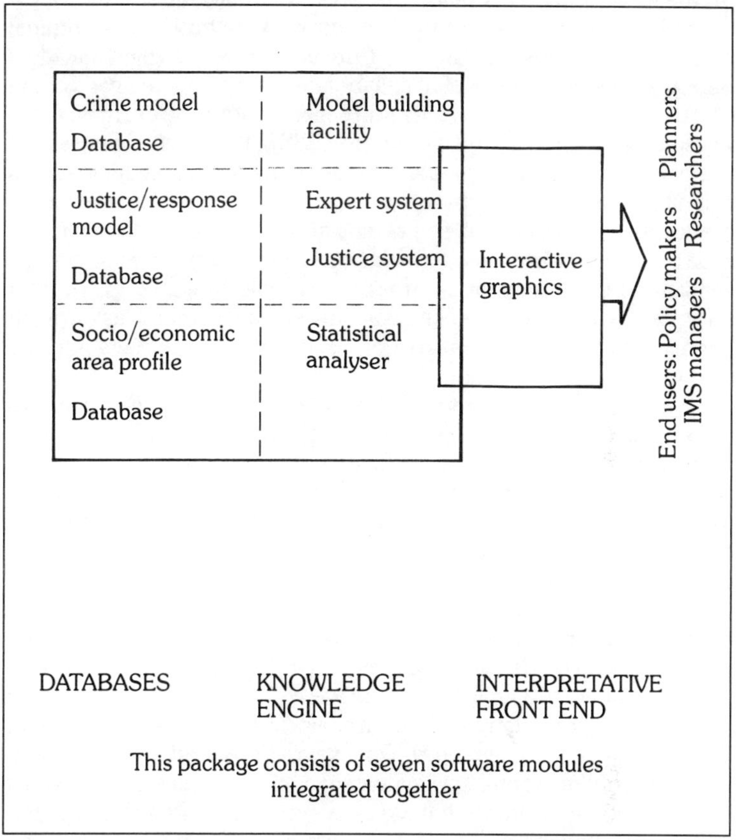

Figure 6.7 Advanced strategic information package for criminal justice planning

Jackson, 1987, p 129]. The imperative of this transformation is that the planning of information systems must be integrated into the organisation's strategic planning process [op cit, p 121]. The evolution from data bases has, it is suggested, also been towards *knowledge-bases* [Waters, 1989] as we noted above. It should not be assumed that computers can replace the need for strategic planning as a human activity; their contribution is to enhance it.

Planning information systems

The design of information systems (ISs) requires that there is a model of the organisation's operations (this is usually referred to as a 'business model', if we can think in terms of the business of criminal justice). In planning ISs for local areas, whether within individual organisations or at the level of collaborative systems, the needs of the end user – the consumer of the information – should be the main focus (a useful text on this theme is Gunton [1988]). ISs within organisations are often planned and operated by research staff in conjunction with senior management. Where no interagency infrastructure exists, however, the location of responsibility for planning and operating collaborative systems poses problems. Agencies can of course engage in bilateral exchanges of information and this already happens. An information audit of the kind suggested above might assist each agency to analyse the needs of its external consumers for the information that it produces.

Planning the development of crime and response models at interagency level poses difficulties since end users are spread over a range of organisations. A local polytechnic or university could perhaps be contracted to survey an area's information needs. In areas where there is a high level of collaboration, a group of research staff from each of the collaborating agencies could form a working party to carry out this task. If collaborative ISs are to be developed, as a support for corporate strategic planning across an area criminal justice system, then clearly responsibility for their organisation and control, evaluation and operational planning needs to be located somewhere. A development strategy for ISs needs to assess cost and resource requirements, operating logistics, management requirements and so on. That is not something which could be added on to already overburdened existing R&I staff within agencies. Many organisations have *information centres* that are responsible for holding information resources, managing ISs and undertaking a range of servicing functions for users. If information is as important to the development of effective strategic planning in local criminal justice systems (as this chapter suggests it is) then the creation of corporate information centres would be a good thing.

Both within organisations and at the collaborative level, assessments need to be made of the effectiveness of ISs. An approach to doing this has been suggested by King [1988]. Strategic planning for ISs is used by King to cover both the planning of information systems and of the broader informational resources of the organisation. To paraphrase his argument in public domain language, he explains that ISs planning needs to be driven by the organisation's operational strategies. Elements from organisational techniques – such as critical success factors, strength-weakness and opportunity/threat assessments can also be included in inputs to the planning process. Resources such as time, funds, computing, etc. provide another set of inputs [op cit, p 104]. Finally, goals of the IS planning process should be added. A primary output of the process is the IS strategic plan – 'a document that describes a set of choices that have been made during the planning process' [ibid]. In effect, he is saying that the same strategic planning processes that would be applied to an organisation as a whole could equally be applied to its ISs. He goes on to describe the methodology for conducting an IS evaluation, and concludes that the IS evaluation approach he describes is a

> 'valuable diagnostic tool, since it permits the direct identification of potential IS planning weaknesses as well as the identification of elements of the planning system that are particularly productive or useful' [op cit, p 111].

Evaluations such as this confer wider benefits to the organisation than simply the improvement of its information flows; similar evaluations can be made of the policy formulation and operational planning functions and these all contribute to the effectiveness of the organisation in meeting its mission and goals.

Finally, IS planning does involve an information technology strategy but this is secondary to the planning of the system as a functional contribution to overall strategic planning. The first stage of IS planning is not about computers; it is about identifying consumer's needs and what information is to be supplied from various sources. Once that has been established, an ISs technology can be developed to make that happen efficiently. Means are not ends.

Strategic information systems

As operations progress, planners will want to assess the degree to which goals are being accomplished and a variety of information sources can be used. In particular, the monitoring of *critical success factors* (CSFs) will be of central importance. Where CSFs are being used in management, information will need to provide detailed and accurate indications of how they are performing. It has been suggested that it is difficult to specify, when CSFs are introduced, exactly what information will be required to monitor them. The choice of data and how it will be used might need to be evolved on a trial-and-error basis [Gibson and Jackson, 1987, p 99]. However, the use of CSFs requires information in support of decision making by providing data on key performance indicators. This also requires the *means* to use that data. The selection of CSFs, according to the person who developed the idea, depends on the objectives and perceptions of individual managers (usually chief executives) rather than on the working of the organisation as a whole [Rockart, 1979, referred to in Gunton, 1988, p 40]. However, studies of the application of CSFs suggest that they appear to succeed best where there is an open management culture and a history of formal planning [Gunton, 1988, p 40]. This might suggest some lessons concerning their introduction for the first time into criminal justice organisations.

CSFs are commonly applied within organisations; but will they be capable of being applied at the collaborative level in order to assess the effectiveness of a local criminal justice system? I think this is possible, since large corporations are analogous to local systems, though some modifications might be needed in the design process and choice of relevant factors. Some analysis might be undertaken of how sets of CSFs in several criminal justice agencies relate together and how these contribute to the success of the system as a whole.

Conclusions

Planning is required to put policy into practice. Planning is needed in order to integrate responses to crime and to develop and enhance the effectiveness of the criminal justice system. Planning procedures must be carefully designed if they are to be effective. Planning requires the utilisation of knowledge of and application of techniques available to planners. Information is an important element of the planning process. Those in control of planning require a strategic information system to provide them with regular and detailed accounts of the system's performance. Planning should and does involve all of the people engaged in a system and not just the managers. There is however a role for specialists in planning. What planning offers to crime prevention, diversion and sentencing is a process for realising goals and achieving targets.

Suggested reading

One of the few UK works that considers the idea of interdependency and systems management in any depth is the collection of papers edited by David Moxon *Managing Criminal Justice* [Home Office Research and Planning Unit, 1985]. Material on criminal justice modelling comes from both United States and United Kingdom sources. A basic introduction (which is now rather dated) is *Modeling the criminal justice system* [Nagel, 1977]. Falkin's often quoted book provides another US source on how modelling has been applied in their criminal justice system [Falkin, 1979]. A general introduction to the work done by the Home Office on the national UK models is given in the Home Office Research and Planning Unit paper *Modelling the criminal justice system* [Morgan, 1985]. A more technical monograph is *Models in quantitative criminology* [Fox, 1981] and a general source on modelling is offered in *Modeling of complex systems* [Vemuri,

1978]. A basic text on crime data, which is also useful in understanding the problems of modelling crime, is *Crime and punishment: interpreting the data* by Bottomley and Pease [1986].

The relationship between policy and information (including planning) is discussed, in the context of juvenile justice, in *Policy and information* [Britton et al., 1988] published jointly by NACRO and Save the Children. A number of practical guides to monitoring have been produced, including those relating to juvenile crime (but probably also as relevant to adult systems): *Monitoring community alternatives to custody and care* [NACRO, 1985] and *Juvenile cautioning: a monitoring guide* [NACRO, 1988]. Judith Unell's series of booklets on Voluntary action and young people in trouble will also be of interest to those in the youth field, particularly, in this context, the one on local surveys. They are published by the National Council of Voluntary Organisations, London.

Material on costings and economics in crime, justice and social care systems is available from the Personal Social Services Research Unit at the University of Kent. Martin Knapp and others at the Unit have written extensively on these subjects. Material relevant to area profiling often comes from the discipline of geography and one of the standard works is *The geography of urban crime* [Herbert, 1982]. Paul Ekblom's paper for the Crime Prevention Unit *Getting the best out of crime analysis*, 1988, published by the Home Office, provides a practical guide, full of useful technical information.

APPENDIX : Example of a local area profile (template)

Section 1 : Community Profile

Common factors: age, gender, race, area/local comparisons

1.1 Demographic data

(a) Age banded population trends
 14 - 16
 17 - 20
 21 and over
(b) Year banded population trends
(c) Ethnic composition of population
(d) Socioeconomic structure

Demographic maps

1.2 Urban characteristics

(a) Population of urban centres
(b) Distribution of population density
(c) Centres or urban transition
(d) Housing characteristics

Mapping of key urban characteristics, transportation routes etc.

1.3 Crime prevention
(a) Description of crime prevention schemes
(b) Crime prevention policies
 Police Force
 Probation
 Local authority
  Local authority Departments
 Others
(c) Crime prevention targetting (neighbourhoods, crime types, age groups, domestic/commercial etc.)
(d) Details of any crime-type specific prevention schemes
(e) Locations and details of any crime prevention projects relevant to young people
(f) Index of local organisations currently involved in crime prevention practice

Mapping of crime prevention schemes against crime rates

1.4 Economy
(a) Description of local economic profile
(b) Labour force breakdown
(c) Age banded labour force breakdown
(d) Area distribution of labour force
(e) Unemployment data by age groups
(f) Length of unemployment for age group

(g) Unemployment status of offenders in age groups
(h) Social security statistics
(i) Selected indicators of poverty

1.5 Voluntary sector
(a) Intermediary bodies
Council for Voluntary Service
(b) Local voluntary organisations
Unemployment
Homelessness
Drugs
Alcohol abuse
Other voluntary bodies
(c) Voluntary youth service

1.6 Local Government
(a) Names of local authorities in area
(b) Selective indictators of performance and policy
(c) Committee structures for each authority (Name of Authority, name of committee, current chair)
(d) Departmental structures for each authority (Name of Department, address, name of Chief Officer)
(e) Costs of local criminal justice agencies

1.7 Local media
(a) Newspapers
(b) Local radio
(c) Local/regional television
(d) Other

Section 2 : Diversion from prosecution

2.1 Cautioning
(a) Policies on cautioning
Police Force
Social Services
Probation Service
(b) Cautioning statistics
By age group, trends, comparisons
(c) Procedures for cautioning
(d) Existing cautioning schemes

2.2 Bail and remand
(a) Bail and remand statistics
(b) Probation bail hostels
(c) Bail and remand procedures
(d) Bail support/information schemes
(e) Informal work with ‘potential offenders’
(f) Results of research into bail and remand in the area
Mapping of cautioning rates

Section 3 : Justice system

3.1 Courts
(a) Magistrates Courts, PSD names and names and addresses of Clerks to Justices
(b) Crown Court centres serving the area, name of courts and circuit
(c) Juvenile court sittings
(d) Research into local courts
(e) Stated goals and performance indicators

Map of PSD boundaries

3.2 Police
(a) Force headquarters and Chief Constable
(b) Annual report (current - selected items of interest)
(c) Relevant specialist sections (e.g. statistics)
(d) Stated goals and performance indicators

Map of police divisions/beats

3.3 Crown Prosecution Service

(a) Name and address of Chief Prosecutor
(b) Local prosecutor's offices
(c) Particular statements of local policy
(d) Goals and performance indicators

3.4 Prison Service
(a) Names, addresses, govenors of local prisons
(b) Regional Prison Service office
(c) Probation service involvement

3.5 Legal organisations and services
(a) Law Society
(b) Other organisations representing lawyers
(c) Organisations providing legal services

3.6 Probation Service
(a) Name of service, address of Headquarters, Chief Probation Officer
(b) Policy statements or policy profile
(c) Systems and procedures relevant to juveniles, young adult offenders, other groups
(d) Professional interests/specialisms within service
(e) Resources and provision: key indicators
(f) Practice characteristics
(g) Inter-agency cooperation and external relations
(h) Patterns of referral to outside organisations
(i) Use of volunteers by service
(j) Performance indicators

3.7 Social services
(a) Policy on child care/juvenile justice
(b) Details of schemes, projects for juvenile offenders
(c) Local research into juvenile crime/offenders
(d) Details of inter-agency liaison, projects
(e) Monitoring schemes, performance indicators

Map of probation divisions Map of social services areas

Section 4 : Crime

4.1 Types breakdown of reported/detected crime
4.2 Types breakdown of sentenced offenders
4.3 Spatial distribution of offences/residence of offenders
4.4 Ethnic composition for offenders
4.5 Offence/sentence
4.6 Details of local research/monitoring of crime
4.7 Cost studies
4.8 Seasonal trends in crime
4.9 Studies of timing of specific offences
4.10 Special studies e.g. commercial crime

Maps of crime distribution

Section 5 : Sentencing

Common factors: absolute numbers of persons, proportionate use of sentences

5.1 General sentencing statistics
5.2 Non-custodial sentences
5.3 Custodial sentences
5.4 Social Inquiry Reports
5.5 Race and sentencing
5.6 Gender and sentencing
5.7 Sentencing by type of court (juvenile, magistrates', Crown)
5.8 Spatial distribution of sentences
5.9 Urban and rural sentencing
5.10 Reconviction rates
5.11 Details of local research/monitoring of sentencing
5.12 Known costs of local sentence options

Mapping of distribution of various types of sentence

7 A strategy for the 1990s

The prospects for controlling crime in the 1990s

We are now in the last decade of the twentieth century; there is nothing mystical about this, though it does have a certain monumental significance. If we look at the trends in crime over the past century and the responses we have made, we can find little to feel satisfied about. In the opening chapters I tried to sketch out the extent of our failure to control crime and argued that this was due to fragmentation, a narrowness of vision and the failure to understand and manage the interdependent nature of crime response systems.

Almost ten years ago an article appeared that reflected what was then current thinking about crime control [Clarke, 1981]. This article acknowledged that crime had been increasing, partly because opportunities for crime had increased as affluence and consumer goods had become plentiful. Whilst no exhaustive analysis of the possible reasons for increasing crime was attempted, some of the more prominent factors were mentioned, including the post war 'baby booms' which resulted in greater proportions of the population being in the age group for peak offending (10-21). It also noted that as the population gets older there might be some decrease in crime.

In discussing the impact of the criminal justice system, it was suggested that 'criminologists now seem to be reaching agreement that the scope is limited for improving the system's effectiveness' and it went on to say that 'there is considerable doubt about the reductions in crime to be achieved by alterations in policing or by sentences intended to deter, contain or rehabilitate convicted offenders' [op cit, p 14]. Ten years ago the view was forming that policies of diversion and decriminalisation offered little scope for reducing crime. It added that 'most criminologists, as well as an increasing number of politicians, administrators and practitioners, now accept that there is little promise in attempts to reduce reconviction either through therapeutic intervention or through the effects of punishment' [op cit, p 15]. This somewhat pessimistic assessment can be seen to reflect the 'nothing works' attitudes prevalent in the penology of the late 1960s and 1970s. Although it poured cold water on rehabilitation and punishment, this dousing has done little to reduce faith in those measures, as evidenced by the green paper of 1988 'Punishment, custody and the community' [Home Office, 1988b]. The shibboleth of punishment has not waned in the litany of conservatism although its definition has been changed from punitive retribution to constructive control. The article ended with four conclusions: there is a lot of crime but ours is still a remarkably law-abiding country, there is little scope for reducing crime through criminal justice system policies, not too much can be expected of crime prevention and more needs to be done to reduce the fear of crime. To paraphrase the argument still further, it seems, in a nutshell, to be saying: don't worry about crime, there's not a lot we can do about it anyway.

Either these views were wildly incorrect or no one took very much notice of them. Only a few years later the Home Office was taking major initiatives to encourage the greater use of diversion from criminal justice, was devoting considerable resources to all forms of crime prevention, was pouring ever greater quantities of its resources into the prison building programme and was ensuring that resources for police services were increased. Many of the current developments in criminal justice thinking seem not to have been initiated at the time of that article; there was no inkling of the emergence of strategy, no reference to the management of interdependence, an almost dismissive reference to the effects on crime of non-criminal justice policies, certainly none of the faith in community based measures that characterises government thinking now was portrayed in the 1988 green paper. Whilst the prospects for controlling crime ten years ago were decidedly bleak, now they are much more confident. We have over the 1980s witnessed a resurgence of commitment to responding proactively to the problem of crime.

Strategic thinking seems to have moved away from being satisfied only with controlling crime, towards an albeit tentative confidence that crime can in fact be reduced. The machinery of criminal justice policy is still dominated largely by lawyers, with their traditionally myopic visions of how to respond to crime. This domination has been increasingly challenged by magistrates, probation officers, voluntary organisations, police officers and by those in local government. The view that the criminal justice system alone cannot effectively respond to crime has by no means been displaced. To offer one example of this view, the Director of NACRO has commented that

> 'there is no reason why the flawed criminal justice process of the late twentieth century has to be carried on into the twenty-first. It is clearly

unjust to many of those caught up in it. It brings scant comfort or satisfaction to the victims of crime. It consumes valuable resources. It is more likely to engender than discourage criminal behaviour in those who are recipients of its ultimate sanction – custody. And it is now widely seen as ineffective' [NACRO, 1989g p 9].

What has been added to current thinking is a clearer idea of what needs to complement the workings of the criminal justice system – crime prevention, diversion and community based measures. The prospects for responding to crime in the 1990s are those of reduction rather than simply control.

The need for a new crime response strategy

If our responses to crime have been marked by failure over the past century, what then are the prospects for controlling, or better still reducing, crime over the next ten years and beyond? In this chapter, I attempt to use the theoretical framework developed in earlier chapters to develop proposals for the creation of more effective response strategies at the local level.

I would suggest that criminal justice in this country now lies on the threshold of a quantum leap from being an ineffective, ramshackle, unsystematic and costly set of reactions to becoming a strategic system of responses that *will* be able to reduce the problem of crime. I have read or heard comments in many places that the criminal justice system is 'crying out for change'. That kind of sea change does not happen without fears and anxieties being expressed and there are no shortage of these at present in criminal justice agencies. If fundamental changes are to occur in the way we respond to crime, what kind of strategy will be required for those changes to result in improvements?

A strategy of reduction

Strategic thinking would seem to demand that there be one central, keystone purpose from which all other goals can be derived. Where crime response strategies are concerned, the central strategic goal must surely be to reduce crime. Having a keystone purpose of this kind confers a degree of unity that otherwise might not be achieved. There is some evidence that the need for such a central purpose is recognised by the government. It is reported that the Home Secretary is 'trying to unify the criminal justice system behind a set of shared objectives' [Guardian, 27th September 1989]. In the Green Paper issued in 1988, it was clearly stated that 'a major objective of the criminal justice system is to reduce crime as well as to punish offenders' [Home Office, 1988b, p 1]. To take another example, the Minister of State at the Home Office has written that 'we would like to see the criminal justice services in each area co-operating to work out policies for reducing crime by young people' [Patten, 1988, p 563]. It would be easy to get widespread support for crime reduction; the substance of policy debate is how best to do this.

We noted, in chapter one, that there is still, it would seem, some doubt that crime can be reduced, despite potential widespread support for this as a policy goal. Strategic thinking, particularly at the Home Office, appears to accept that, if crime is to be reduced, then there are a set of conditions that must be met; these include broadening the response strategy out from the criminal justice system and seeking a closer partnership between the response agencies. The argument offered in this book is that crime can be reduced through adopting a strategic approach based on integration and enhancement of the response planning process.

In the section on 'a strategic approach to crime' in chapter three, I suggested that the overall architecture of a strategy requires us to think about the choice and blend of its substrategies. Since crime is affected by a wide range of social, political and economic influences, a response strategy needs to have a comprehensive structure, bringing together a variety of social policy ingredients. The current strategy of the government acknowledges the significance of these social policies. Poverty, unemployment, homelessness, drug and alcohol abuse and many other factors influence offending behaviour and come together in the urban environment to produce concentrations of crime. A strategy to reduce crime therefore needs to be formulated within the broader context of urban regeneration, addressing the problems faced by those who live in urban concentrations. This aspect of strategy requires distribution of resources away from those responses that are known to contribute little to crime reduction to those that are more likely to be effective. A strategy of responding to crime must be one of crime reduction.

Decriminalisation

One of the strategic factors in responding to crime should be, as has been suggested for a long time, the limitation of growth in criminalisation. This requires that we set clear and purposeful boundaries around criminal jurisdiction, to ensure that only those acts that genuinely need to be controlled by the criminal justice system are controlled by it. The considerable growth in the number of criminal offences was referred to in the opening chapter. Allied to this has been the increasing range of powers made available to agencies of crime control and indeed to those concerned with other forms of social intervention. One of the effects of this growth in intervention has been the drawing of an increasing number of people into the network of crime responses. The process of criminalisation has long been studied and in a variety of ways; sociologists and criminologists, for example, have paid considerable attention to this theme [see for example the work of Hartjen, 1978]. The need for the state to intervene in certain types of behaviour is, fundamentally, a political decision and one which, for some types of behaviour, is subject to political debate. In strategic terms, where there is a need for the state to intervene, other systems of control should be considered before any decision is made to bring yet more people or behaviours into the criminal law. Likewise, careful consideration should be given to decriminalising those people or acts that need no longer be controlled by the criminal justice system.

Setting appropriate boundaries around the law of crime would seem to require that its purpose is clearly established. Currently this is by no means the case:

> 'Our criminal law has grown up over many centuries and the purposes of those who have framed it, and those who have enforced it, have undoubtedly been many and various. Consequently, it is not easy to state confidently what are the aims of the criminal law at the present day' [Smith and Hogan, 1988, p 3].

Those countries that have established fully written and consolidated criminal codes are, one could argue, in a better position than we are to set clear objectives for their criminal jurisdiction and to formulate a body of law that seeks to achieve these goals.

One of the central issues of criminal justice in the next decade could well be that of narrowing the net of criminal jurisdiction. The criminal law, I would argue, has become an over used means for the regulation of society. Two sets of attitudes have become established amongst the public in general and amongst some legislators: criminalisation and penalisation. Two figures of everyday speech which are often heard are 'there ought to be a law against it' and 'they ought to be locked up'. The advocates of these attitudes are responsible for the massive encroachment of the criminal justice system into more and more aspects of society. This encroachment has overloaded the system and its organisations with so many responsibilities and problems that its capacity for responding to common crimes has diminished. Such encroachment also requires an ever increasing volume of resources to be devoted to the system in order to meet demands placed on it. In consequence it has become overburdened and ineffective and thus has failed to meet the moral or ethical objectives of those whose demands have resulted in its over use in social control.

Before committing a behaviour to the statute book, legislators should think carefully about why such behaviour needs to be governed by the criminal law and what other systems of control could be used instead. There is too often a presumption that the criminal law is the best and most effective system for dealing with certain social problems and for the control of individual or corporate conduct. The nature of criminal acts is difficult if not impossible to adequately define; this being so, it is equally difficult for legislators to decide whether or not an act or omission should be made subject to criminal law. Criminalisation could perhaps be explained by the inadequacy of alternative means of dealing with problematic behaviours. Some conflicts between or injuries inflicted between parties can be dealt with under civil proceedings but

> 'any attempt to distinguish between crimes and torts comes up against the same kind of difficulty encountered in defining crimes generally; that most torts are crimes as well, though some torts are not crimes and some crimes are not torts' [Smith and Hogan, 1988, p 21].

It would therefore seem that there is no completely clear distinction between criminal and civil proceedings as far as their purposes are concerned. Recent history appears to suggest that the predilection of legislators for introducing criminal powers in the control of social problems is driven by the desire to exercise political and governmental control. There has been a marked diminution in the state's confidence that private individuals can, either through informal or civil actions, remedy the problems they face without the assistance of the state. The contribution brought by strategic approaches is to develop a clear sense of purpose in the organisation of justice.

Depenalisation

Two forms of decriminalisation have been suggested: *de facto* decriminalisation which involves reducing the activities of criminal jurisdictions over certain offences even where there has been no change in the competence of the system, and *de jure* decriminalisation which aims at full legal and social recognition of the activity that was previously defined as illegal. Allied to this, *depenalisation* involves either reducing the seriousness of the offence or replacement of custodial penalties attached to it by less intrusive measures [Council of Europe, 1980].

Decriminalisation might involve the transfer of some offences from the criminal to the civil law or the development of ways of exerting control without recourse to the criminal law. This would mean finding or developing methods of dealing with problems other than through the criminal justice system. The principle that should be applied is that criminal proceedings should not be widened but should be reserved for behaviour that cannot be regulated by any other means.

Another method of decriminalisation is the removal of certain categories of people from criminal jurisdiction. The most obvious category for decriminalisation is very young people. It has been suggested that the minimum age of criminal responsibility should be raised to fourteen [see for example NACRO, 1987b, p 25]. Very few children under this age are currently being prosecuted so that this reform would best be tackled now. Local authority child care services present a more appropriate means of responding to offending by children than the machinery of criminal justice. Offenders aged fourteen to eighteen could be dealt with by local authority juvenile justice systems under the jurisdiction of an expanded juvenile court. Those aged eighteen and over would continue to be the responsibility of probation as they are at present [NACRO, 1989e].

There is however a counter argument that the powers invested in the justice system make it a more reliable custodian of individual rights than social welfare or administrative bureaucracies. Do mental patients have their rights protected more or less than criminals? Does the Immigration Service or the Customs and Excise pursue their duties more fairly than do the police? These questions pose similar problems to those that we find associated with the care and welfare issue in juvenile justice.

The view has developed, most strongly over the 1980s, that the criminal justice system intervenes in the lives of offenders more intrusively that it needs to or ought to. There is, certainly in probation and social services, a growing acceptance of the principle of minimal intervention. One can trace the origins of this principle back in several directions, in social work, in mental health and in penology. One variant on this theme is that of 'radical non-intervention', expounded most notably by Schur [1973]. One writer has drawn attention to the degree to which prison, the most interventionist penalty, intrudes deeply into the lives of prisoners in this country [Downs, 1988]. Many of the debates that followed the green paper of 1988 [Home Office, 1988b] centred on the issue of just *how* necessary it would be to create alternatives to custody, in the form of intensive probation programmes, that would strongly intervene in the lives of offenders. Such debates are by no means resolved either in theory or in practice. One of the issues confronting strategists is that of choosing the level of intervention that would be required given the resources made available (in time, staffing, finance and so on) to keep offenders out of custody. Minimising intervention also minimises resource consumption in probation services but, in a crime reduction approach, the impact of the intervention is clearly important. If the intervention is minimalised too rigorously it may not be possible to achieve reductions in reoffending.

A substrategy of depenalisation therefore commands clear thinking about how to set a level of intervention in offender programmes that achieves effectiveness and economy in the use of resources whilst achieving targets of reducing reoffending. This does of course suggest a shift in penal philosophy away from retributive justice towards justice based on the primacy of reducing crime. The emphasis laid on punishment by the 1988 green paper must be evaluated against the criteria of its likely success in stemming recidivism. The principle of minimal intervention carries with it the danger of over use; if it is pursued too enthusiastically, negative consequences might well result, not least a declining respect for the justice system on the part of offenders. An alternative concept is that of *optimum* intervention, in which the degree of intrusion into an offender's life is assessed against the criteria of the degree to which his or her future behaviour is likely to be affected by that intervention.

Increasing the integration of responses

A crime response strategy for the 1990s should take, as its prime purpose, the reduction of crime; this should be included in the strategic goals of all the organisations that contribute to crime responses and particularly of the organisations that make up the criminal justice system. The centrality of crime reduction is already a part of Home Office policy (as cited above). As was argued in the opening chapters, responses to crime have been ineffective and this has been because those responses have become fragmented. The solution to this problem, it was argued, lies in the formulation of a comprehensive and integrated strategy for responding to crime. At national level this requires that all policies and measures of central government are evaluated for their contribution to crime reduction. Certainly no policy or measure undertaken by government should be likely to increase the level of crime. The discussion went on to look at how the application of strategic planning offers to make these response systems more effective by increasing the degree to which they are collectively organised, by targeting their resources and by increasing systematic monitoring and evaluation of their tasks. This approach, it was argued, needs to happen at both the national and the local level and both these levels require effective coordination.

If fragmentation of responses to crime lies at the root of the ineffectiveness of current responses, then integration of policies and operation, through collaborative strategy, provides a basis for controlling the problem of crime. Of central importance to the development of a crime reduction strategy is the successful management of interdependency. There needs to be a managed relationship between crucially related responses: between cautioning, prosecution, sentencing and offender programs and between policing and crime prevention. The relationship between custodial and noncustodial sentencing might be more tightly defined. The legal criteria for custody, introduced for young people by the Criminal Justice Acts of 1982 and 1988, should be extended to cover adults. There is a strong possibility that this measure will be included in the criminal justice legislation that is currently predicted for 1990/91. It has however been suggested that a more significant principle that would govern the relationship between custodial and noncustodial penalties would be that 'legislation should create a clear presumption in favour of community based sanctions in all cases' [NACRO, 1989c, p 51]. The impact of crime prevention on rates of offending and on the internal dynamics of the justice system must be fully researched and understood. There needs to be coherence between the crime control and security measures that are operated in the public domain and those that are provided in the private sector. Such research and evaluation will enable organisations to integrate their policies and their operational planning.

Integration through collaboration

Since there are a number of organisations involved in the prevention, control and processing of crime and offenders, collaboration adds another function to the equation of effectiveness in reducing crime. Collaboration is an essential function in integrating strategic responses at both national and local levels. Whilst a degree of collaboration already takes place at both levels, increased effectiveness requires it to be pursued in the context of strategic planning. In chapter two it was suggested that various levels of collaboration could be defined, ranging from simple liaison through to the hypothesised fully corporate approach. These levels of collaboration were seen to have different patterns of policy formulation, planning and operational relationships. The degree of collaboration amongst the agencies in a local area could thus be analysed using the framework provided. The level of functional integration is therefore dependent on the level and patterns of collaboration being practised within an area. This will depend on there being policies and structures through which that practice can be developed. The aim of promoting collaborative responses at local level is to integrate the agencies and functions into a strategic rather than a fragmentary response to the local crime problem.

National/local integration of strategies

In our opening chapter, we depicted the criminal justice system as, roughly speaking, a two tier system comprising national and local agencies; this depiction flows from the model in which the system is governed partly at national level, partly at local level (depending on the agency concerned) but in which most of the operation or service delivery is made at the local level. Currently, the government seems to be effecting an incremental shift away from local to central management of the system as a whole. This is a reflection of a broader trend towards the general centralisation of government. This might, on the face of it, appear to satisfy some of the requirements of integration; centralisation does not, however, necessarily create functional integration, since the interdependences of the system largely operate at the local level, however much the framework is set nationally, not least through law and policy. We have recognised that strategies are emerging at both national and local levels and have considered arguments favouring complementary strategy development at both levels.

Since national and local crime response strategies are interdependent they should be integrated or at least coordinated. If locally organised strategies are to be successful then they need to be supported by the national strategy on which they will depend. Local strategies cannot be developed by central government. Only local people, who are responsible for the management of their local organisations and know the communities of which they are a part, are in a position to devise the most effective strategy for responding to the problem of crime in their area. A national strategy depends on local strategies being developed that will take forward in an area the framework presented by central government.

How then can national government support local crime strategies? The task of central government is to ensure that resources are available to local organisations to enable them to meet their policy objectives. In the chapter on policy, the point was made that policies need to be related to resources and vice versa. Central government's role is therefore to provide sufficient resources directly or to allow local authorities to raise sufficient funds locally in order to put policies into practice. Strategic planning processes suggest that there is a cycle of consultation between those who make the fundamental strategic choices and those who are concerned with the detailed tactics of operations. This approach would therefore necessitate central government monitoring local strategies and consulting with local policy makers and planners in the formulation of a national strategy for responding to crime. Resource allocation is thus driven by this process of collaborative strategy development.

Structures for local planning

If a strategic approach to responses to crime is to be effectively practised, then structures need to be created that will bring people and organisations together to pursue that task. If integrated and comprehensive responses to crime are to be developed at local level appropriate groups of people must be able to work collaboratively towards that end. Bringing such groups into being will allow responsibility for the strategic planning of responses to crime to be located *somewhere*. At present such responsibilities are diffused throughout a plethora of organisations in a fragmentary fashion.

Criminal justice organisations can and do engage individually in strategic planning; what is currently missing is the means for them to do so collectively and in an organised way. A structure will not of itself create a strategic approach but a correctly designed structure would provide a framework for collective planning. This collective, interagency approach to crime is of fundamental importance to effective response planning. This is not to suggest that a layer of bureaucracy should be created; we must be able to distinguish between structures that enable processes to happen effectively and bureaucracies that simply engage in routine functions.

The idea of interagency planning is not new to criminal justice; a number of experiments have already been tried in particular arenas of criminal justice. Reference was made earlier to NACRO's Juvenile Crime Consultative Groups; these provide an example of a range of organisations being brought together to review, evaluate and plan responses to juvenile crime. Although they were created initially as time-limited groups, some of them have led to the establishment of permanent review bodies and these provide examples, on a limited scale, of what local strategic planning groups might look like. The creation of specialised working parties that looked at specific aspects of the juvenile justice system – such as prevention, diversion and alternatives to custody – was found to very useful as a way of breaking down into manageable segments a large and complex area of work. Each of these reported back to the main consultative group and, at the end of the initial process, a review was produced that included a range of recommendations to the participating agencies.

In the field of crime prevention, crime reduction groups have already been suggested by the agency *Crime Concern* and crime prevention panels frequently draw their members from a range of backgrounds. In juvenile crime responses, the interagency approach has received considerable attention; the project management groups set up under the 1983 DHSS intermediate treatment initiative brought together a number of local agencies and this theme continues to receive attention as a central component in the management of juvenile crime [Cooper, 1989].

Clearly, a multiagency strategy is required if the developing theme of the management of justice systems and agency interdependency is to be pursued. The need for a comprehensive strategy in the reduction of crime requires the integration of responses being made by a wide range of local bodies and groups. Much of this interagency work happens routinely and informally but if comprehensive strategies are to be developed, the interagency dimension will require systematic organisation. This can best be achieved through the creation of local strategic planning groups.

Crime response commissions

For the purposes of this discussion, these local strategic planning groups will be called *crime response commissions*. I realise that the term 'commission' is not wholly satisfactory and there is no reason why such groups *should* be so called. But I prefer this term to 'committee' which smacks somewhat of bureaucracy. A commission is simply a body of people constituted to discharge a task and I see such groups as being task oriented.

The reduction of crime in a local area is something that is contributed to by a number of organisations. More broadly, community groups, networks of people and the general public share with organisations the task of responding to crime. The idea of a commission is based on the need to enable a range of criminal justice, local government organisations and interest groups to engage in collective strategic planning of the way that crime is responded to in their area. The commission therefore offers a structural framework for collaboration in the development of collective policy and planning.

The functions of commissions

The mission of the interagency group would be to develop a comprehensive strategy for responding to and reducing crime in the local area. As argued in previous chapters, policy and planning are the main components of strategy and a commission would therefore have the aims of developing a collaborative operational policy and of enabling coordinated planning of its implementation.

That does not mean that each of the organisations represented on the commission would have to surrender its own policy and planning functions. What it means is that the collaborative strategy will provide an anchorage to which organisational policies and plans can be moored. In the same way, commissions would not be required to take over the operational planning of constituent organisations but to enable the coordination of planning functions across agency boundaries. The objective of a commission would be to integrate response systems and to ensure that the overall pattern of response to crime is consolidated within the framework of a corporate strategy.

The formulation and implementation of an operational response strategy must be founded on a well established public policy, as was argued in chapter four. A broad national strategy for dealing with crime is formulated by central government but the implementation of that strategy at local level requires the active involvement of local agencies and people. There is always the possibility that local people will want to mould the national strategy to their own values and circumstances. That integration between national and local strategies is required for effective responses has already been argued and, as will be considered later, commissions could in fact improve the coordination between national and local levels.

Local public policy formulation has not been encouraged by national governments and many councils have failed to address this aspect of policy in any degree of detail. Crime and justice issues have by and large been left to representatives on police authorities and probation committees. There is a need to redress this policy vacuum at local level and to encourage councils to develop crime response policy and this encouragement could well come from commissions through processes of policy analysis and the provision of well analysed information. The concept of the local commission is not one of taking over the creation of public policy but of supporting policy formulation by clarifying the key decisions that operational agencies require policy makers to address.

Another function of the commissions should be that of evaluating current policy and practice and of assessing how effectively resources are being used. This is of course a similar task to the evaluations made internally by any individual organisation. The commission's level of evaluation is therefore that of looking at the response system as a whole. The bottom line of such evaluation is analysing crime rates to see if they are being affected by current approaches. If the strategic purpose of responding to crime is to reduce it, then the principle goal of a crime commission would be to coordinate a strategy of crime reduction in a local area.

A crime response commission would be both a product and producer of enhanced collaboration. Without a pre-existing level of collaboration a commission might never be developed; where collaboration can be developed and a commission set in place, it would further enhance collaborative approaches. A successful commission would possibly give rise to the corporate level of collaboration envisaged in chapter two. A further function of local commissions is to act as a bridge between national and local strategies.

Since information will undoubtedly place an increasingly important role in strategic responses, commissions can function as bridges between local and national strategies in reporting to central government on their activities and in receiving information from the national level about policy and planning initiatives. Local commissions could provide central government with a channel of communication to local agencies; they could also assist in the implementation of national strategic objectives in their local areas. Most importantly, the commissions would be able to provide implementation of national strategy that is geared to the conditions and circumstances of the local area.

Finally, I feel bound to emphasize that crime response commissions should not be restricted to one aspect of response; their mission needs to cover prevention, diversion, prosecution, sentencing and offender programmes in probation, social services and the voluntary sector. This is a prerequisite for achieving integration and comprehensiveness.

The membership of commissions

Our previous discussion, in chapter two, of the components of collaborative action suggested that strategic choices need to be made about level of representation and choice of agency in constituting groups of this kind. In the following discussion it will be clear that I lean towards a top down model, with chief officers forming the apex of the commission structure. This is not to deny that modern strategic planning methods generally emphasize a bottom up approach or a process in which there is coordination between those making the key strategic choices (at senior management level) and those who are operating at the service delivery end (the practitioners). The model of commissions that I offer here is rooted in the corporate concept of response strategy. My approach has been to assume an incremental approach to the development of such commissions; starting with the chief executives would seem to be easier than trying to construct vertical commissions which attempt to consolidate an interagency strategy across several agencies.

The representation on commissions of certain organisations will be essential: these being the magistracy and judiciary, the police, the Crown Prosecution Service and the probation service. Local government representation should also be seen as essential if a comprehensive strategy is to be established. This could be achieved through the inclusion of the chief executive of each local authority included within the commission's boundaries. Each commission could comprise a core of chief officers of criminal justice agencies and local authorities who would be responsible for the formulation of strategic policies and a wider group of senior officers responsible for strategic planning. Below this central commission there would be several working groups concerned with specific aspects of responses according to local needs and circumstances and focusing perhaps either on age groups or on aspects of the strategy such as prevention, diversion and community based programmes.

The issue of whether or not commissions should include political representation is more complex. It could be argued that, since such commissions would have an impact on the public, they should be accountable to the public through being composed of elected representatives. The involvement of elected members might also enhance the public credibility of commissions. Since the public policy element of strategy development is important, the involvement of elected representatives is essential but the method of their involvement requires consideration. It could also be argued that since commissions are unlikely to be given executive powers then there would be less need for them to include politicians.

A commission composed on the whole of politicians would resemble a public authority, similar to a Health Authority or Police Authority. But, Councils currently fulfil this function and there would seem not to be a strong case for removing responsibility for public policy away from Councils to yet another political forum. If Councils are seen to be the appropriate forum for the formulation of public policy on crime and justice at local level, the commissions would be reserved for the implementation of that policy. Councils can also continue their representation on police authorities, probation committees and so on, providing channels of accountability for individual agencies in a way that a commission would not.

Councillors could be engaged in policy formulation without necessarily having to become members of the commission itself. Is there a case for saying that commissions should in fact be in effect subcommittees of the local authority? Part of this issue is concerned with accountability and partly it is about addressing the importance of public policy. What puts the issue into context is what is currently happening to local government: its powers are being curtailed or transferred to Whitehall and the trend is towards local authorities as being service contractors rather than service providers. One view of local authorities sees them as being strategic planning bodies that eventually will simply coordinate and regulate a range of services that are provided by private enterprise [Stewart and Stoker, 1989]. Many analysts of local government foresee its doom if the current policies of central government continue. A general election could in any case reverse this trend and redirect power back to the local level. It is therefore difficult to place the innovation of crime response commissions in local authorities that face an uncertain future.

The membership of commissions could be very large if every organisation or interest group were to be included. This might overburden meetings and make detailed planning unworkable. For this reason and because the scale of the task is great, a commission might need to set up a series of working parties concerned with particular aspects of local responses, through which a wider body of interests could be involved and consulted. Existing crime prevention panels, juvenile crime liaison groups and so on could thus provide inputs to the commission without their members having to attend all of its meetings.

The main purpose of the commission would be to develop coordination and planning; it would then be up to each of the constituent organisations to implement the resulting strategy and it is through operational organisations that accountability might be achieved. The issue of whether or not there should be a lead agency poses a number of difficulties. Experience of interagency working on a smaller scale suggests that, where interagency politics might be an inhibiting factor in the development of a collaborative approach, there might be some benefit in allowing agencies to come together on neutral ground. In some cases, cooperation amongst statutory agencies has been enabled by a voluntary body offering a neutral setting in which various statutory agencies could meet. Strategic interagency groups might require a round table approach in which no one agency has a leading role and all participants have an equal status.

Commission secretariats

In order for a commission to undertake its work effectively a range of support services will be required. As we saw in chapter six information is of central importance to all aspects of strategic planning. A primary support service would therefore be the provision of information about what crime is being committed and how local organisations and the community are responding to it. Crime and response information would be used by members of commissions but the need to provide freely accessible statistics on all aspects of crime responses is an allied need. The development of joint information systems therefore would support collaborative policy and planning. In order for the information and support functions to be provided, each commission would need a small secretariat staffed by people who have the requisite knowledge and skills to coordinate information and service the commissions. Since the support services required would be more than just administration of meetings the staff should include people skilled in information, research, technology and policy analysis.

The secretariat would provide centralised research and information services to enable effective strategies to be developed. Some of the developments in criminal justice computing, referred to in chapter six, could be located in the work of commission secretariats. They could act as clearing houses for research results and provide a range of statistical services for local and national consumers.

Information on its own, as we saw in the previous chapter, is relatively inert; only when information is digested and interpreted (that is, when it becomes knowledge) does it begin to take on power, meaning and significance. Interpretation requires a policy and planning framework. The work of those providing support services might therefore need to go beyond the provision of information, to include policy analysis and this requires specialised expertise. Policy analysis does not set out to decide the results of policy evaluation or formulation but to enable those functions to be performed effectively by policy makers. Those providing support services to the commissions must therefore be able to practice a range of skills, preparing a variety of briefing papers and analyses so that commission members are fully up to date, well informed and able to base their judgement on well presented briefings. Also, strategic planning has become a highly developed technique and one which has, allied with it, a range of management and organisational methods, as for example critical success factors, performance indicators, scenario planning, environmental scanning and so on. Commission members need to be able to draw on knowledge and expertise from a field that is rapidly developing.

If secretariats are to be established, the question arises of where they could be based. Placing a secretariat within any one of the criminal justice agencies might be seen as giving that agency an undue degree of influence over it. As a possible solution to this issue of neutrality, the secretariat could be annexed to the local authority chief executive or, if a more neutral territory is thought to be desirable, could be set up as an independent trust managed by representatives of organisations represented on the commission.

It will be important that commissions should not become mere discussion groups but have a planned programme of work. Specific aspects of local responses will need to be considered, such as crime prevention, the management of justice processes, the development of offender management programs and so on. The work programme therefore will need to prioritise particular aspects of the response system for consideration. But in order to achieve integration and comprehensiveness, overall reviews of the local area would need to be made. The preparation and use of area profiles, as outlined in chapter 6, could be undertaken by secretariat staff. These would provide an accessible information base to support policy and planning by commission members.

NACRO has, in its juvenile crime work, suggested that each local authority should publish an annual review of juvenile crime and justice. Each year, chief constables publish reports that provide details of what crime has been committed in the area and how the police have responded to it. It would aid public awareness of measures to control crime if a corporate annual report on crime and crime responses were to be published by commissions. This would allow each of the organisations involved in an area to put its own annual review into a wider context. It would also allow both central and local governments to assess the development of and progress in implementing crime reduction strategies. An annual report on crime and responses in the local area might also include the strategic plan for crime response for the next year. Collected together by central government, these annual reports would provide a comprehensive picture of what is happening in crime responses throughout the country. The drafting of these annual reports would be a secretariat duty. It would also help central government if there was a national planning schedule with all the reports being published in the same month.

The Home Office papers on criminal justice [Home Office, 1986 and 1989c] provided a national level review of crime, prevention, enforcement, policing, sentencing, probation, imprisonment and other aspects of policy. Clearly presented statistics and information were given in appendices. These provided a very useful snapshot of government policy and national responses to crime and would, if published annually, provide a very useful reference to what is intended and what has happened at national level. If each local commission or first tier local authority would do the same kind of annual report, public opinion would be better informed and central government would have a clearer view of what was happening at local level, moreso than through each agency providing a separate report of its own. This would aid the harmonisation of national and local responses.

The cost of commissions.

Adequately serviced commissions would cost money; the secretariat services alone would involve considerable costs. Such costs would however be an investment and should be based on an economic analysis of the costs of crime in the local area and the benefits being derived from local responses. If a corporate and strategic response to crime does succeed in reducing crime by a significant amount, then investment in such an approach would be cost-effective. The work of commissions would provide a return only in the long term; in most areas, it would probably be at least five years before any fundamental reductions in the costs of crime could be demonstrated.

This would depend to some extent on the development of local economic profiles of the cost of crime and the cost of responding to crime. As with many other aspects of public service, it is often necessary to spend in order to save [Metcalfe and Richards, 1987]. Secretariats could commission research into and coordinate monitoring of economic data on crime and responses. Expenditure on commissions should be viewed therefore as an investment. Resources devoted to commissions might in the long term be 'self-financing' and this could be a strategic goal in creating such commissions.

Since commissions will require extensive support services, the provision of central government pump priming funds would enable them to get started more readily than if their development were to be dependent on scarce local resources. The cost of setting up the commissions (including piloting of the idea) should be borne by central government, possibly through a direct specific grant system. The on-going costs could be shared by the local authorities and the criminal justice organisations at local level.

Apart from grant-aiding the development of local commission, central government might also fund a national resource centre to provide developmental services to local commissions. Such services might include making available information about the models that could be used, exchange of ideas and experience of setting up commissions, monitoring the growth of commissions and providing expertise in the form of consultants who could be engaged by local areas. The interchange of local ideas and experience through conferences, seminars and the publication of case studies will also be of help in evening out the rate of growth and might help to set standards of excellence.

The concept of commissions, as set out here, does not envisage them as having many executive powers. There is however a case for saying that commissions should be able to fund particular local initiatives that will contribute to the development of strategic responses. Such initiatives might include innovatory projects that will develop and demonstrate good interagency practice. There should also be the means to fund and commission local research. Most of the funding for development work has, up to now, come from central government (with some also coming from trusts and charities). The value of such work has been great but could be increased if funding were available on a local basis, rather than from central departments. Much of this work supports local developments and any findings or lessons have generally been made available nationally.

The way forward

I would not wish to underestimate the difficulties and problems that could be associated with the idea of local commissions. The traps, barriers and pitfalls confronting the establishment of a commission are considerable; but then so would be the payoffs if the initiative is successful. A commission could easily become simply a talking shop or an arena for fighting interagency battles. Those who have ventured into the potentially stormy waters of interagency work know only too well the rough passages that must be navigated. The task of setting up a local commission therefore requires great skill and ingenuity and a grasp of the art of development work. More will be said on this later.

Local crime response commissions are, in my view, an exciting development for the future. They could offer a potentially powerful basis for winning the fight against crime. But resistance to such an idea will be considerable; the autonomy syndrome is a deep-seated force within the conscience of criminal justice agencies. It might well be that the currents of professional independence run deeper than the desire to collaborate in responding to crime. If such resistance is to be overcome a high level of commitment to the corporate approach will have to be promoted. Much lip service is paid to the need for innovation in tackling crime. But innovation means change and change is something that is often feared. If change is to take place and innovation is to flourish then the fears in which the autonomy syndrome is rooted must be addressed.

There is a case in favour of incremental growth, with each area choosing to develop its own commission or not as the case may be. There are many preconditions for this to happen, not least the acceptance of and commitment to a collaborative approach to crime responses. Will the development of commissions require legislation? The funding of commissions is one aspect that might demand legislation. Legislation might also provide a mission to local agencies to engage in a commission; some agencies, the courts in particular, often feel that their independence restrains them from engaging in interagency initiatives of any kind. Parliament might be able to devise a framework where the positive aspects of autonomy are protected but where the barriers against engagement in policy and planning functions of criminal justice system are largely removed. There might also be a need for legislation to free up the supply of aggregate crime and justice statistics and to enable the free flow of non-confidential information. The issue of accountability is another aspect of the need for a legislative basis to commissions.

It is perhaps unlikely that commissions will be inaugurated as a national initiative. A process of incremental development might be more likely to bring them into existence though the consequence of this is likely to uneven development, with some areas having them, some having well resourced and effective commissions and others having none at all. If central government accepts the need to foster local collaborative responses, there are a number of measures that it could sponsor to aid this. More research needs to be done on the management of interdependence; this could take the form of action-research projects in local areas where the criminal justice agencies are moving towards a managed system of interdependence. The 'theory' of interdependence has been established, what is less clear is exactly how the management of interdependence can take place effectively at local level.

Strategic planning of local responses

The development of permanent crime response commissions offers a way forward for reducing crime in local areas. This is, of course, a long term development, a vision of the future. What is already beginning to emerge in some localities are collaborative and coordinated approaches to crime based on meetings of chief officers of criminal justice agencies and supported by interagency work at management and practice levels. It would be judicious therefore to consider an alternative to the creation of commissions that might go some way to achieving the same result in the immediate future. If criminal justice organisations cannot at the present time fully share in a collective approach to crime, then the next best thing would be for each to engage individually in strategic planning that takes account of other agencies. This is, if you like, a sort of *unilateral corporatism.* An essential feature of any intraorganisational planning is analysing the relationships that an organisation has with others on which its functions depend. For example, strategic planners in police forces would only be able to develop an effective strategy for policing if they were able to integrate the various functions of policing with those of private security, community crime prevention, prosecution and sentencing. Likewise, probation services need to include, within their strategic plans, policy and operational relationships with policing, prosecution and sentencing.

A comprehensive and integrated strategy for responding to crime in a locality could therefore result from effective strategic planning within each of the organisations involved in the overall system of response. Criminal justice agencies already engage in this form of interrelation though, as I have argued, insufficiently and ineffectively. This is partly because such initiatives are not fully supported and serviced by research and policy analysis and partly because such interorganisational meetings tend to lack a developed technique of strategic planning. Personnel from many local organisations currently talk to each other about how their organisations are responding to crime and there are some opportunities for interagency study and research. These processes of interagency collaboration are however currently too fragmentary to result in the development of a comprehensive corporate strategy.

Interagency policy development and planning needs to be more highly organised. Hence my argument for a structure to enable this to happen. However, though it is far more difficult and less reliable, a corporate approach to strategic crime response planning could be achieved without the creation of a commission. The development of coordinated planning needs to be studied in order that the process of development can be understood. This could be enabled by a programme of research, or a series of practical development projects, funded by the Home Office.

A considerable amount of work is required to establish an appreciation of exactly what strategic planning means in the context of crime and criminal justice. As pointed out in chapter 3 strategic planning is currently enjoying a renaissance in the business sector and a new set of methods for practising it are being developed. Various criminal justice organisations currently engage in strategic planning; police forces, for example, are showing an interest in it and some now have strategic planning units or committees as part of their internal management structure. For example, the Chief Constable of Leicestershire has written, in one of his Annual Reports, that

> 'planned policing could not be introduced without some central assistance and guidance. As Chief Constable, I determine the Force Objectives but only after the fullest consultation within and outside the Force. To assist in this process a new committee has been established - the Strategic Planning Committee' [Hirst, 1986].

The function of the committee is 'to prepare an annual development plan, to identify appropriate Force Objectives and to suggest priorities for organisational development' [ibid].

A strategic planning approach to the reduction of juvenile crime was developed in the United States [Falkin, 1979]. This resulted from a research programme funded by Federal government but nothing like it has ever taken place in this country. More recently the US Department of Justice has published a series of papers under the title 'Perspectives on Policing' and two of these are directly relevant to our present discussion: 'Corporate Strategies for Policing' [Kelling and Moore, 1988] and 'The Evolving Strategy of Policing' [Moore and Trojanowicz, 1988]. These papers indicate that US thinking about strategic planning in law enforcement agencies has moved on some way from where Falkin left it in 1979 but that the Federal Government is still at least promoting strategic approaches as a central element in increasing the effectiveness of policing.

The creation of a local strategy for reducing crime can only be effective if national and local policy and plans are integrated, if certain strategic policies are developed and if the discipline of local development work is learnt and fully utilised. These considerations form the remainder of this chapter but before I move onto them I wish to look briefly at two further aspects of local strategic planning that deserve some attention.

Central government has laid some stress on the setting and use of performance indicators in all public sector agencies. Performance indicators have been developed for most criminal justice agencies, particularly for the probation and police services. They might also be developed for the courts service, though this might be limited to their administrative rather than their sentencing functions [Hurd, 1986 and Biggin, 1988]. As a management and organisational technique, performance indicators can help agencies to achieve their objectives. What concerns me at this point is the interagency dimension of such indicators. The systems analysis on which the interdependence thesis rests, views the criminal justice system as having certain goals that its various functions are intended to achieve. Performance is in simple terms what an organisation or department does in pursuit of its goals; the performance of the criminal justice system as a whole is, to some extent, an aggregate of the performances of each of its constituent agencies. If indicators can be set to measure the performance of say the police forces or the probation services, then why not have a set of performance indicators for the criminal justice system as a whole? The bottom line indicator might be the success of the system in reducing crime but a number of other indicators could also be set, as for example, reducing discrimination, increasing proportionality, making more effective use of resources and so on.

If, as has already been argued, a corporate approach to crime responses is required, then how do the performance indicators of each of the criminal justice agencies relate to each other? As far as I can tell little or no attempt has been made to tackle this question. Should there be some attempt to secure a degree of harmonisation of performance indicators among the various criminal justice agencies that have them? I recently put this question to some strategic planners from one of our larger police forces. The reply I got, roughly speaking, was that the practice of performance indicators in management was relatively new and there is enough trouble getting harmonisation of indicators within organisations without moving on to seeking harmonisation across and among agencies. It is understandable that this should be so but the issue of interagency harmonisation should, I would argue, be considered before organisational practice becomes entrenched.

I appreciate that performance indicators are, to a certain extent, being imposed by central government as part of its political programme of seeking cost-effectiveness in the public sector and the political implications of this process are also appreciated. But the technique of performance indicators is not new, even to public sector organisations and certainly pre-dates the present government. As a technique it can be a valuable management device and is becoming widely adopted in private sector companies. If we wish to have clear goals for criminal justice organisations and if we wish those agencies to operate more systematically, then it is possible and certainly desirable to formulate a set of indicators by which the performance of that system can be assessed. That surely would lead us to considering the value of harmonising at least some of the indicators that are common to the various organisations within the system.

The missions of crime response agencies

The mission of crime response agencies at local level turns on the need to reduce crime. The promotion of fairness and equality and the eradication of discrimination are equally important though these two purposes are in many ways inseparable. We have already seen that a local strategy requires a comprehensive and integrated approach to crime management, based on public, corporate and organisational levels of policy and planning. The organisation of information, research and evaluation systems and procedures is necessary to support this collaborative approach. In developing a successful strategy, local planners need to identify the key factors in crime and justice and to prioritise these in terms of actions and resources.

Defining missions

What kind of mission would be appropriate to police forces? Strategic planning of law enforcement and crime control has already emerged in some police forces and is being encouraged by the government. What would help police officers to utilise the potential of strategic planning would be its inclusion in the training, support and professional development facilities offered by the police colleges and national bodies. Other national organisations can and do also offer expertise and knowledge to the police. The importance of information in strategic planning has been stressed in previous chapters and in all aspects of the development of a local strategy, access to crime data collected by the police will be of central importance.

What I would particularly stress about policing strategy in the 1990s is the need to relieve the police of the burden of some of their duties that do not at present contribute to crime reduction and which moreover divert their resources away from that task. The development of annual objectives for police forces is very much in the vein of a strategic approach. But objective setting and achievement will not in itself increase the effectiveness of the police in reducing crime until more police time is given to crime and less to those duties which could be transferred to other organisations. Crime prevention work will always need to remain part of the police officer's duty to some extent but by its nature it is a response that could be as effectively led, in the future, by local authorities or, perhaps, by local crime response commissions.

If the work of the police in controlling crime is to reach its full potential then its resources need to be more fully targeted on crime than at present they appear to be. The boundaries between the police and other agencies, such as social services, education, health authorities, the voluntary sector and community groups, should be more clearly delineated. There has been a tendency to overload police forces with more and more duties and for them to elect to take on responsibilities that could equally well be assumed by other organisations; crime prevention, the education of young people, youth work, community relations and various aspects of road traffic are examples I have in mind.

What kind of mission would be appropriate to the courts? The need for aggregate data about sentencing and court practices to be made available has been widely stressed. The same argument about the police providing a statistical service applies equally to the courts. Currently, data about sentencing is filed with the Home Office for the national criminal statistics by the police. But this data arrives too late and in too little detail to allow it to be used effectively in local strategic planning. Given the emphasis currently being placed on efficiency in court administration and the growing availability of computers, the production of a statistical service on sentencing and other aspects of the justice process should not be an undue burden for local courts. The collection and processing of criminal statistics is being computerised and this will increase the speed and efficiency of the service.

The need to reduce delays in bringing people to trial has already been taken on board by the government [Home Office, 1986]. If diversion from prosecution begins to work, the reduced workload on the courts will allow cases to be processed more speedily. Government policy acknowledges the need for the police, the Crown Prosecution Service and the courts to work together so that cases are heard more quickly.

The sentencing decision is at the heart of the justice system and thus many other response mechanisms relate to it. The involvement of magistrates and judges in the planning and management of the justice system, as broadly defined, is therefore a prerequisite for the development of a fully integrated and comprehensive response system. However, opportunities to engage in such work have been greeted by sentencers with a mixed response. Many magistrates and most judges seem to have rejected such opportunities on the grounds that they might be subjected to unwarranted influences. Thus their involvement in the management of community service and intermediate treatment schemes has sometimes not gone ahead. Some of these objections to being too closely involved in particular schemes and projects are understandable. But the involvement of sentencers in policy and the broader aspects of strategic planning is essential for their sakes as well as for other people in the system.

Sentencers need to engage in the policy and planning processes required in the criminal justice system as much as police officers, probation officers or any other group who contribute to crime control. National bodies, such as the Home Office, the Lord Chancellor's Department, the Magistrates' Association and the Board of Judicial Studies would do well to study the needs and problems involved in sentencers' participation in the local strategic planning and should offer clear guide-lines particularly since the current situation appears not to be clearly understood. Practice varies considerably: some magistrates do play an active part in the management of local schemes and a few judges do participate in the development of local initiatives. But the legitimacy of such participation is not universally accepted.

If judges and magistrates are to play their part in local strategic planning then central government should enable them to do this, firstly, by removing any impediments that might unnecessarily inhibit their involvement and secondly by positively encouraging their involvement in appropriate bodies and initiatives. This is particularly important if local crime response commissions are to be set up; they would not be able to function without the involvement of magistrates and judges.

Development work and local initiatives

I said earlier that the development of corporate approaches to crime reduction, whether through commissions or through the less corporate approach of interagency strategic planning, requires the exercise of knowledge, skills and techniques. Development work will be required to establish strategic responses to crime. Once commissions have been established, they might continue development work, particularly through the secretariat staff. Some thought however needs to be given to what is meant by *development work*. My experience in NACRO has led me to think about this and what skills are required by those who are engaged in it.

In straightforward terms development work is 'being able to make things happen'; usually this means being able to bring about change. Let me unpack that seemingly simple idea. What is 'being able'? Firstly, there is the perspective of the *individual*. In order for individuals to engage in development work a range of requirements can be identified: knowledge, skills, techniques and commitment. Developers need to *know* how the local criminal justice system operates if they are to change it in any way. That knowledge-base includes criminal law and procedure, a working understanding of each of the organisations in the local system and information from which new knowledge can be generated.

In order to engage in development practice a range of *skills* will be required, such as motivating people, being able to communicate effectively, being able to solve problems, analysing policy issues and so on. *Techniques* are methods through which skills can be applied effectively; they are conceptual 'tools for the job'. Strategic planning requires a tool box of techniques and the same can be said of management. Successful development work requires knowledge of what techniques are available and skills in being able to practice them artfully. Finally, developers need to be *committed* and need to be able to pass that commitment on to others. If a development task has been clearly defined and has goals and targets, then the developer must stick to the task and not be side tracked. A single minded commitment to achieving results is what makes things happen.

Secondly, there is the perspective of the *group*. Bringing about change in local crime responses relies on a collective effort as much as on campaigns by individuals. A development work team should be able to cover the range of *knowledge* required for the task. Specialisms need to be blended together within the context of a collective and shared knowledge-base. Where there are gaps in knowledge, learning and study needs to be planned. A team of people might have a portfolio of *skills*, each member having strengths and weaknesses. For the team to perform well, skills should be deployed appropriately according to the demands of any particular task. Gaps in the team's portfolio of skills can be remedied through training.

If a programme of tasks is to be completed then there needs to be an analysis of what skills will be required. One of the fundamental skills is being able to work in and as a team. Some might offer leadership skills; some technical and supportive skills. Groups need to work, at times in a programmed way, at others in a creative way. There are *techniques* that can be applied to creative working, such as synectics and these can be used to enhance the more usual intuitive approaches. Finally, a team requires equality of *commitment*; they must share in the initiative and be dedicated to it both individually and as a group.

'Making things happen' necessitates strategic thinking and this requires a working understanding of what strategy is and how it can be used to tackle a range of problems and the achievement of goals. The art of good strategy is being able to select the correct priorities, to see in what is the right direction to move, to manoeuvre large numbers of people into position (metaphorically) and to pursue objectives with a single minded dedication. Development work is about being able to formulate an effective strategy for change and this will frequently require gaining the commitment of large numbers of people.

Development work is not therefore about being a charismatic leader, a born entrepreneur or a great dictator. Development work is not an intuitive faculty that people are born with; people can learn to do development work just as they can learn to drive a car. For great things to happen in the field of crime response, there needs to be a body of people around the country who can act as developers, who can make things happen and bring about change through the practice of development work.

There is also a need for development groups and for projects which can perform development functions. Central government has operated a number of 'initiatives' and 'action plans' designed to foster changes in the way things happen at local level. Two of these that come most readily to my mind are the DHSS's initiative to develop intensive intermediate treatment for juveniles [DHSS, 1983] and the Home Office's action plan promotion for young adult offenders [Home Office, 1988c]. In both cases, the accent was on development at local level and centralised facilities were provided through NACRO to support local development work. National development agencies have played and should continue to play a key role in the improvement of crime response services and practice. More however needs to be done to train those engaging in development work and to establish the practice methodology for this kind of work. This might be achieved by universities or polytechnics offering courses in development work across a number of disciplines.

Innovation and the creation of new services and schemes can be achieved, in some cases, more quickly and flexibly by voluntary agencies than by those in the statutory sector. Development groups can enable change in the statutory sector through offering a *neutral ground* for interagency initiatives. Some have done this through the provision of services and some through promoting service delivery and change in other agencies. Once needs have been identified, voluntary agencies have been able to meet those needs themselves or have played an enabling role in fostering other agencies to meet those needs. This has been particularly true where voluntary agencies have tackled needs or problems that cut across local authority departmental structures (such as unemployment or drugs) or which fall outside of local authority responsibilities (such as counselling services).

The creation of new services *on behalf* of statutory bodies is also an area where voluntary agencies have played a prominent role. Far from being in competition with the statutory sector, there has been a long history of partnership and mutual interdependence between voluntary and statutory sectors. Local crime commissions could therefore be seen as development bodies whose tasks might include

- improving communication between agencies;
- increasing interchange of ideas and expertise in tackling specific problems;
- identifying key areas where improvements in the management of interdependence are required;
- facilitating the sharing of resources;
- bringing new resources into existence;
- provision of multidisciplinary training schemes;
- review and evaluation of criminal justice systems and processes;
- commissioning research into aspects of interdependency;
- promoting standards of practice.

Well constituted and constructed commissions would provide an overview of the response strategy that will remedy the organisational myopia often found in agencies that concentrate exclusively on their own functions to the exclusion of the broader system of which they are a part. There is already an increasing awareness amongst those who work in the criminal justice system of how they fit into the system of responses as a whole; such awareness needs to be encouraged as part of the move towards a more integrated approach to crime.

Crime and justice policy for the 1990s

The orientation offered in this book is that of a strategic approach to crime and justice. Planning and information play a supportive role to policy implementation. The strategic approach overlays all of these aspects of organisation. I would not wish it to be assumed that I am advocating that there can be a *technocratic* response to crime; there is a very important role to be played by technical solutions to problems but that role is seen to be subservient to policy considerations. If we are to reduce crime then policy issues must be of focal concern.

I conclude by considering some of the policy initiatives that could contribute to a strategic approach to crime in the 1990s. Most of these issues are currently being debated and might well dominate crime response legislation or practice over the years ahead. They are offered, partly because they are causes which many in the field of criminal justice reform would espouse and partly as examples of the kind of policy subjects that would contribute to the strategic goal of reducing crime. There are innumerable policy issues in the arena of crime responses: if a crime reduction strategy is to be the key to how we respond to crime, then these issues should be analysed in terms of their contribution to that strategy.

The criminal justice system in the 1990s will face a series of challenges, the response to which will have a profound effect on the society of the twenty-first century: the challenge of maintaining the quality of justice, the challenge of deciding where the boundaries should lie between public and private responses to crime and the challenge of building a realistic replacement for imprisonment as the main means of dealing with persistent offenders. These are not presented in a prescribed order of importance, since they are in many ways equally important.

Maintaining the quality of justice

The British system of justice has for a long time exemplified a good model of fairness and equality that has been copied by many countries. This is not to say that our system of justice is perfect or operates to perfection. There are some fundamental issues of fairness and equality that we must face over the next few years if we are to be seen to take the principles of our approach seriously. The issue of facing up to racial discrimination has already been mentioned. The problem is that many judges and magistrates strenuously deny that such discrimination is practised within the courts of Britain. How do we explain that proportionately more black people are being given imprisonment and less are being given noncustodial penalties than their white counterparts? And how do we explain variations in treatment between black and white defendants? Should the courts assume a share of the responsibility for researching the causes of variations in the treatment of white and black people in the criminal justice process?

If we begin with the concept of institutional racism, we can see that discriminatory treatment has already imposed differential justice on the black offender before he or she arrives for trial. The 'discriminatory' sentencing of black offenders is not necessarily due to racial prejudice on the part of the sentencer. It is more likely to be an outcome of a process of institutional disadvantage that began at the moment of arrest and which involved a number of people working in a range of agencies and professional settings: the arresting police officer, the prosecutor, the solicitor and the probation officer. The process of justice is more than what individuals think, decide or do. The institution exerts an influence on the individuals that work within it. The disadvantages that black people face, in being dealt with by the system, are more systemic than personal in origins.

If the quality of justice is to be maintained, then there is a real need to eradicate racial discrimination from our system of justice. Evidence for the existence of racial discrimination has been put forward by a range of bodies, not least by NACRO in its reports on black people in the criminal justice system [NACRO, 1986 and NACRO, 1989f]. Exactly how such discrimination operates within the system is still subject to research and debate but its existence and extent has been quantified and examined to the extent that many would concur that discrimination against black people does take place within all organisations involved in criminal justice. One of the priorities of the 1990s should be to deepen our knowledge of how such discrimination occurs in criminal justice organisations.

The strategic planning of criminal justice offers a potentially powerful means of increasing the impact of our systems of social control. It would be unwise therefore to ignore the dangers that this might pose for the rights and liberties of the individual or to overlook the need for planners to be accountable for what they do. Similarly, if strategic planning can offer effective techniques for change, then it could be used to address the issues of discrimination and injustice that we find throughout all parts of the criminal justice system. In the chapter on policy, emphasis was laid on principles and one of the most important principles must surely be that of equality before the law.

Privatisation of criminal justice

The current policy of the government is to engage in either wholesale or incremental privatisation of many public services. Many would argue that the health service, for example, is being subjected to incremental privatisation. It has been suggested that the government is to introduce a 'free-market penal policy' [Independent, 1989]. The

Home Office have announced that private companies will be allowed to provide imprisonment for offenders on remand and might well allow commercial involvement in the use of electronic 'tagging' experiments. Already almost as much security is provided by private companies as is provided by the police: in some respects it is the private sector that provides property security more than do the public police forces.

Since the police spend only a proportion of their time on public security work, it might be that the government will want to consider the privatisation of certain elements of policing. The wholesale privatisation of the police is very unlikely to become politically feasible, even for the Conservatives, but some marginal and incremental privatisation of their less crucial functions is likely over the next ten years (or as long as the Conservatives remain in power). Our discussion of the relationship between economy and effectiveness bears on these issues; it would not be a strategic move to reduce the effectiveness of the police by seeking economies that, in the long term, would not contribute to crime reduction.

Another aspect of the privatisation issue concerns the probation service. The long term future of the probation service is currently in some doubt. It has been suggested that the Home Office is considering a plan to privatise offender services. Electronic tagging programmes, drug and alcohol groups, day centres, employment schemes and community service would be put out to tender [Indepedent, 1989]. There has been widespread anxiety among probation officers about the extent to which bodies could be contracted to provide services that are currently part of probation's responsibilities. NACRO is viewed by some probation officers with suspicion as being an organisation that is trying to take over the probation service either wholly or in part. NACRO responded to such fears by assuring NAPO that 'it has no wish to take on statutory supervision tasks now seen as the responsibility of the probation service or to displace the work of probation officers in any respect' [NAPO, 1988a, p 2].

The transfer of functions to the voluntary sector is often regarded as being part of the privatisation process, though I prefer to draw a clear distinction between the commercial, profit making sector and the non-profit, non-governmental voluntary sector. Probation has had a long standing experience of working in partnership with the voluntary sector. If community approaches are more effective than custody in reducing crime, then the probation service should play a considerable role in the provision of community based services for offenders. In this scenario, we should expect to see a considerable relocation of resources, in the long term, from the prison to the probation service.

But will the Government be able to demonstrate that the privatisation of public crime responses contributes to the reduction in crime? I suspect that they will respond to this question by saying that privatisation is not intended to achieve that objective but to make law enforcement measures more cost effective. In my view privatisation is unlikely to contribute to crime reduction; if anything it is more likely to inhibit it because it will add to the fragmentation of criminal justice systems. The current system of public criminal justice organisations is already fragmentary; the introduction of private companies into this system will further increase this fragmentation and thus make the system even more difficult to plan. Profit making companies are and must be autonomous organisations and, as I have already argued, the autonomy syndrome is one of the major obstacles to increasing the effectiveness of crime response strategies. Because private, profit making companies are driven largely by market forces, it will be very difficult, if not impossible, to bring them within the network of collaboration required for strategic responses to crime. The strategic goal of private enterprise companies is to achieve a return for their investors. Such an aim would be incompatible with the strategy required by effective responses to crime.

The challenge of reducing imprisonment

Britain has the highest rate of imprisonment in Western Europe and a higher proportion of its population in prison than Turkey [Prison Reform Trust 1989, NACRO, 1989c]. What needs to be done to reduce imprisonment? Several suggestions can be drawn from the considerable body of writings and debates about this subject: the need to provide effective noncustodial alternatives, the need for local action planning to reduce custody, the need for national government to extend criteria for custody to adults and the involvement of the judiciary in integrating probation with sentencing policies. Sentencing policy and the legislation on which it is based should create a clear presumption in favour of community based sanctions [NACRO, 1989e]. We have in this country, the largest and best resourced probation service in the world. This country, it has been said, leads the world in the proliferation of diversionary and noncustodial provisions. This lends a certain degree of irony to the fact that we are also one of the most punitive countries in Western Europe.

Reducing imprisonment will continue to be one of the most urgent criminal justice issues facing this country in the 1990s. A strategic response to crime requires imprisonment to be curtailed for two reasons: one is that prison conditions and regimes are inhumane and brutalizing and thus do little or nothing to rehabilitate prisoners; the other is that prisons are not cost effective measures in crime reduction. Prisons contribute to rather than decrease levels of crime. Whilst they are necessary for offenders who cannot be maintained in the community, they do not offer effective facilities to crime reduction strategies.

A reduction in the prison population would enable the prison service to develop its professional practice in the rehabilitation of prisoners. In the event of this being possible, a greater proportion of available resources should be devoted to in-service training and practice development. The purpose of imprisonment, in a crime reduction strategy, should include the need to reintegrate offenders into the community and to support a decrease in their tendencies to offend. A crime reduction strategy therefore demands a much reduced prison population.

A sentencing strategy

Arguments about how best to reduce imprisonment generally centre on sentencing, since it is the courts that send people to prison. Such arguments acknowledge the role of probation officers and social workers in making recommendations for custody in their social inquiry reports and much work is underway to reduce this factor in the custodial sentencing equation. The imposition of short custodial sentences has widely been supported as a measure that would contribute to reducing imprisonment. There has for a long time been a trend in this direction though its success in reducing the numbers in prison has often been called into question. The size of the prison population depends on how many people are placed in custody and on the length of time they remain there.

Another method of reducing custodial sentencing is to reduce by statute the maximum length available to the courts. It has been suggested that maximum penalties should be reduced along the lines of the 1978 report from the Advisory Council on the Penal System [Prison Reform Trust, 1988]. The present government has traditionally fought shy of this method. It has preferred the technique of stipulating criteria for custody (in relation to young offenders) and this has met with a moderate degree of success. Such criteria must needs be applied with equal strength to both magistrates' courts and the Crown Court, since it is the latter that contributes most to the size of the prison population.

The green paper of 1988 suggested that sentencers would use community-based alternatives to custody if they could be confident that such options would work and would not just be 'soft options' that would only allow offenders to continue with crime. The proportion of first time offenders in prison and those who are there for property crimes of relatively low values suggest that many sentencers, particularly those in the Crown Court, do not hold much faith in the reformative value of these alternatives. Either that or they regard punishment as being the primary function of sentencing and see prison as being the only realistic method of punishment available to them. Given the richness of what the probation services have to offer as alternatives to custody, we might be drawn to conclude that what is needed to make more use of them is a fundamental change on the part of sentencers in the attitudes and beliefs that they hold about the purpose of sentencing.

One of the foremost problems, for many sentencers, is that of trying to decide where the threshold should lie between short sentences of imprisonment and engagement in community based disposals. The criteria laid down for young offenders has gone some way to defining this threshold but much still depends on judicial discretion in the application of the criteria. It has been suggested that the judiciary alone is unable to formulate satisfactory sentencing guide-lines and that any sentencing council that might be formed would need to be widened beyond judges and magistrates [NACRO, 1989e]. This presupposes that a clear sense of purpose can be established for sentencing. We referred earlier to the confusions surrounding the goals of the criminal law and the lack of a clear mission for the criminal justice system. If the purpose of sentencing is clearly established as flowing from the need to reduce crime then the task of the court would be to find the disposal that will contribute most to this objective. Sentencing therefore becomes an exercise in finding the option that is most likely to reduce the chances of reoffending. The task of reducing custody and of improving the effectiveness of sentencing therefore becomes wedded to that of formulating a strategy for the criminal justice system as whole.

It is possible that strategies designed to tackle the problem of custody have focused too narrowly on sentencing at the expense of the broader potential offered by systems management. Reducing custody is a task that needs to be applied to the criminal justice system as a whole. Cautioning (possibly in tandem with prosecution practices) could help to reduce the intake into the criminal justice system of certain categories of offenders and this will affect the rate of custodial sentencing. Cautioning-plus schemes, in which support is provided after a caution has been given (but not as a condition of receiving a caution), have been tried with juveniles, are now being developed for young adults and could be of value for certain categories of adult offenders. Stringent criteria must be applied to their use. Diversion from prosecution will have an indirect but nevertheless noticeable impact on the level of custody.

In many continental justice systems, prosecutors are empowered to waive prosecution if this is in the public interest. It has been argued that the Crown Prosecution Service plays a strategic role in the criminal justice system [Justice of the Peace, 1989d]. It acts as a decision making gateway to the sentencing process and its position in the system allows it to promote and develop coordination among justice agencies. Prosecutors could play a very central role in reducing the remand population, as is evidenced by the experience in West

Germany [Feest, 1988]. It is widely accepted that the reduction of custodial remands is an essential component in the strategy to reduce the prison population and the use of imprisonment generally. There is much potential in using diversionary measures, not just for the intrinsic benefits they confer on the justice process, but as part of the strategy to reduce the imprisoned population.

One further aspect of the sentencing process is its preoccupation with punishment. The government appears to have reacted to this by proposing to develop methods whereby offenders are 'punished' in the community rather than in prison. What has not been so widely acknowledged is the interests of the victims in all this and the relationships between the functions of retribution and compensation. Many victims would agree that the courts should have greater powers to ensure that they are adequately and properly compensated for the harms that have been done to them. Compensation can come from private insurance policies but where these have not been taken out other methods of compensation need to be available, such as offender restitution or provision from state resources. The relationship between victim compensation and punishment of the offender should be clearly developed, allowing victims some degree of contribution to the outcome of a trial. Retribution is of little practical value to victims of property crime; the notion of punishment, as retribution, would serve the interests of society if it were to be replaced with the notion of criminal justice as a means of mediation between those who offend and those who have been offended against.

In all other aspects of crime response planning, evaluation has been given emphasis and sentencing does not differ in this respect. Both legislators and sentencers should address the contribution to crime reduction in their evaluation of sentencing options and policies. If sentencers are to be involved in the development of local crime response strategies then the current restrictions placed on their doing so should be lifted. It would be helpful if the Lord Chancellor were to offer guidance to sentencers on how they may engage in developing criminal justice policies, locally, without compromising their need for independence in dealing with individual offenders. It is easier for magistrates to be involved in their local probation service than for Crown Court judges but the active involvement and support of judges in community-based alternatives is vital to their success.

One key factor in current crime trends is that ours is now the aging population foreseen by Clarke ten years ago. Young people constitute a relatively diminishing proportion of the population and therefore their contribution to crime is likewise going down. Of those offences that are traced to offenders about thirty per cent are committed by juveniles [Home Office, 1986]. Added to this natural decline in the age group, cautioning and juvenile justice programmes based on diversion from reoffending, have grown and have lessened the propensity for offending amongst many juveniles, particularly the more persistent. The decline in the custodial sentencing of young people has and will continue to contribute to the lessening of their crime rate. These decreasing rates of custodial sentencing of young offenders provides us with what Dr. Henri Giller has called a 'window of opportunity' to abolish custody for those aged 14 to 16 [Giller, 1989]. We must however watch population trends carefully and ensure that the advances that have been made in the 1980s are not lost once the age group begins to expand again.

Too many people are sent to prison unnecessarily. A more effective system of diversion and sentencing policies that are geared to reducing reoffending are characteristics of a strategic approach. It is essential that the courts be freed of a wide variety of minor offences, thus allowing resources to be targeted at the more serious categories of persistent offenders. Ashworth has argued that it is the persistent offender that causes the greatest problem in the criminal justice system [Ashworth, 1983, pp 5-7]. A large proportion of those in our overcrowded prisons are persistent offenders. If just 7 % of males are responsible for 65% of all offences committed by males [Home Office, 1989c p 13] then a reduction strategy would clearly target this group. Similarly, if most crime is committed by young males, then this would also present a strategic target for reduction.

Conclusions

There is at present a fairly wide consensus about criminal justice strategy. The differences between the criminal justice policies of the various political parties relate more to specific issues than to any fundamental variations in approach. The goals of reducing and preventing crime, reducing imprisonment and making more effective use of criminal justice resources are widely accepted both by politicians and those who work within the criminal justice arena.

What I have attempted to do in this book is to emphasize some of the weaknesses of the criminal justice system – its fragmentation, its lack of local planning structures, its preoccupation with independence rather than collaboration – and I have suggested ways in which these problems can be resolved. I have argued that strategic planning can make a significant contribution to increasing the effectiveness of crime responses and have set out a theoretical framework for the practice of strategic planning.

What lies at the heart of this approach is the need to view criminal justice as a total system and to plan and develop its operations as a whole. Allied to this is the need to consolidate criminal justice policies with those that affect crime and offenders in a broader way. If crime, as a problem, is to be reduced, there must be an integrated set of strategies governing many of the responses that we make to crime. Many would retreat from the scale and complexity of this task. But, armed with a strategic planning approach the challenge becomes less daunting.

Crime is not the only problem that afflicts all developed societies: health, employment, the environment are other aspects that present equally challenging problems and strategic planning is being used in meeting these challenges, so why not use it in responses to crime? The foremost challenge facing those concerned with crime in the 1990s will be that of reducing the size and impact of the problem. To meet that challenge, a more highly developed approach to policy, planning and information will be required. This development is already underway but will require a more extended appreciation of what strategy is before its potential can be fully realised.

Crime is a problem that poses a social, economic and political threat to society. We have so far suffered more crime than we have needed to. The next decade will, I hope, see a reduction in the scale of that threat.

BIBLIOGRAPHY

Abbreviations
CVS (Councils of Voluntary Service)
DHSS (Department of Health and Social Security)
D of E (Department of the Environment)
ed, eds (Editor, editors)
HMSO (Her Majesty's Stationery Office)
NACRO (National Association for the Care and Resettlement of Offenders)
NAPO (National Association of Probation Officers)
NCVO (National Council of Voluntary Organisations)
SOLACE (Society of Local Authority Chief Executives)

Alderson, John (1979) *Policing freedom: a commentary on the dilemmas of policing in Western democracies.* MacDonald and Evans.

Andreano, Ralph and Siegfried, John J (eds) (1980) *The economics of crime.* John Wiley and Sons

Ashworth, Andrew (1983a) *Sentencing and penal policy.* Weidenfeld and Nicholson.

Ashworth, Andrew (1983b) Reducing the prison population in the 1980s, the need for sentencing reform. In *A prison system for the 80s and beyond, the Noel Buxton Lectures 1982-83.*

Ashworth, Andrew (1988) Criminal justice and the criminal process. *British Journal of Criminology* 28(2), pp111- 123

Ashworth, Andrew (1989) *Custody reconsidered – clarity and consistency in sentencing.* Policy Study No 104. Centre for Policy Studies.

Audit Commission (1989) *The probation service: promoting value for money.* HMSO.

Bainbridge, David (1988) Sentencing of offenders using a computer-based expert system. *Justice of the Peace* 28.5.88, pp344–346

Balmer, D, Goodman D and Doukidis, G (1989) *Integrating expert systems and simulation for decision support.* Chap 7 In Doukidis et al 1989 q.v.

Barrett, Susan and Fudge, Colin (eds) (1981) *Policy and action: essays on the implementation of policy.* Methuen.

Barton, A C F (1984) *The criminal justice system model, police sub-model.*

Home Office Scientific Research and Development Branch Publication 39/84. Home Office.

Bauer, Raymond and Gergen, Kenneth J (eds) (1968) *The study of policy formation.* Free Press Collier Macmillan.

Baynes, Peter (ed) (1973) *Case studies in corporate planning.* Pitman Publishing.

Beck, Peter W (1988) The importance of strategic vision, in *Successful strategy making in public and non-profit making organisations*, report of a joint conference of the Strategic Planning Society and the Royal Institute of Public Administration. London, Strategic Planning Society.

Biggin, S J (1988) The wind of change - the direction of change in the court service. *Justice of the Peace* 12.11.88 pp 734–735.

Birley, David and Bright, Jon (1985) *Crime in the community: towards a Labour Party Policy on crime prevention and public safety.* Alperton, Middx. Labour Campaign for Criminal Justice.

Bish, Robert L (1976) The assumption of knowledge in policy analysis. In Gregg, Phillip H (1976) *Problems of theory in policy analysis, q.v.*

Bishop, Norman (1988) *Noncustodial alternatives in Europe.* Helsinki Institute for Crime Prevention and Control (Publication series number 14).

Blaber, Anne (1979) *The Exeter community policing consultative group, a study of the first year.* NACRO.

Blagg, Harry; Pearson, Geoffrey; Sampson, Alice; Smith, David; and Stubbs, Paul (1988) Inter-agency co-operation: rhetoric and reality. Chapter 12 in Hope, Tim and Shaw, Margaret (eds) (1988) *Communities and crime reduction.* Home Office Research and Planning Unit.

Blagg, Harry and Smith, David (1989) *Crime, penal policy and social work.* Longman.

Blumstein, A and Larson, R (1969) Models of a total criminal justice system. *Operations Research* 17 pp 199–232.

Bohigian, Haig (1977) *What is a model?* Chapter 1 In Nagel Stuart (ed) (1977) q.v.

Bottomley, Keith and Coleman, C (1980) Understanding crime rates. In Clarke, R V G and Hough, J M (eds) (1980) *The effectiveness of policing.* Farnborough, Gower.

Bottomley, Keith and Pease, Ken (1986) *Crime and punishment interpreting the data.* Open University Press.

Bradley, David, Walker, Neil and Wilkie, Roy (1986) *Managing the police: law, organisation and democracy.* Wheatsheaf Books.

Brehny, Michael and Hall, Peter (1984) The strange death of strategic planning and the victory of the know-nothing school. *Built Environment,* 10(2) pp 95–99.

Britton, Bruce, Hope, Barry, Locke, Trevor and Wainman, Liz (1988) *Policy and information in juvenile justice systems.* NACRO and Save the Children.

Bryson, John M (1988) A strategic planning process for public and non-profit organisations. *Long Range Planning* 21(1) pp 73–81.

Burch, Martin and Wood, Bruce (1983) *Public policy in Britain.* Martin Robertson.

Burney, Elizabeth (1985) *Sentencing young people. What went wrong with the Criminal Justice Act 1982.* Gower.

Burris, Rhys (1989) The Le Vay scrutiny *Justice of the Peace* 14.10.89 pp 655–659.

Butler, Sid (1982) Mathematical modelling of the criminal justice system. *Home Office Research Bulletin* No 14 pp 16–20.

Carley, Michael (1980) *Rational techniques in policy analysis.* Policy Studies Institute/Heinemann Education Books.

Chancellor of the Exchequer (1989) The Government's expenditure plans 1989-90 to 1991-92 Chapter 11 – Home Office and Legal Departments Cm 611. HMSO.

Chapman, B (1980) *The police state.* Pall Mall.

Clarke, Michael (1987) *Politicians and professionals – the changing management of local government.* Luton, Local Government Training Board.

Clarke, Ronald (1981) The prospects for controlling crime. *Home Office Research Bulletin* No.12, pp 12-19.

Clarke, Ronald (1983) Urban crime, fear and stress. *Home Office Research Bulletin* No 15 pp 5-7.

Clinnard, Marshall B (1978) *Cities with little crime: the case of Switzerland.* Cambridge University Press.

Cohen, J et al (1973) Implementation of the JUSSIM model in a criminal justice planning agency. *Journal of Crime and Delinquency* July 1973 pp 117-131.

Committee of Public Accounts (1982) 22nd report of the committee, Cmnd 339. HMSO.

Cooper, Barrymore (1989) *The management and prevention of juvenile crime problems.* Home Office Crime Prevention Unit.

Council of Europe (1987) Interactions within the criminal justice system. Reports presented to the 17th criminological research conference 1986, Council of Europe collected studies in criminological research Volume XXV. Strasbourg: Council of Europe.

Council of Europe (1980) Report on decriminalisation. Strasbourg: Council of Europe.

Croft, John (1982) Planning. *Home Office Research Bulletin* No 14, pp 5-8.

Crown Prosecution Service (1988) Annual Report 1987/1988. HMSO.

Crown Prosecution Service (1989) Annual Report 1988/1989. HMSO.

Curtis, Sarah (1989) *Juvenile offending, prevention through intermediate treatment.* B T Batsford Ltd.

Cushman, Robert C (1980) *Criminal justice planning for local governments.* Washington, National Institute of Law Enforcement and Criminal Justice, United States Department of Justice.

Davidoff, Paul and Reiner, Thomas A (1982) *A choice theory of planning.* In Faludi Andreas 1973, q.v.

Davidson, R N (1988) *Local area profiles of crime.* Paper presented to the 'Crime and policing: new geographical perspectives' conference, Cambridge, 1988. Royal Institute of Geographers.

Denning, Basil W (1971) *Corporate planning: selected concepts.* McGraw-Hill.

DHSS (1972) *Intermediate treatment - a guide for the regional planning of new forms of treatment for children in trouble.* DHSS.

DHSS (1977) *Children and Young Persons Act 1969 - Intermediate treatment* (Local Authority Circular LAC(77)1, 27th January 1977. DHSS.

DHSS (1983) *Further development of intermediate treatment* (Circular LAC(83)3). DHSS

Ditton, J (1979) *Part-time crime: an ethnography of fiddling and pilferage.* Macmillan.

Doukidis, G I; Land, F and Miller, G (1989) *Knowledge-based management support systems.* Chichester UK, Ellis and Horwood Ltd.

Downs, David (1983) *Law and order, theft of an issue.* Fabian Society.

Downs, David (1988) *Contrasts in tolerance: penal policy in the Netherlands and in England and Wales.* Clarendon Press.

Dror, Yehezkel (1973) *Public policy making re-examined.* Leonard Hill Books.

Dror, Yehezkel (1975) *From management sciences to policy sciences.* In Pollitt, C et al 1979 q.v..

Dunn, William H (1981) *Public policy analysis: an introduction.* Englewood Cliffs Prentice Hall.

Dye, Thomas R (1972) *Understanding public policy, 4th edition. Prentice Hall.*

Ekblom, Paul (1988) Getting the best out of crime analysis. Crime Prevention Unit Paper 10. Home Office.

Etzioni, Amital (1968) *The active society.* Free press.

Falk, Nicholas and Lee, James (1978) *Planning the social services.* Saxon House.

Falkin, Gregory (1979) *Reducing delinquency: a strategic planning approach.* Lexington Books, DC Heath & Co.

Faludi, Andreas (ed) (1973) *A reader in planning theory.* Pergamon Press.

Farrington, David P and Gunn, John (eds) (1985) *Reactions to crime: the public, the police, courts and prisons.* Wiley and Sons.

Faulkner, David (1983) *Crime and the criminal justice system.* Lecture to the Howard League for Penal Reform. Unpublished.

Faulkner, David (1989) *Future of the probation service: a view from the government. Justice of the Peace* 23.9.89 and 30.9.89 pp 606-626.

Feeny, Floyd (1985) Interdependence as a working concept, chapter 2 in Moxon, David (ed) 1985, q.v.

Feest, Johhannes (1988) *Reducing the prison population: lessons from the West German experience?* NACRO.

Fitzgerland, Mike and Muncie, John (1983) *System of justice, an introduction to the criminal justice system of England and Wales.* Basil Blackwell.

Floyd, Michael (1984) *Policy-making and planning in local government, a cybernetic approach.* Gower.

Fowles, Tony (1989) Monitoring expenditure on the criminal justice system: the search for control. Paper presented to the British Criminology Conference, Bristol, 1989. University of York.

Fox, James A (1981) *Models in quantitative criminology.* Academic Press.

Friend, John and Hickling, Allen (1987) *Planning under pressure, the strategic choice approach.* Pergamon Press.

Friend, J K and Jessop, W N (1977) *Local government and strategic choice,* 2nd edition. Pergamon Press.

Froman, L A (1970) The categorisation of policy contents. In Ranney *A Political science and public policy.* Chicago, Markham.

Fulton, (1968) The Civil Service Vol I (report of the committee 1966 - 1968, Fulton Report), Cmnd 3638. HMSO.

Gibson, Cyrus F and Jackson, B B (1987) *The information imperative: managing the impact of information technology on business and people.* Lexington Books.

Giller, Henri (1989) Crisis for the young adult offender - strategies and solutions. Address to the Prison Reform Trust lecture series on prison policy in the 1990s. London, Prison reform trust.

Gladstone, F J (1980) *Co-ordinating crime prevention efforts.* HMSO.

Goldsmith, Michael (1980) *Politics, planning and the city.* Hutchinson.

Gordon, P (1984) Community policing: towards the local police state? *Critical Social Policy* 10 pp 39-58.

Gottfredson, D M and Tonry, M (eds) (1987) *Prediction and classification. Criminal justice decision making.* University of Chicago Press.

Green, Allan D (1987) *Strategy for the Crown Prosecution Service.* Lord Chancellor's Department.

Greenly, Gordon E (1986) Does strategic planning improve company performance? *Long Range Planning* 19(2) pp101-109.

Gregg, Phillip H (ed) (1976) *Problems of theory in policy analysis.* Lexington Books, DC Heath & Co.

Guardian, (1989) 'Hurd calls Judges to talks on criminal justice reforms' by John Carvel, 27 September 1989.

Gunton, Tony (1988) *Business information technology: end user focus.* Prentice Hall.

Hambleton, Robin (1986) *Rethinking policy planning, a study of planning systems linking central and local government.* School for Advanced Urban Studies, University of Bristol.

Hambleton, R L (1978) *Policy planning and local government.* Hutchinson.

Hambleton, R L (1979) *Towards theories of public learning.* In Pollitt C et al 1979 q.v.

Hamilton, John F (1976) Computer simulation as a technique in policy analysis. In Gregg Phillip H 1976 *Problems of theory in policy analysis*, q.v.

Harding, Philip and Jenkins, Richard (1989) *The myth of the hidden economy: towards a new understanding of informal economic activity.* Open University Press.

Harris, Robert (1989) *Probation officers still social workers? Probation Journal* 36(2) pp 52 - 57

Hartjen, Clayton (1978) *Crime and criminalisation*, 2nd edition. US, Holt, Rinehart and Winston/Praeger.

Hartley, T C and Griffith, J (1981) *Government and the law*, 2nd edition.

Heal, Kevin (1987) Crime prevention in the United Kingdom: from start to go. *Home Office Research Bulletin* No 24, pp 9 - 15.

Heclo, Hugh (1972) Review article: policy analysis, *British Journal of Political Science*, Vol.2. pp 83 - 108.

Henry, S (1978) *The hidden economy: the context and control of borderline crime.* Oxford, Martin Robertson.

Herbert, T (1982) *The geography of urban crime.* Longman.

Heywood, I and Hall, N (1988) Is there a role for geographical information systems in formulating multi agency crime prevention strategies. Paper presented to the 'Crime and Policing: new geographical perspectives' conference, Cambridge, 1988.

Hirst, Michael (1986) Chief Constable's Annual Report. Leicestershire Constabulary.

HMSO (1972) The new local authorities: management and structure. Report of the study group appointed jointly by the Secretary of State for the Environment and Local Authority Associations. HMSO.

Hogwood, Brian W and Peters, B. Guy (1983) *Policy dynamics.* Wheatsheaf Books.

Hogwood, Brian W and Gunn, Lewis A (1984) *Policy analysis for the real world.* Oxford University Press.

Hogwood, Brian W and Peters, B Guy (1983) *Policy dynamics.* Wheatsheaf Books Harvester Press.

Home Office (1965) Report of the Committee on the prevention and detection of crime (Cornish Report). Home Office.

Home Office (1968) Children in trouble (White Paper, Cmnd 3601). HMSO.

Home Office (1976a) A review of criminal justice policy 1976. Home Office.

Home Office (1976b) Children and Young Persons Act 1969, Observations on the eleventh report from the Expenditure Committee, (Cmnd 6494). Home Office, Welsh Office, DHSS, DES, HMSO.

Home Office (1978) Juveniles: co-operation between the police and other agencies (Home Office circular 211/1978 19th December 1978). Home Office, DHSS, Welsh Office. HMSO.

Home Office (1980a) Young offenders (White Paper Cmnd 8045 October 1980). Home Office, Welsh Office, DHSS. HMSO.

Home Office (1980b) Statistics of the criminal justice system, England and Wales, 1968 – 1978. Home Office.

Home Office (1983a) Crime prevention – a co-ordinated approach. Home Office.

Home Office (1983b) Manpower, effectiveness and efficiency in the police service. Home Office Circular No 114/1983. Home Office.

Home Office et al (1984) Crime prevention (Circular 8/1984). Home Office, DES, D of E, DHSS, Welsh Office. HMSO.

Home Office (1986) Criminal justice, a working paper, revised edition. Home Office.

Home Office (1987) Special European Edition, *Home Office Research Bulletin* No 24.

Home Office (1988a) Prison statistics England and Wales 1987, Cm 547. HMSO.

Home Office (1988b) Punishment, custody and the community Cm 424 (Green Paper). HMSO.

Home Office (1988c) Tackling Offending: an action plan (Action Plan Circular). Home Office.

Home Office (1989a) Magistrates' courts, report of a scrutiny 1989, Volumes 1 and 2. HMSO.

Home Office (1989b) Ministerial group on crime prevention, *Crime Prevention News*, Jun/Sep 1989, p 4.

Home Office (1989c) Tackling Crime. HMSO.

Hood, Roger and Sparks, Richard (1970) Key issues in criminology.

Weidenfeld and Nicholson esp Chap 5 Understanding the sentencing process.

Hope, Philip (1981) *Voluntary organisations and intermediate treatment.* London, National Council for Voluntary Organisations.

Hope, Barry (1988) Dynamic modelling using STELLA In Britton Bruce et al 1988 q.v.

Hope, Tim and Shaw, Margaret (1988a) Community approaches to reducing crime. Chapter 1 in Hope, Tim and Shaw, Margaret (eds) (1988) *Communities and crime reduction.* Home Office Research and Planning Unit.

Hope, Tim and Shaw, Margaret (eds) (1988b) *Communities and crime reduction.* Home Office Research and Planning Unit.

House of Commons (1975) Eleventh report from the Expenditure Committee, session 1974-75, The Children and Young Persons Act 1969, Volume I, Report. HMSO.

House, Peter W (1982) *The art of public policy analysis: the arena of regulations and resources.* Sage Publications.

Huss, William R and Honton, Edward J (1987) Scenario planning - what style should you use. *Long Range Planning* 20(4) 21-29.

Hurd, Douglas (1986) Justice's Clerks Society annual conference. Home Secretary's speech: justice and good management. *Justice of the Peace* 14.6.86 pp 379 - 380 and p 398.

Independent (1989) Home Office draws up free-market penal policy. Article by Sarah Helm, 24.7.89.

Johnson, Gerry and Scholes, Kevan (1988) *Exploring corporate strategy*, 2nd edition. Prentice Hall.

Justice of the Peace (1988) Article in issue dated 17.12.88 p 886 reviewing Uglow's Policing liberal society.

Justice of the Peace (1989a) Axing a tier of management, 7.10.89 p 633.

Justice of the Peace (1989b) The week in parliament, criminal offences, 18.3.89 p 172 (referring to a question in the House of Commons on 3rd March 1989).

Justice of the Peace (1989c) Managing the criminal justice system. 14.10.89 p 649.

Justice of the Peace (1989d) The strategic role of the Crown Prosecution Service, 8.10.89 p 641.

Kahn, Alfred J (1969a) *Studies in social policy and planning.* Russell Sage Foundation.

Kahn, Alfred J (1969b) *Theory and practice of social planning.* Russell Sage Foundation .

Kelling, George L and Moore, Mark H (1988) The evolving strategy of policing. Perspectives on policing No.4. Washington USA, United States Department of Justice.

Kilroy-Silk, Robert (Chair) (1981) *Young Offenders - a strategy for the future* (Parliamentary All Party Penal Affairs Group). Barry Rose Ltd.

King, Michael (1981) *The framework of criminal justice.* Croom Helm.

King, William R (1988) How effective is your information systems planning? *Long Range Planning* 21(5) pp 103 - 122.

Kinsey, Richard, Lea, John and Young, Jock (1986) *Losing the fight against crime.* Basil Blackwell.

Lang, Douglas W (1977) *Critical path analysis*, 2nd edition. Hodder and Stoughton.

Lasswell, H (1970) The emerging conception of the policy sciences. *Policy Sciences* I, 3-14 (quoted in Hogwood and Gunn 1984 q.v.).

Locke, Trevor (1982) The range of strategic and practical options in work with young people in trouble, background paper for a group discussion at the CVS Conference in Bath. September 1982.

Locke, Trevor (1983) Inter-agency collaboration in I.T., *Intermediate Treatment Mailing* No.13, March 1983, pp 7 - 9. Leicester, National Youth Bureau.

Locke, Trevor (1989) Leicester case study: the economic impact of crime on a local area (student essay). Leicester Polytechnic Business School. Masters course in Urban Policy Studies. Leicester, the author.

Locke, Trevor (1989) What is policy? Student essay, Leicester Polytechnic Business School. Leicester, the author.

Lockyer, K G (1969) *An introduction to critical path analysis*, 3rd edition. Pitman Publishing.

Maclean, Doug (1987a) Evaluation of the use of computers in magistrates' courts - the way forward (main phase report). Home Office.

Maclean, Doug (1987b) *Computers in criminal justice: the promise and the reality*. Home Office.

Maddox, Nick Anthony, William, P and Wheatley, Walt (1987) Creative strategy planning using imagery. *Long Range Planning* 20(5) pp 118 - 124.

Magistrates Association et al (1978) The children and young persons Act 1969 - report of a joint working party of the Magistrates Association, the Association of Metropolitan Authorities and the Association of County Councils, July 1978. London, Magistrates Association.

Mars, G (1983) *Cheats at work: an anthropology of workplace crime*. Allen and Unwin.

McEwen, Neil, Carmichael, Colin, Short, David and Steel Ashley (1988) Managing organisational change - a strategic approach. *Long Range Planning* 21(6) pp 71 - 78.

McGill, Ronald (1988) Planning for strategic performance in local government. *Long Range Planning* 21(5) pp 77 - 84.

Meltsner, Arnold J and Bellavita, Christopher (1983) *The policy organisation*. Sage Publications.

Metcalfe, Les and Richards, Sue (1987) *Improving public management*. Sage Publications.

Millett, Stephen M (1988) How Scenarios trigger strategic thinking. *Long Range Planning* 21(5) 61-68.

Mockler, Robert J and Dologite, D G (1988) Developing knowledge-based systems for strategic planning. *Long Range Planning* 21(1) pp 97 - 102.

Moir, Esther (1969) *The Justice of the Peace*. Penguin Books.

Mood, Alexander M (1983) *Introduction to policy analysis*. Edward Arnold.

Moore, Mark H and Trojanowicz, Robert C (1988) Corporate strategies for policing. Perspectives on policing No.5. Washington USA, United States Department of Justice.

Morgan, Patricia M (1985) Modelling the criminal justice system. Research and Planning Unit Paper 53. Home Office.

Morris, R M (1980) Home Office crime policy planning: six years on. *Howard Journal* Vol XIX pp 135 - 141.

Moxon,David (ed) (1985) *Managing criminal justice: a collection of papers.* Home Office Research and Planning Unit/HMSO .

Moxon, David (1988) *Sentencing practice in the Crown Court.* Home Office, Home Office Research Study No 103. HMSO.

Murphy, J J (1989) Identifying strategic issues. *Long Range Planning* 22(2) pp 96 - 105.

NACRO (1974) *Architecture, planning and urban crime.* NACRO.

NACRO (1985a) *Juvenile crime: co-ordination and the community.* NACRO.

NACRO (1985b) *Monitoring community alternatives to custody and care.* NACRO Juvenile Offenders Team.

NACRO (1986) Black people and the criminal justice system, report of the NACRO Race Issues Advisory Committee. NACRO.

NACRO (1987a) *Local authority action on juvenile crime, a role for Chief Executives.* NACRO.

NACRO (1987b) *Time for change: a new framework for dealing with juvenile crime and offenders.* NACRO.

NACRO (1987c) *Working with prisons*, NACRO.

NACRO (1988a) *Juvenile cautioning: a monitoring guide.* NACRO Juvenile Crime Section.

NACRO (1988b) *Factsheet: the probation service.* NACRO.

NACRO (1988c) *Growing up on housing estates, a review of the play and recreational needs of young people.* NACRO.

NACRO (1988d) *Northern Region Area Profiling Scheme Review.* NACRO Juvenile Crime Section.

NACRO (1988e) *Punishment, custody and the community* (response to the Green Paper). NACRO.

NACRO (1989a) Control and management of probation services. *NACRO News Digest* No. 57 July 1989 pp 11 - 12.

NACRO (1989b) *Crime prevention and community safety: a practical guide for local authorities.* National Safe Neighbourhoods Unit, NACRO.

NACRO (1989c) *Imprisonment in Western Europe: some facts and figures.* NACRO Briefing No. 25. NACRO.

NACRO (1989d) *Police* (NACRO fact sheet). NACRO.

NACRO (1989e) *The real alternative: strategies to promote community based penalties.* NACRO.

NACRO (1989f) *Race and criminal justice.* The second report of the NACRO Race Issues Advisory Committee. NACRO.

NACRO (1989g) Annual report 1988-1989. NACRO.

NACRO/SOLACE (1987) *Local authority action on juvenile crime, a role for the chief executive.* NACRO and SOLACE.

NACRO/SOLACE (1988) *Crime prevention and community safety: a new role for local authorities.* NACRO/SOLACE.

Nagel, Stuart (ed) (1977) *Modeling the criminal justice system.* Sage Publications .

Nagel, Stuart S (1980) *The policy-studies handbook.* Lexington Books, D C Heath & Co.

Nanus, Bert (1974) A general model for criminal justice planning. *Journal of Criminal Justice*, Vol.2, pp 345 - 356 (quoted in Cushman, 1980, q.v.).

NAPO (1988a) NACRO assurances. *NAPO News* August 1988 No 2. p 2.

NAPO (1988b) *Punishment, custody and the community, the response of the National Association of Probation Officers.* NAPO.

Narchal, R M et al (1987) An environmental scanning system for business planning. *Long Range Planning* 20(6) pp 96–105.

Nash, M R (1987) What influences offenders to give up crime? - A snapshot of opinion. *Justice of the Peace* 31.10.87, pp 697 - 698.

Noam, Eli M (1977) The criminal justice system: an economic model. Chapter 3 In Nagel 1977 q.v.

Ostrom, Vincent (1976) Language theory and empirical research in policy analysis In Gregg Phillip H 1976 *Problems of theory in policy analysis.* Lexington Books DC Heath & Co.

Patten, John MP (1988) *Punishment, custody and the community. Justice of the Peace* 3.9.88 pp 563 - 564.

Parliamentary All Party Penal Affairs Group (1981) *Young offenders, a strategy for the future.* Barry Rose Ltd.

Parston, Greg (ed) (1986) *Managers as strategists, health service managers reflecting on practice.* Kings Fund Publishing Office.

Pepinsky, Harold E (1980) *Crime control strategies, an introduction to the study of crime.* Oxford University Press.

Personal Social Services Council (1977) A future for intermediate treatment, report of the intermediate treatment study group London. PSSC.

Pollitt, Christopher et al (1979) *Public policy in theory and practice.* Hodder and Staughton.

Prison Reform Trust (1988) *A manifesto for penal reform.* Prison Reform Trust.

Prison Reform Trust (1989) Justice (editorial) *Prison Report* No. 8 September 1989 p 2.

Pullinger, Hugh (1985) The criminal justice system model: the flow model. Research and Planning Unit Paper 36. Home Office.

Raine, John (1986) Do magistrates courts give value for money? In Harrison A and Gretton (eds) 1986 *Crime UK 1986.* Newbury, Policy Journals.

Research and Planning Unit (1987) *Research Programme 1987-88.* Home Office.

Rice, A S (1984) The criminal justice system: magistrates' court sub-model. Research and Planning Unit Paper No. 24. Home Office.

Richardson, Nigel (1987) Justice by geography: a review of six local juvenile justice systems monitored by Social Information Systems. Manchester, Social Information Systems.

Rockart, J F (1979) Chief executives define their own data needs. *Harvard Business Review* Mar-Apr 1979 pp 81 - 93.

Rockart, J F and Treacy, M E (1982) The CEO goes on-line. *Harvard Business Review* Jan-Feb 1982 pp 82 - 88.

Rutherford, Andrew (1986) *Growing out of crime, society and young people in trouble.* Penguin Books.

Saunders, Peter (1981) *Social theory and the urban question.* Hutchinson.

Scarman, Lord (1981) *The Scarman report: the Brixton disorders, April 10 - 12 1981.* HMSO.

Schur, Edwin (1973) *Radical nonintervention.* Prentice Hall.

Scott, Tony and Miller, Clive (1987) Doing it by the book. *Community Care* 23.4.87 pp 20-21.

Smith, Brian (1976) *Policy-making in British government: an analysis of power and rationality.* Martin Robertson.

Smith, Stephen (1986) *Britain's shadow economy.* Oxford, Clarendon Press.

Shaw, Stephen (1987) Crime prevention: a counsel of despair? In Harrison Anthony and Gretton J (eds) 1987 *Crime UK, an economic, social and policy audit.* Policy Journals.

Smith, David (1988) The limits to interagency co-operation, in: Harrison A and Gretton J *Crime UK 1988, an economic, social and policy audit.* Newbury, Policy Journals.

Smith, J C and Hogan, Brian (1988) *Criminal Law,* sixth edition. Butterworths.

Smith, Lorna and Laycock, Gloria (1985) *Reducing crime: developing the role of crime prevention panels.* Crime Prevention Unit paper 2. Home Office.

Smithies, Edward (1984) *The black economy in England since 1914.* Dublin, Gill and Macmillan.

SOLACE/NACRO (1986) *Crime prevention and community safety, a new role for local authorities?* SOLACE/NACRO.

Stein, Morris (1975) *Stimulating creativity.* Volumes 1 and 2. New York, Academic Press.

Stern, Vivien (1987) *Bricks of shame, Britain's prisons.* Penguin Special.

Stewart, John and Stoker, Gerry (eds) (1989) *The future of local government.* Macmillan.

Stockford, Dick (1988) *Integrating care systems, practical perspective.* Longman.

Tormedd, Patrick (1987) Can crime be controlled through planning - new perspectives and critical observations. *International Annals of Criminology* 25(1) pp 193-211 .

Train, C J (1977)The development of criminal policy planning in the Home Office. *Public Administration* Winter issue pp 373-384.

Tsichritzis, Dionysios C and Lochovsky, F H (1982) *Data models.* Prentice Hall .

Unell, Judith (1983) 'Constructing an area profile', Chapter 3. In *Voluntary action and young people in trouble: local surveys.* NCVO.

United States Department of Justice (1980) *Delinquency prevention: theories and strategies* (revised edition). Washington US Justice Department.

United States Department of Justice (1981) *Delinquency prevention – selective organisational change in the school* (revised edition). Washington US Justice Department.

Vemuri, V (1978) *Modeling of complex systems, an introduction.* Academic Press.

Vickers, Sir Geoffrey (1965) *The art of judgement - a study of policy making.* Chapman and Hall.

Vincent, Dr. Jackie (1980) *Planning resources for community based treatment of juvenile offenders* (published in three sections). London, Social Policy Research Ltd.

Walker, Nigel (1971) *Crimes, courts and figures, an introduction to criminal statistics.* Penguin Books.

Waters, Sam (1989) From data-bases towards knowledge-bases, chapter 21 In Doukidis G I et al 1989 q.v.
White, Robin C (1985) *The administration of justice.* Basil Blackwell.
Wildavsky, Aaron (1979) *The art and craft of policy analysis.* MacMillan.
Wilner, Daniel (1974) Evaluation: the state of the technical art. (Quoted in Carley M 1980,q.v.).
Windesham, Lord (1987) *Responses to crime.* Clarendon Press.
Young, W (1986) Influences upon the use of imprisonment. *Howard Journal* 25(2).
Zander, Michael (1985) *The lawmaking process 2nd edition.* Weidenfeld and Nicholson .
Zellick, Graham (1983) Justice and accountability in prisons, In *A prison system for the 80's and beyond.* NACRO.